A
History
of
Bloxham School

The chapel, about 1890.

A
History
of
Bloxham School

by
Brian S. Smith

Published by Bloxham School
and the Old Bloxhamist Society
1978

Printed by H. E. Boddy & Co. Ltd., Banbury, for the publishers, Bloxham
School and the Old Boxhamist Society

ISBN 0 9506231 0 5

In memory of

PHILIP REGINALD AND HARRIET EGERTON

CONTENTS

Preface

ILLUSTRATIONS

MAPS

PREFACE

The beginning of All Saints' School, Bloxham, has been described by its Founder, the Revd Philip Reginald Egerton.

'I had been for the first two years of my clerical life one of the curates of the parish of Deddington, close to Bloxham, which I was obliged, in common with the other curates, to leave on the return of the then vicar to his parish. It happened that on a Monday morning, in the autumn of 1859, my fellow curate and myself walked over to Banbury to see the vicar of Banbury, Mr. Wilson. After seeing him, my friend proposed that we should return by way of Bloxham, instead of going back the way we had come, viz., through Adderbury. It was this change of route that led to my beginning the School at Bloxham. As we approached the village, I saw, for the first time, that portion of the buildings, which had already been erected by a Mr. Hewett, and solemnly dedicated to the service of the Church. This school had failed, and had been broken up, and for two years there had been no school existing, and the property was to be sold by auction on the Thursday following that Monday.

We went to the vicar of Bloxham, obtained the keys of the building, and went over it — lamenting that it had been abandoned and the work given up — the more so as there was talk of its falling into the hands of those who were opposed to the Church.

The idea of re-starting the school was suggested to me by my friend and rejected promptly by myself, as I said that it was the very last thing in the world that I should think of, to become a schoolmaster. However, as we walked back to Deddington the matter was discussed again and again, and as I had then no immediate plans for the future, I at last began to think that it would be a work to which I might devote my life and do some good in'.

In fact, the story, which appears almost miraculous in the simplicity of this version, was much more complex, and was related in greater detail in the school's first *History,* published in 1910 to mark its jubilee, later extended by a *Supplement* to 1925. That *History* has been unobtainable for some years and in any case is now over fifty years out-of-date. In the last half-century the school has experienced success, decline and recovery with its reputation now standing at a new peak of achievement. There have also become available old records and papers unknown to the earlier historians, permitting a new assessment of Egerton's foundation.

CHAPTER I

J. W. HEWETT
1853-1857

The first half of the nineteenth century was a period of rapid and profound change in England. The country was transformed from a predominantly rural society to an urban and industrial one. The population doubled from nine million in 1801 to eighteen million in 1851. The government of the nation was radically overhauled at both national and local level by the Whigs in the 1830s. Yet amid all these changes and their social consequences the influence of the Church of England was in relative decline and in particular it was failing to supply the religious needs of the great new urban middle and working classes.

The Church of England was reinvigorated by reformers of both the evangelical party and the Oxford Movement. The latter originated in the introspective discussions, debates and political manoeuvres of the university with a call for the revival of ecclesiastical authority within the state accompanied by a return to ordered and disciplined forms of worship and private life and a reminder of the historic links with the pre-Reformation universal, or catholic, church. The leaders in Oxford, John Keble (fellow of Oriel, 1812-35 and professor of poetry, 1831-42), Henry Newman (fellow of Oriel, 1822-45) and Edward Pusey (fellow of Oriel, 1823-29, canon of Christ Church and regius professor of hebrew, 1828-82) were in a position to inspire the young men at the university. Among those who came under their influence were Samuel Wilberforce (Oriel, 1823-26), later successively bishop of Oxford and Winchester, George Moberly (Balliol, 1822-25), headmaster of Winchester before preferment as bishop of Salisbury, and W. E. Gladstone (Christ Church, 1828-31), who as prime minister in 1869 appointed Wilberforce to Winchester and Moberly to Salisbury and recommended Nathaniel Woodard as sub-dean of Manchester in 1881.

Even more in need of reform than the Church of England was the dismal state of schools to educate the new Victorian nation. From early in the century the National Society and the British Society had been providing elementary schools of either an Anglican or nonconformist bias, and these were supplemented by a variety of charity and dame schools or needy clergy taking a few pupils. The town grammar schools were largely moribund and distributed unevenly throughout the country on a ratio of about one to every 25,000 people; few of their masters were capable or willing to teach 'grammar' as their statutes demanded. One or two, like Rugby or Shrewsbury, possessed rich endowments which ranked them with the ancient endowed (and therefore 'public') great schools of Winchester, Eton, Westminster, Harrow, Charterhouse, St Paul's and Merchant Taylors'. Others survived to be reformed in the 1850s, as Berkhamsted, Sherborne, Felsted and Uppingham. It was Uppingham's reforming headmaster, Edward Thring, who formed the Headmasters' Conference to counter the recommendations of the Taunton Commission of 1864-68, the latter having proposed to Gladstone's government the establishment of a national system of secondary education which would have limited the independence of the endowed grammar schools. Membership of the Headmasters' Conference became the prime qualification of any school claiming to be a 'public school', whatever its origin. The seven original public schools had been examined and found wanting by the Clarendon Commission in 1861; those outside London catered almost exclusively for the sons of the aristocracy and landed gentry, giving a strictly classical education and providing the most appalling living conditions for their boys. Their reform was due largely to the example of Thomas Arnold of Rugby (1828-42) who established a new pattern of school life and educational theory, introducing Christian morals and religion into his scheme of the school as a character-builder. He imported to Rugby both the prefect system and houses for boarders, and these, together with his popular appeal to Christian manliness, spread both to the other old-established schools and the new foundations of mid-Victorian England. The educational demands of the growing numbers of lesser gentry, clergy and professional men were too urgent to wait for the reform of the existing schools, and therefore despite the enormous cost there was no alternative but to found new schools either by joint-stock companies or public subscription. First was Cheltenham in 1841 where a rapidly growing population of retired army officers and civil servants had only the town's decayed grammar school for their sons. It was soon followed by others, Marlborough in 1843 for the sons of the professional classes and clergy, Rossall in 1844, Brighton in 1845, Radley, the first Oxford Movement school, in 1847, Glenalmond and Bradfield in 1850.

There still remained few schools of any description for the fastest growing section of the population, the middle classes. The term covered a wide social range from wealthy and successful businessmen or junior and poorer branches of gentry families at one end to small-town tradesmen, clerks and lesser farmers at the other. These were the men calling for a wider parliamentary franchise, seeking a greater part in municipal affairs and acquiring experience of organisation and management in their business affairs and in the administration of nonconformist chapels. Before the 1870 Education Act the state gave little practical encouragement to education, and even after the act the elementary schools were inadequate for training boys for business, the grammar schools continued to teach purely academic subjects and the middle classes had no desire for their sons to go to the aristocracy's public schools and universities. It was this gross deficiency of schools for the middle classes which Nathaniel Woodard recognised and sought to overcome.

Woodard had been at Oxford from 1834 to 1840 and was a disciple of Keble, Newman and Pusey. He believed in Arnold's idea of the Christian state and in the duty of the church towards education, already carried out at elementary level by the National Society. It was his aim to bring the church's education to the middle classes, especially their lower ranks who, from the evidence of the 1851 census, showed a marked lack of interest in the religion of the established Church of England. By forming a fellowship of priests he had the vision of founding at least

2

one middle-class school in every diocese, and when at the age of 35 he became curate of Shoreham in Sussex he started to put his ideas into practice. In 1848, two years after his appointment, he opened 'Shoreham Grammar School' and founded the Society of St Nicolas College, Shoreham, composed of seventeen men all in holy orders. His recognition of the breadth of the term 'middle classes' led him to classify and divide his school on different sites, and this was the origin of Lancing (1848), Hurstpierpoint (1849) and Ardingly (1858). Despite his flair and ability for fund-raising his hopes of extending his system took longer than expected and not until the 1870s could Canon E. C. Lowe, the headmaster of Hurstpierpoint, be freed to found a Midland division of Woodard schools with Denstone (1868) and Ellesmere (1884). King's College, Taunton, bought by Woodard in 1879, was the only other school dating from before Canon Woodard's death in 1891. He was therefore a long way from achieving his ambition of a network of middle-class diocesan schools, and even had he succeeded the diocesan schools would have satisfied only a small proportion of the demand. As it happened, the Taunton Commission's recommendations heralded state intervention in education and therefore effectively checked the development of a system of diocesan schools. However, since the Liberal government for political reasons did not adopt the Commission's advice, for the time being middle-class and secondary education was left to the grammar schools reformed under the Endowed Schools Act of 1869, a few post-1870 school board schools with higher grades above the purely elementary, private urban commercial schools and the boarding schools like those of Woodard, his opponents and imitators. Among the latter were the two men who founded Bloxham.

————————— • —————————

The seventeen members of the Society of St Nicolas College, Shoreham, in 1849 included an assistant master, the Revd John William Hewett.[1] From Barnstaple Grammar School and Trinity College, Cambridge, he had joined Woodard's Society at the age of twenty-five. He was an enthusiastic Anglo-Catholic of extreme views, urging for example that confession should be made systematic and regular, if not compulsory. Such an outlook was not received with much sympathy at Shoreham, but Hewett was not prepared to be over-ruled, and after being rebuked by Woodard for 'a flagrant piece of insubordination' he left in 1852.

There followed an unedifying episode in which Hewett claimed in correspondence with a parent of a new boy that systematic confession was practised. The parent took the matter up with the bishop of Chichester and with Woodard's willing cooperation an official enquiry was held. Although Hewett now repeated his charges openly, the bishop found that there was no substance in them and the College was cleared. The row was embarrassing and with a former master providing evidence it seemed to confirm Protestant fears about Woodard's schools. Lancing's historian attributes a check in its growth to the

---

[1] His name is frequently mis-spelt Hewitt. The spelling that he used was Hewett.

publicity given to Hewett's accusation, which, he claims, was brought out of spite. Perhaps this overstates the importance of Hewett's ill-conceived action, though certainly the young man displayed both impulsive thoughtlessness and a singular obstinacy. On the other hand the experience did not destroy his determination and enthusiasm to promote the Anglo-Catholic cause in education, and since on his own telling he was a competent teacher he decided that in future he would have to take the risks and do it his own way.

In January 1853 the new Anglo-Catholic vicar of Bloxham, the Revd J. Hodgson, appointed Hewett as his curate. The large north Oxfordshire village stands on the hilly banks of a brook, about three miles south-west of Banbury, its brown stone farms and cottages dominated by the tall and slender spire of its fourteenth-century parish church. In the mid nineteenth century the parish had a population of about 1,350, chiefly farmers and country tradesmen living in the village with its web of narrow lanes and in the smaller hamlet of Milcombe, a little over a mile farther south-west. As curate Hewett was chiefly responsible for Milcombe, where stood a small dilapidated medieval chapel. He received a stipend of only £34 a year, but gave the impression of having considerable private means as well as good expectations on the death of his mother. He took up residence in the vicarage, opposite the church, and there in February 1853 he began a small school.

By the end of the summer he had worked out **optimistic plans for the** enlargement and proper establishment of his school, **now boldly named** All Saints' Grammar School, stating in his first prospectus that 'This School is designed, under God's blessing, for the liberal Education of the Sons of the Clergy, Naval, Military and Professional Men, and others'. The school was to comprise 100 commoners, 40 scholars and an unspecified number of choristers, with a staff of twelve graduates teaching a traditional curriculum of theology, classics, mathematics, history and geography, writing and drawing, French and singing. The year was divided into four quarterly terms with five-week holidays at midsummer and Christmas, the fees for a commoner being £40 a year, an excessively high figure compared with Lancing at 30 guineas and Hurstpierpoint at 18 guineas. The fees for commoners were increased in 1856 to 50 guineas a year, but in practice it is likely that many of the boys paid the reduced fee of 25 guineas as choristers. Scholarships, of which two were given at the school gaudy in 1853, were worth £20 each. By these rather high fees Hewett hoped to make sufficient profit to pay for the acquisition of a site and cost of buildings, and in his advertisement of 12 September 1853 he also appealed for benefactions.

A month later, following Woodard's example of calling public meetings and seeking good publicity, Hewett issued invitations for his first school gaudy. Considering that he had few pupils — and in 1907 an Old Boy, Admiral Sir Gerard Noel, K.C.B., recalled in a prize-day speech at Bloxham that in 1854 it 'was then a very small school' — it was an ambitious programme. The day started with holy communion in the parish church at 8 a.m., followed by breakfast for the visitors and the admission of two boys to scholarships. At 11 a.m. there was morning service in the church, the clergy being asked to wear surplice, stole and

4

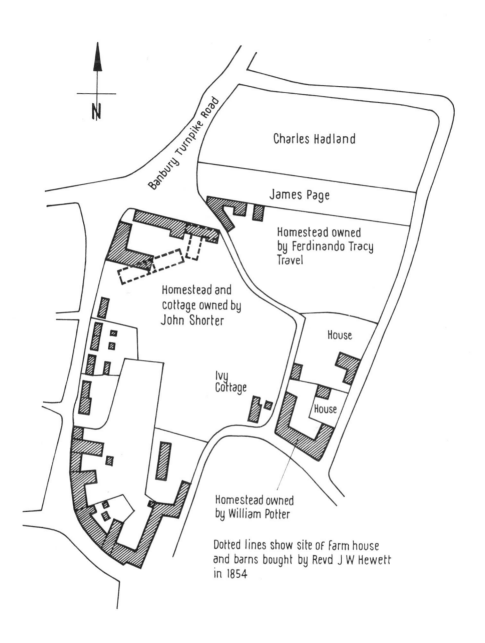

Charles Hadland

James Page

Homestead owned
by Ferdinando Tracy
Travel

Homestead and
cottage owned by
John Shorter

House

Ivy
Cottage

House

Homestead owned
by William Potter

Dotted lines show site of farm house
and barns bought by Revd J W Hewett
in 1854

Banbury Turnpike Road

BLOXHAM IN 1802

5

hood, with a lunch for first the visitors and then the parish choir. Significantly the date of the gaudy was 1 November. Already Hewett had firmly fixed on All Saintstide as the principal school festival.

The death of his mother in July 1854 came fortuitously for Hewett's plans. He inherited £2,700, not a large sum, but the amount was probably not generally known and he continued to give the impression of possessing an ample private fortune. He now had enough ready cash to seek a site and start building his school, and his manner and his hopes inspired confidence. First, he paid £1,100 for a farmhouse and outbuildings on the northern edge of the village from Thomas and Hannah Barrett, and then in February 1855 he established a trust with the bishop of Oxford, Samuel Wilberforce, the archdeacon, Dr. C. C. Clerke, the rural dean, the Revd Edward Payne of Swalcliffe, and the vicar of Bloxham, the Revd James Hodgson, as trustees. The terms of the trust echo the earlier advertisement — 'to the intent and purpose that the same [property] may be applied as and for a Grammar School for the liberal education, in the principles of the Catholic and Apostolic branch of Christ's Church now established in this Kingdom — of the Sons of the Poorer Clergy and Gentry, Naval, Military and professional Men and others'. Hewett was prepared to give the school his furniture and large personal library, and assign to it his life insurance policies of £1,200.

The property, legally not a freehold one but copyhold of the manors of Bloxham Fiennes and Bloxham Beauchamp, consisted of the farmhouse built within the previous fifty years, which was later the headmaster's house and still stands in the heart of the school buildings, with a miscellaneous range of outbuildings to its north-east. Hewett immediately designated the farmhouse as the master's residence and, true to his ideals, allocated a site for a chapel. Probably on the recommendation of bishop Wilberforce, who was enthusiastic for the school, the diocesan architect, G. E. Street, an eminent Victorian architect much favoured by High Churchmen, was engaged to draw up plans for the school, the first of a series of commissions that he carried out in the neighbourhood. Copies of the 'Anastatic View' of Street's proposed buildings survive among the school's archives and with a description of the proposals in the *Banbury Guardian* give a good idea of Hewett's ambitions and Street's design for 'one of the most beautiful modern Gothic buildings ever devoted in England to a scholastic purpose'.

In place of the old farmhouse Street planned two cloistered quadrangles with ranges of tall stone buildings. An imposing college gateway faced north, leading on the left to the chapel and on the right to the larger quadrangle containing the only part to be built according to the original plan (later named Wilberforce house). Around this quadrangle were spread the other buildings, a hall, two big schoolrooms in the traditional style, library, museum, common room, oratory, singing school, VIth-form rooms and six dormitories. The chapel, to which Street's 1871 building bears some resemblance, was on one side of the smaller and more richly decorated quadrangle which was to enclose a burial ground.

In March Thomas Barrett contracted to pull down some of the outbuildings

6

and erect the first part of the new school at a cost of £2,000, and the scheme was sufficiently well advanced for the foundation stone to be laid amid a great three-day celebration on Thursday 7 June 1855. The festivities began with evensong on the Wednesday when Hewett preached, and reached their climax on Thursday when bishop Wilberforce, after preaching at holy communion in the parish church, went in procession down the village street to bless the foundation stone. The large and colourful procession of robed clergy and masters interspersed with banners — one with the school motto *Justorum semita lux splendens,* another with Hewett's motto, 'Be just and fear not',[2] and a third with the arms *argent a cross flory gules,* wound down the village to the platform on the site of the building. The bishop opened the ceremony,

'My brethren, you who have been with us in church know well the purposes we have in view in laying this first stone. You are aware that we desire to lay the foundation of a building which will be for God's glory and for the good of his Church . . . for the seed that may be sown here, by God's blessing, will undoubtedly be carried without these walls, so that those children who are taught in this place, the knowledge that they may here receive will unquestionably flow upon all that are round about them'.

Then in a cavity beneath the foundation stone were placed a bible, prayer book and service of office, with a brass plate over them inscribed *'Justorum semita lux splendens. Scholae Grammaticalis Omnium Sanctorum de Bloxham Fundamentum posuit Samuel Episcopus Oxoniensis, die vii mensis Junii. MDCCCLV'.* With a silver trowel the bishop laid the stone with its three consecration crosses, saying,

'The School that shall be raised here is hereby dedicated to Almighty God; and in praise of his Holy Saints it is now called All Saints' Grammar School'.

The stone with its three consecration crosses can still be seen at the north-west corner of the building on the outer wall of the masters' common room.

There was a lunch in the temporary dining hall, where in view of the later history of the school it was extraordinarily prophetic of the bishop to remark that 'he trusted that the time might come that the ancient glory of William of Wykeham would descend upon that Grammar School'. The next day the builders were given a dinner at the Joiners' Arms and on the Saturday the village was invited to remember the occasion by the distribution of a dole of meat to the poor and a concert by the boys singing choruses from *Messiah* and entertaining light songs. The sale of tickets for these events, copies of Street's design, sermons and service sheets went towards the building fund.

With construction work begun, Hewett's school started to take its place in the life of the neighbourhood. The village Cottage Gardeners' Club held its first annual show in the school grounds, an English summer scene of marquee and country crowds, the Banbury town band and the flags of the allies in the Crimean

---

[2]This is the motto of the Hewitt family, Viscounts Lifford, from whose arms Hewett also took his crest of an owl, which he used on his notepaper. I have not been able to trace his connection, if any, with this Irish peerage family. The arms of a red cross on a white background displayed on the third banner are borne by various families with no connection with either Hewett or Bloxham, and would appear to have been of his own devising unauthorised by the College of Arms.

7

War. A few days later, on 21 September, the school played its first recorded cricket match against Magdalen College School at Banbury. Bloxham won by 58 and 47 runs to 34 and 34 runs.

As the building advanced Hewett incurred more expenditure, negotiating for the two adjoining cottages in the street to house assistant masters, together with a small orchard, buying furniture and engaging staff. By August 1855 his debt on the school amounted to £5,977 with very little income from fees. This was, of course, part of the risk in starting the venture, but it now began to become apparent that perhaps he did not have the ample private capital to carry the business through the inevitable heavy outlay of the first few years.

The new school, built of the tawny-coloured local Hornton stone with Bath stone dressings, was finished during the summer of 1856 and the builder, Barrett, who had underestimated the costs, started to press for payment of his first £1,000, as agreed, the second £1,000 being spread over the next three years. Hewett was £250 short and when he tried to borrow on the security of the school he discovered that because he had conveyed it to trustees he could not raise any money on it personally. The sum of £250 was not a large one to borrow, but this was not the limit of his needs and the news was spreading fast that he was in difficulties. In September he wrote to bishop Wilberforce, admitting that 'your Lordship bade me look carefully to money matters', and seeking a loan of £1,200 to £1,500. This would have been sufficient to pay Barrett, purchase the cottages which he had contracted to buy for £300, and clear some of his other debts. In reply, the bishop, restrained by his registrar, J. M. Davenport, merely advised mortgaging the school or raising small loans to pay off the creditors by instalments. The last device held off disaster a little longer while Hewett sought desperately for other means to ensure the school's survival even if he had to sacrifice himself. First he suggested cancelling the trust so that he could borrow on the security of the school before resettling it in a new trust, and when that was turned down by the bishop's legal advisers he offered to withdraw entirely so that he might be replaced by someone else 'to take up my School & make it what I designed it to be — the same to the poorer Clergy & Gentry as Radley & Bradfield are to the richer'.

His creditors would not wait for such manoeuvres. All autumn Barrett had been calling daily to demand his money and in December the Banbury traders were also pressing hard. On 20 February 1857 a meeting of creditors was held in Banbury at which it was reckoned that Hewett owed about £5,300, and on 27 February he filed his bankruptcy petition. The end was rapid, and proved even more disastrous than Hewett or his bishop had imagined. Within the week Hewett announced his intention of resigning at midsummer in the hope that a proprietary college with shareholders, like Cheltenham, would continue his school. Until then it had been assumed that it was Hewett who was insolvent, not his school which was the subject of the trust and therefore protected. Then at this critical stage the legal experts discovered fatal flaws in the trust deed which completely destroyed any chance of saving the school. Not only did an omission in the deed allow the sale of Hewett's furniture and books, but it was now proved that far from being as wealthy as everyone had been led to believe he was already insolvent when he signed the trust deed in 1855. The trust was therefore invalid and the creditors could obtain the property. On 19 March Hewett wrote again to the bishop to say that if the school were not continuing he must send the boys home and resign at Easter. With the creditors in unrelenting mood no one would save him. On Thursday 2 April he proposed dismissing the boys by Saturday, on which day the vicar, James Hodgson, wrote to Oxford that the boys were nearly all gone and the stragglers would have departed by Monday.

The trustees and creditors were now left to salvage what they could. Understandably Hodgson commented, 'I wish we had never had anything to do with it', but he went on to express a desire that the school should survive, fearing that it would otherwise fall into the hands of either Roman Catholics or Quakers. On the Sunday that the school actually closed Lewis Gilbertson of Jesus College, Oxford, a friend of one of the assistant masters, wrote to Nathaniel Woodard to tell him that Hewett would be glad to sell and had reckoned in his ever-optimistic way that it was worth £5,000. Later, in April Hodgson suggested that the trustees, on behalf of the creditors, should directly offer the school to Woodard and he himself wrote at least once to try to persuade him to accept it. This was the first of several occasions when the Corporation of SS. Mary and Nicolas College was given the opportunity to acquire Bloxham. The offer was refused.

The creditors' bailiff had seized Hewett's possessions, including his fine library and the school furniture, among which were some things belonging to the unfortunate assistant masters and boys. The particulars of their sale on 4-9 May reveal a little more evidence about the school. One of the outbuildings was used as a temporary chapel, furnished with an organ and silver gilt communion plate, including a chalice mounted with pearls and precious stones; the 42 kneeling mats and 25 surplices give an indication of the size of the school, which from other clues seems not to have risen above 30 boys. The dormitories contained 50 bedsteads and 80 blankets (not an over-generous provision for north Oxfordshire winters!), and the schoolroom had three thirteen-foot long writing desks. Hewett's library was that of a cultured country gentleman with a wide selection of antiquarian books, supplemented by the works of the Oxford Movement by Pusey, Keble and Newman. Woodard's *Public Schools for the Middle Classes* (1852) was on the shelves, and a good schoolmasterly collection on the classics, languages, mathematics and accountancy. The *Guardian* and *London Illustrated* afforded some lighter relief and there were also, according to its catalogue published in 1854, a few boys' story books.

The internal layout of the building is difficult to re-create owing to the extensive alterations since the 1850s.[3] It contained a porter's lodge with sitting room and bedroom, the fireplace of the former still plainly to be seen on the right hand side of the north entrance to the buildings until the modernisation of the entrance in 1977. On the ground floor was the school dining room and probably the singing room and some of the masters' quarters. Both of the upper floors

[3]Hewett's school building is now occupied by the masters' common room and Wilson house. Until 1962 it was known to earlier generations of Bloxhamists as Wilberforce house.

Hewett's school building of 1855 from the south-east.

contained a large dormitory which remained relatively unchanged as the Wilberforce house dormitories until 1962, each with a master's bedroom, clothes room and washing room adjoining. An indication of the up-to-date character of Street's design was the presence of three water-closets, then a rare feature even in large houses.

The farmhouse, used by Hewett for his own residence, also apparently had the rooms of the second master and French master, and its two kitchens must have supplied the school dining room, which was linked by a covered passage; this suggests that the present masters' dining room was originally the school one. The schoolroom was one of the outbuildings, like the chapel. In Lewis Gilbertson's letter in 1857 and in the particulars of the first proposed sale on 27 April 1859 there is reference to an unfinished chapel which is not mentioned in the particulars of the sale actually held on 15 September that year. Instead there appears an 'Unfinished portable building . . . admirably adapted for a Granary or Store Room' of brick and timber construction. The school also possessed the two cottages in the High Street used by the assistant masters, apparently sold at the April auction, part of the playing field area which was used as garden allotments, and some surrounding land which Hewett had planted with shrubs at the high cost of nearly £200. It is doubtful if any of these survive; the largest and oldest Bloxham tree is the wellingtonia on the headmaster's lawn planted by Egerton in 1863.

The school trustees recognised that the trust deed had been invalidated by Hewett's insolvency on its creation, but felt that they could not abandon the trust without the authority of a decree in chancery. Not until this was obtained in July 1858 were they able to put the school up for auction for the benefit of the patient creditors, chief of whom were Thomas Barrett, who claimed £1,614, later proved at £1,440, the architect, G. E. Street for £140, a Banbury bookseller for £150 and an Oxford tailor for £150. The village butcher (£220), baker (£80) and Hunt Edmunds, the Banbury brewers (£75 for beer) were also sufferers. The total claims amounted to about £6,000. On the credit side Hewett's assets were valued at £2,210, chiefly his life insurance policies, the cottages and land at Bloxham held in his own name and worth £590, and a house at Bishops Tawton near Barnstaple, which had presumably been his own home. Even after the auction the creditors could not expect much more than half their outstanding bills. As the trustees prepared to sell the school early in 1859 there was a renewed attempt to interest Woodard, holding out to him the prospect that Bloxham was the only private school surviving in the neighbourhood, except for an old-fashioned one in Banbury which could not compete with a rival on the Hurstpierpoint pattern 'provided the people around could overcome their extremely Protestant tendencies'. The Revd Edward Payne with three or four friends also considered reviving the school themselves, but nothing came of either proposal.

The venture totally ruined Hewett who 'went forth as literally bare as the bailiffs could wish'. Looking back on his failure he admitted, 'I was too sanguine. Too blindly sanguine. I ought to have known it was impossible. I ought to have known that no promise of success justified incurring debt, especially on so large a scale, or the involving friends, though I am sure I never reckoned that they would be losers by me'. Had his creditors been less swift to demand repayment, or had he drawn up the trust deed more carefully or completed its provisions more closely, his school might have survived. No doubt his financial worries, aggravated by family responsibilities following his marriage and the birth of his eldest child in 1856, contributed both to the bad relationship with his staff and irritability with the boys. The episode of the Friday fasting early in 1856 is an example of his lack of schoolmasterly understanding. He encouraged the boys to fast on Fridays when the food was 'good, nourishing and sufficient', but plain. The inevitable complaints were made and he abandoned the practice, preaching a sermon in which he confessed that the rule 'was one of great economy to the school . . . the recent changes in our weekly meal will increase the cost of our living by £20 a year' but went on to appeal for a voluntary abstinence so that the money saved might be given to charity.

Throughout he was obviously filled with high ideals and romantic ideas, but hopelessly lacked the business acumen to run a school successfully. Ever optimistic he had written to the bishop in September 1856 that the number of boys was slowly increasing, a more rapid expansion only being held back by local prejudice against his extreme brand of High Churchmanship. One boy had matriculated at Exeter College, Oxford, and an examiner's general report had been favourable. He had a large staff and would need no more for additional new boys, a statement which itself betrays his unbusinesslike approach in building up his staff too quickly. He was negotiating with the Revd H. C. Levander (later headmaster of the proprietary grammar school founded at Devizes in 1859 and of University College School, London, from 1866 to his death in 1884) to join his venture, and possibly he was right in his claim in 1862 that given the right partner the school could have been profitable enough to pay off its debts within four years. However, the later record of the school suggests that this, like his earlier statements, was over-optimistic.

Hewett never recovered from the Bloxham debacle. He moved to Ashby de la Zouche where he wrote a series of religious tracts, verses and antiquarian booklets and, to supplement his small income as a curate at Whitwick, he also continued to teach a few pupils. He seemed to attract misfortune. In 1862 his wife was ill and his eldest daughter had diphtheria so that his pupils were kept away. In one undated letter, probably of 1866 when he moved to Derbyshire, he wrote that his wife, four children and two pupils were all suffering from scarlatina, the epidemic resulting in heavy doctor's bills and driving away his other pupils. In 1870 he went to live in central London, and again had three of his children ill, and in 1875 he himself had been ill and was appealing for money to take a holiday. He died at Claybrook, Leicestershire, in 1886 at the age of 62.

His death was hardly noticed at Bloxham, receiving in *The Bloxhamist* a mere passing mention in the long obituary notice of his former vicar, James Hodgson, who by coincidence died the same week. Owing to the prejudices which had been aroused Egerton could not afford to have reminders of Bloxham's failure under Hewett, and not until 1907 did *The Bloxhamist* publish an appreciation of his work by one of his friends, the Revd W. D. Macray. Bloxham, however, owes its origin to him, together with its tradition as an Anglo-Catholic school. 'He had great enthusiasm but he had not some of the other qualities necessary for carrying out such a work', was Macray's verdict. 'In faith he gave literally his *all* and died poor, disheartened, and what the world would perhaps call a failure. In spite of all, however, the School *is* there and but for his devotion would never have been'.

Hewett chose its name and its motto, both of which are still in use. He chose and bought the site and erected there the first range of school buildings, in stone and built by one of the best Victorian architects. Still today it is the most prominent school building seen from the main road approaching the school, and most boys have entered the school for the first time through its doorway. For two and a half years it stood empty, damp and derelict while the lawyers wrangled over its future. This was the building which attracted the attention of Reginald Egerton and his fellow curate from Deddington one autumn morning in 1859.

CHAPTER II

P. R. EGERTON
THE YEARS OF RISK, 1859-64

The Egerton family lived at Adstock in Buckinghamshire as gentry and rectors of the parish for four successive generations in the sixteenth and seventeenth centuries before a junior branch became established as London merchants. Charles Egerton (1686-1747) and his son John (1724-89) were haberdashers, the latter being a freeman of the Company of Haberdashers of London. Among preferments in the gift of the Haberdashers' Company was that of preacher or lecturer at Bunbury in Cheshire, to which first John Egerton's son, John (1763-1847) and then the latter's nephew John (1796-1876) were appointed. This last John Egerton married Ellen Gould in 1828 and they had a large family of six boys and four girls, one son and two daughters dying in childhood. Their third son was Philip Reginald Egerton, born at Bunbury on 14 July 1832.

Through his grandmother Mary Coker, wife of the Revd Charles Egerton (1765-1845), Reginald Egerton, as he was always known to his family and friends, could trace descent from William of Wykeham, founder of Winchester College and New College, Oxford, and therefore had the right to enter Winchester as founder's kin. His elder brother, Charles C. Egerton, did so but Reginald won a scholarship. He was at Winchester from 1845 to 1850, becoming senior prefect, or head of the school, during the headmastership of George Moberly. Winchester had a profound and lasting influence on Reginald Egerton, and through him on Bloxham. It was at Winchester that he received his early training in the Anglo-Catholic beliefs of Dr Moberly, who was a friend of John Keble, by then vicar of nearby Hursley and his co-editor of *The Anglo-Catholic Library*. For years Bloxham boys sang the Winchester school song *Dulce domum* at the end-of-term concerts, and in the days before the adoption of generally recognised football rules Bloxham's 'were founded on Winchester and common sense'. More fundamental, Egerton resisted all early attempts to call him 'Founder'. Mindful that William of Wykeham had 'founded' Winchester in the sense of providing it with a foundation endowment he insisted that Bloxham was his private school with no future beyond that of his own active lifetime. Not until after he had successfully formed the school trust in 1884 did he allow himself to be called Founder, a title which he enjoyed and appreciated, writing sharply on one occasion in 1897 that he was not to be referred to in *The Bloxhamist* as 'the Revd P. R. Egerton' but as 'the Founder'. Indeed, the Winchester influence persisted an extraordinarily long time, for in 1951 the bursar of the Woodard Corporation claimed that there was still some resemblance to Winchester in the character of Bloxham.

About the time that he left Winchester in 1850 his parents moved from Bunbury to a large eighteenth-century house at Bexley in Kent called Vale

Mascal. In those days it had extensive park-like gardens with tennis and croquet lawns bounded by the river Cray with weirs and cascades where the children had a little canoe. With a butler and servants in the house, Reginald Egerton's home was that of a big and lively well-to-do clerical family. Their wealth apparently came through the Goulds on his mother's side, but Reginald as a third son among so many children could not expect to inherit any large share.

From Winchester he proceeded to New College in 1851, where he took the degree of bachelor of civil laws in 1857, and was subsequently, as a scholar transmitted from Winchester and so long as he remained unmarried, elected to a fellowship worth £200, a useful source of income for a young man which did not require residence in college. His upbringing led naturally to the decision to be ordained and to this end he entered Cuddesdon theological college in 1855. Cuddesdon, near Oxford, had been founded by bishop Samuel Wilberforce only two years earlier and was the chief training ground of the second generation of Anglo-Catholic clergy. Its vice-principal was the Revd H. P. Liddon, an associate of Keble and Pusey and only three years older than Egerton. The two young men formed a lifelong friendship.

It was probably this personal friendship which led to Egerton's appointment by Wilberforce as one of the 'Cuddesdon curates' at Deddington, where he was licensed on the day of his ordination as a deacon, 20 December 1857. It was not the happiest place to work. Ever since the appointment in 1836 of the High Churchman, the Revd W. S. Risley (who was present at the laying of the school's foundation stone), the parish had been violently split between high and low church factions, heightened by the wretched behaviour of Risley's successor from 1848, the Revd James Brogden. The vicar's stipend was insufficient to support his large family and his drinking habits, and the living was soon sequestered to pay off his debts. Parishioners and bishop were powerless to get rid of him, but during his enforced absences the bishop appointed Anglo-Catholic curates to look after the divided parish. In 1857 Reginald Egerton and Ambrose Cave-Browne-Cave arrived in Deddington the same day, fresh from theological college, to join a third senior curate, the Revd John Burgess.

Egerton settled uneasily into life at Deddington. As a newly ordained young parson with high ideals he missed the support and advice available at Cuddesdon, and in the loneliness of parish life was intensely introspective and self-critical. The two new curates confided in each other, aggravating their spiritual worries until Egerton seriously doubted whether he had been right either to enter the ministry or to serve the unresponsive country people of Hempton and their newly-built church for which he was particularly responsible. His bishop gave him some reassurance before ordaining him priest in 1859 and Liddon was constant in his comfort and advice. Soon after his arrival at Deddington, for instance, Egerton considered becoming a missionary in Australia, a choice which Liddon strongly urged him to postpone for at least three years. However, when his absentee vicar announced his intention to return to the parish, which he did in November 1859, Egerton again seriously considered going overseas to New Zealand. That he did not do so was partly due to the advice of Father A. H. Mackonochie, who reminded him that there was a need for work at home as well as in the colonies, offering him a post with the East London mission. He declined this offer and a similar curacy at All Saints, Margaret Street, London, but he had no prospects when he and Cave-Browne-Cave, the son of a baronet who in 1860 became rector of Stretton-en-le-Field, Leicestershire, decided to walk into Banbury to see the vicar there on Monday 12 September 1859.

According to the Founder it was Cave-Browne-Cave who suggested returning home by way of Bloxham village, and that this was the first occasion that he saw the school building. It is hard to credit, however, that the Deddington curates had not heard tales of Hewett's venture or were unaware that the building was about to be auctioned a few days later. It seems that Cave-Brown-Cave was the more curious and, having obtained the keys and viewed the building, the more enthusiastic about it, pressing Egerton to take on the school. By the time that they had walked the last four miles back to Deddington Egerton was converted to the idea. He wasted little time, instructing his solicitor to attend the sale on the following Thursday, when Thomas Barrett bought the buildings for £1,500, then negotiating his purchase from Barrett on the Saturday for £1,615, and arranging a mortgage. There then ensued a wait while the legal formalities were concluded. It was a nerve-racking two or three months and not surprisingly he wondered whether he had done the right thing. The reaction of those from whom he sought advice and encouragement, like his bishop, the warden of New College, the headmaster of Winchester and Nathaniel Woodard, can have done little to reassure him.

His first action a fortnight after the auction had been to introduce himself to Woodard by writing for advice and to ask whether he might stay at Hurstpierpoint to gain first-hand experience of Woodard's system and how to run a similar school. The visit was quickly arranged and Egerton spent the next two or three weeks there with Dr E. C. Lowe, its first headmaster who had been with Woodard from the beginning at Shoreham. Lowe was greatly impressed and his description of Egerton to Woodard is testimony of the very remarkable character of Bloxham's Founder.

'I have seldom made the acquaintance of a more agreeable person. His honestness & his simplicity of character, together with his resolution & desire to do just what is right make him a very promising adherent. He seems to have great manliness of mind — with fixed ideas of his own — tho' not an intellectual man. He has been a great leader in all active sports & games including boxing, tho' he has given them all up. He has great gravity of character, with abundance of humour & cheerfulness, when the first acquaintance has been made'.

Lowe was not alone in his high opinion for the Revd Edward Payne of Swalcliffe, a man apparently not given to over-enthusiasm, also provided Woodard with a good report, adding that Egerton had the financial backing of his father 'and the cooperation of an extremely well disposed and cautious Solicitor of Deddington'; this was H. Churchill, who later sent his sons to the

Revd Philip Reginald Egerton, about 1870.

school.

Egerton's rising hopes were dashed by Woodard. His promised interview was put off although Woodard, despite his prejudice against Hewett and all his works, did come to look at Bloxham on 1 December. His verdict was swift and blunt.

'I have just returned from Bloxham and Swalecliffe, and after a personal inspection I have no hesitation in advising you not to purchase the buildings if you have not done so already'.

His own formula for success, which he passed on to Egerton, was to use his money instead to buy a site of 25 to 50 acres within a mile or so of a railway station and to start modestly with half a dozen pupils in a small cottage. It was sound advice and twenty years later, when the two were again corresponding about Bloxham joining the Woodard Corporation, Woodard reiterated that Bloxham's site was too limited. More recent headmasters and school Councils would agree that the layout of the buildings and playing fields has been hampered by the school's position, a defect shared with other public schools situated in

16

towns or villages, especially those which developed from ancient grammar school foundations. It was a handicap which Woodard himself took care to avoid whenever he had the choice of a new site. What he did not appreciate in Bloxham's case was Egerton's overwhelming sense of vocation — that it was not a matter of choosing a site for a school, any more than it was a matter of choosing to be a schoolmaster. 'The fact is', he replied to Woodard, 'that my only reason for giving up parochial work or missionary work wh: I had looked forward to, was the preserving of these buildings at Bloxham to the service of our Church. Had it not been for this I should never have entertained the idea of school work at all'.

Egerton evidently met Woodard briefly before his return to Shoreham and impressed the more experienced man so much that he wrote a more heartening letter two days later, saying that he did not wish to dampen his zeal if he were already committed and, although he could not risk a loss, he might consider transfer to the Corporation if Oxford diocese would put up the purchase money. By the same post he wrote more frankly to Liddon that either the diocese should give the building, in which case he would be glad to have Egerton join the Corporation, or his friends should urge him to pay the penalty and get out of the bargain. 'Mr. Egerton's fervent zeal & excellent spirit deserve a better fate . . . I wish I had *fifty* such men as he to work in our Society'.

The suggestion that Oxford diocese might promote the school was a practical development of the scheme of Woodard and other churchmen that there should be a church secondary school in every diocese, just as there was a church primary school in many parishes. Bishop Wilberforce had been officially connected with the Hewett school and disappointed at its failure, though helpless personally to do anything about it. Egerton consulted him soon after buying the buildings and received rather lukewarm congratulations for his courage in taking the risk. The bishop was not going to be stampeded by a second enthusiastic and impoverished curate and made it quite clear that the diocese would not purchase Bloxham in order to give it to Woodard. He merely promised his goodwill. Later, when Egerton had shown by his determination and sensible start that Bloxham could be soundly established, the bishop gave him much good advice and practical encouragement.

With the lack of financial support from the diocese and with Woodard keeping firmly to his conditions for acceptance further negotiations were pointless and Egerton broke them off, expressing his deep disappointment and fear that it was madness to go on against Woodard's experienced advice and criticism. However, the purchase legally had to be completed and there was little likelihood of successfully disposing of the school buildings again so soon, so he had no choice but to persevere. Despite his despair at Woodard's rejection of his proposals, made the greater because they had been earlier so favourably received and advocated by Dr Lowe, the failure of the negotiations cleared away his final hesitation. Bloxham was his and his alone. There were friendly and experienced churchmen to offer him advice and watch his progress with sympathetic interest but he could only depend on himself. He set out with determination to spread the news of his intentions.

Some idea of his original aims for the school may be gathered from his first advertisement, in which he announced that it would be opened on 31 January 1860 'as a Grammar School, for the Education of the Sons of Tradesmen, Farmers, Clerks, and others of the Middle Classes', and that 'It will be called "All Saints School" henceforth, as of old'. His plans were set out at greater length in a letter on 28 December 1859, probably addressed to the Revd Edward Steere, rector of Little Steeping, Lincolnshire, a member of the Anglo-Catholic guild of St Alban and later a bishop in Central Africa. Following Woodard's example he hoped to form 'a brotherhood of men who shall devote themselves to this one object, the thorough and religious education of the Middle Classes'. The notion of a collegiate brotherhood of clergy was even less successful at Bloxham than at Shoreham and the school has never had a collegiate constitution or character, lay or clerical. Quite correctly, therefore, proposals in 1911 and 1951 to re-name it "Bloxham College" were not pursued.

In his second and more important aim Egerton never wavered in his intention to provide a public school type of education for middle-class boys who would normally go straight into business on leaving school. Again and again he repeated this. Towards the end of his time at Bloxham, for example, he wrote, 'The only object I have had in carrying on this school is the Education of boys of the Middle Classes in the Catholic (in the old & true meaning of the word) principles of the Church of England', although in his farewell speech as headmaster he revealed a change of outlook of a most un-Victorian character. Replying to Earl Beauchamp when presenting him with his portrait, he said, 'His lordship referred to the school as one for the middle classes. He (Mr Egerton) had a great objection to talk about classes, and instead of calling the school a middle-class school, he termed it a secondary school'. However, earlier statements are a better guide to his thoughts at the beginning, and two more may be quoted. To Coker Adams of New College he wrote, 'the school is not intended to prepare boys for the Universities — but for going straight out into the business of life after leaving school'; and similarly to a parent, 'I began the school with the simple desire of supplying a need, which I was convinced the ordinary commercial schools could not do — I desired in my little degree to communicate to others the advantages which I myself felt I had received at a Public School'.

So, on 31 January 1860, Reginald Egerton received his first pupil. He was William Pearce, son of a local farmer, who stayed with him for two years. A fortnight later, as he loved to relate, he doubled his numbers. Pearce was joined by Arthur Hodgson, eldest son of the vicar of Bloxham — a singular mark of confidence considering the disappointment and disillusionment that the vicar had already experienced over Hewett's school; later, he sent another son. After Easter, on 4 April 1860 the first boarders arrived, C. J. Wilson and T. M. Evans, both from Haunton near Tamworth, Staffordshire, and Herbert Flower from Wiltshire, together with two more day boys. In later years Wilson used to describe his arrival. How, like many a new boy, he arrived with his father at Banbury station, and with his spirits sinking ever lower they made the journey to

Bloxham by road, in those days by one-horse wagonette. How frightened he was of meeting the other boys, and how when he arrived he was amazed to find no other boys, for the two day boys who made up the school had gone home! In reply to a friendly enquiry from Woodard, Egerton wrote cheerfully, 'I re-open today or I might almost say "begin", for I have had no boarders till now — two have arrived this morning — & I expect another before night. These three with three day-boys make a real beginning. I hear of many others who are inquiring, & I expect perhaps a dozen after this next Quarter'.

The boarders slept in the former farmhouse, not in the school building which 'they looked upon as a playground by day and a place of mystery by night'. In those days the farmhouse had a central door leading into a passage. On one side was a sitting room, on the other the schoolroom, but that first winter Egerton used just the one room, damp and sparsely furnished with only coconut matting, a trestle table, school desk and six cane-seated chairs. Upstairs he furnished in a similar spartan manner one bedroom for himself, and others for the boys and his Deddington housekeeper, Mrs Bliss. The little school grew. Fourteen boys entered that first year; by November 1861 there were 29 and in early 1863 there were 50. Further growth was limited by the buildings which could only accommodate 60 boys.

The establishment and administration of a school is a complex and costly business. It was disregard for a sound business base which had caused Hewett's failure, but Egerton was of a very different disposition. His notebooks and accounts, written with an old-fashioned swan quill rather than the Victorian steel nib, reveal his meticulous and methodical interest in financial affairs. Like Hewett he had few private resources, the £200 New College fellowship being the most valuable, but, as he told Woodard, he reckoned that he could survive two years even if he had no pupils at all. He bought the school with the aid of a mortgage of £1,000 and loans of £800 from relatives and friends, chiefly his father but including £100 from Ambrose Cave-Browne-Cave. He kept the fees low, only £25 4s. 0d. for boarders and six guineas for day boys, so that whereas Hewett had barely 30 boys after four years, Egerton had double that number. And although in those first three or four years the school was not constantly paying its way, at least every year his own gross income exceeded his expenditure by a small margin, his house was furnished and his own household supplied. In comparing his income with that of a parson in a benefice of £400 he reckoned that he was better off. He advanced cautiously, scrapping Hewett's grandiose building plans for much more modest proposals as and when the need arose. Finally, he had the wisdom to ask for advice, and take it.

In this Lowe and the Revd C. H. Lomax, an assistant master at Hurstpierpoint, were generous and practical, and Egerton owed much to their help. The long letters from Lomax ranged over every conceivable topic from the choice and price of joints of meat — 'Pork I think is not always proper for boys as it often gives them the belly ache' — to furnishing the former cowshed as a small temporary chapel. He warned Egerton about the ways of cooks, advising 'Ask your housekeeper to tell you the least she can do with, then make her give up one

Egerton's original buildings, 1863. From the left are the farm house, the barn (formerly Hewett's schoolroom) and the cowshed used as a chapel by Egerton. Behind is Hewett's 1855 school building.

third'. A typical week's menu was roast beef and plum pudding on Sunday; cold beef and suet dumpling on Monday; roast mutton and treacle roll on Tuesday; meat pie on Wednesday; boiled beef on Thursday; soup and bread and cheese on Friday; meat pudding on Saturday; on days without pudding a second helping of meat was given. Breakfast and tea were based on a diet of bread and watered milk. Plain white crockery and simple furniture made by the village carpenter would have been used, and the school lit by common tallow dips.

On the academic side Lomax gave the Hurstpierpoint timetable as an example:

Monday, Tuesday, Wednesday, Friday		Thursday, Saturday
6.30	Rise	
	Prayers	
	Latin exercises gone through	Euclid
7.30	Breakfast	
8.00-9.00	No regular school: singing, drawing, drilling	
9.00-9.45	Chapel	

9.45-10.45	Divinity	
10.15-11.15	Latin, prepared beforehand	English
11.15-12.15	Arithmetic	Book-keeping, arithmetic, algebra, Euclid

1.00	Dinner
2.30-3.30	French
3.30-4.15	Writing and mapping
4.15-5.00	History/Geography alternately

He helpfully added a long list of school text books and the shrewd comment, 'Of course you must sell your own stationery as a shop keeper, making a profit of say nearly 25 per cent'. Further similar letters followed this first one written on 3 January before the school was opened, and Egerton sent his bills to Lomax for scrutiny. Everything seemed to be going reasonably well in those early months. The main problem was to enlarge the number of boys in preference to raising the fees, and Lomax advised judicious advertisement not locally, which should be unnecessary, but in the Birmingham press or *The Times*. The activity and pressure of business kept Egerton fully occupied. His introspective spiritual worries and doubts were submerged to such an extent that when he did write a confessional letter to Liddon in August 1861 the latter was anxious for him on new grounds. 'I wish that your work was of a less secular cast: it is a great evil to be so much engrossed as we are by serving tables. You must make every opportunity of getting at the souls of your boys'.

There was little need for such a caution. Although he had been surprised and reluctant to recognise his calling — to become a schoolmaster rather than a missionary in the colonies or London slums — his purpose was clear, as he reminded his old boys in 1880. 'He was not satisfied, however, if the result of his labours was only the production of an *esprit de corps,* or a kind regard for him or affection for the place, for his aim had been to make them love their religion, as he had striven to teach it in the true spirit of the Church of England.' His first prospectuses did not stress this purpose, perhaps to emphasise the distinction from Hewett's school, but the letters of good will from Anglo-Catholic clergy show where his loyalties lay.

Egerton's own interpretation of Church of England doctrines closely adhered to early Anglo-Catholic practices, still suspect in mid-Victorian times, underlining the links between the Anglican church and the catholic church stemming from its universal Christian origins, keeping strictly to the disregarded rubric of the book of common prayer with its emphasis on the central importance of the holy communion within a setting of discipline, exhortation and proper preparation, including confession. Egerton himself, we are told, was no ceremonialist, but he did stand firm in favour of that most controversial Anglo-Catholic practice, confession before communion and especially before confirmation. Much of the public controversy centred round the dispute whether confession should be regular and systematic or reserved for rare and extraordinary circumstances. In 1869 a Mr Baxter brought a complaint about confession at Bloxham to the notice of the bishop, who ruled that Egerton was to secure parental approval. Like Hewett he learnt that his principles aroused local prejudice against Bloxham. In the *Banbury Guardian* an anonymous correspondent in 1869-70 attacked the school's practice of genuflexion to the altar and went on to criticise the vicar of Bloxham and the bishop for the 'strange dramatic performances' in the parish church. The names of two members of the staff who heard confessions were placarded with abusive threats on every hoarding in north Oxfordshire in one campaign in the 1870s, and a local squire withdrew a divinity prize because 'he could not approve of our religious teaching'. Egerton was unyielding. To the bishop he defended himself vigorously, concluding, 'In submitting thus to your Lordship's guidance, I cannot but say that it is *only* out of deference to your Spiritual Authority that I do it'. He told Canon Woodard that he would rather go on alone than sacrifice his principles in order to give Bloxham a wider appeal, and he refused to accept the resignation of the two masters who thought that their departure might save him embarassment. On that occasion his only action was to deliver one of his most eloquent sermons in chapel, explaining and justifying his beliefs to the boys.

In fact, he rarely preached in chapel and was not a good preacher. Some 70 of his sermons survive to show that he was for Victorian times refreshingly brief: most would have lasted ten to twenty minutes. In addition to the time spent in chapel, however, much class time was devoted to religious instruction (as in the Hurstpierpoint timetable already quoted), and in the late 1860s each form had four one-hour periods of divinity a week. Egerton shared these classes with his chaplain, although his formal teaching was apparently no better than his preaching.

Where he made the lasting impression on his boys was in the example of his personal life. Dignified and handsome, supremely courteous, upright and honest, no one had either the wish or the audacity to do anything that would hurt him. He trusted the boys absolutely and never doubted their word, for which he earned their unqualified respect. A reproachful look by the Founder was enough to make a boy horribly aware of guilt and betrayal: an accusation of favouritism in 1862 brought an apology from the head of the school on behalf of all the boys, to which Egerton wrote a fittingly serious and appreciative reply. He disliked corporal punishment intensely, and clamped down on its abuse by other masters. In the early days he laid down a rule that all punishment was to be inflicted by himself alone, and although he used the cane on hand or 'another part of the body' he thought that it was brutal and unnecessary for discipline and the need to use the cane made him unhappy for days afterwards. As the school grew in size it was less easy to exercise such tight control, but in 1872 he announced to his staff that he was going to abolish the cane and all forms of corporal punishment by any master below the second division; instead, they were to make use again of impositions and entries in the punishment book. His gentle manner did not mean that he was in any way a weak person. He could be forthright and determined. He was a good and active sportsman, and had a great sense of fun, thoroughly enjoying the end-of-term concerts and Old Bloxhamist dinners when he was regularly called on to sing favourite songs, being described as the greatest boy of them all. Clearly he was an outstanding man of exceptional character. His outward display of Christian faith, grace and humility inspired many of the boys that he taught, few of whom were aware of his internal battles with his own conscience.

Throughout those early years he needed frequent reassurance and encouragement. Once he was committed to Bloxham, Woodard and his colleagues had supplied that encouragement in the first decisive weeks. Then in November 1861 he received an unexpected accolade. Woodard had called a public meeting in Oxford to gain support for the proposed new buildings at Ardingly for St Saviour's school, Shoreham. Egerton went and, writing excitedly to his mother afterwards, described the meeting.

'To my surprise I found that Bloxham & myself were better known than I had ever imagined. It appears that some or rather many of the Clergy of the Diocese had rather objected to Mr. Woodard's coming to Oxford for this meeting for fear it should prejudice work wh: was already going on in the Diocese — & my school was especially mentioned.

It appears indeed that letters had passed between some of these clergy & the Bishop & Mr. Gladstone, so that when the speaking began it seemed necessary for the speakers to make a kind of explanation & to say that no disparagement was intended of works already begun in other Dioceses (& indeed Mr. Woodard has no present intention of invading the Diocese but only wants funds for that particular school of his).

Imagine my confusion (for I was present of course) when Mr. Gladstone ended up a long sentence, which I felt was getting strangely personal, with my name — The way in wh: the words were received by the audience, was very gratifying as shewing me that tho' I had not imagined it — the school was more widely known than merely among my own friends.

The Bishop of Oxford alluded also to Bloxham in his speech — so altogether I was so encouraged by the meeting & its results, that I really do believe now that if I can get a scheme which has been running in my head, got into actual tangible practical shape — I shall be able to get it taken up heartily & effectually'.

Gladstone, then chancellor of the exchequer, was indeed warm in his recommendation of Egerton. As M.P. for Oxford University he proposed the motion supporting middle-class education and Woodard's venture, but reminded his audience,

'It is not to claim for Mr. Woodard either exclusive credit or exclusive support. We are bound in justice to recollect that others, too, have conceived the happy idea of which he has become so prominent and so powerful a champion. Others remaining, perhaps, in the shade — labouring within narrower spheres, less happy in their opportunities of addressing themselves to the country at large — have nevertheless confronted the difficulties and perceived and realised the advantages of this important scheme of what may be called middle-class education. In Oxford particularly it would not be just that we should even commend, encourage, and assist Mr. Woodard without remembering that in this diocese itself there are examples of the most noble self-sacrifice, the most wise and early forethought. When I speak of self-sacrifice, I need only refer to the name of a particular clergyman, Mr. Egerton'.

However, Egerton continued to be worried, his anxieties about taking Bloxham and its precarious financial balance being aggravated by fresh worries about marriage. The difficulties there were twofold. He was in love with his cousin, Harriet Gould, daughter of Nathaniel Gould of Tavistock Square, London, but was concerned that they were too closely related for marriage. Bishop Wilberforce had ruled firmly in 1860 that there was no legal impediment and Liddon urged a short engagement, but now Harriet's wealthy father added to Egerton's hesitation by questioning his prospects. The young man poured out his troubles to his bishop, wondering whether to give up Bloxham entirely. Again, the bishop was decisive, applauding his solitary decision to start the school and pointing out that 'even as a matter of mere worldly prudence I think it would be a great mistake — you would by it throw yourself back into the mere common mass of Curates, whereas you now stand on a vantage ground few can reach'. Wilberforce thought that a married headmaster would be good for the school, and hinted that it might benefit from the Gould family wealth. Whether or not Egerton showed his uncle this letter, as the bishop suggested he should, the wedding duly took place on 4 November 1862.

The author of the first school *History,* writing from much nearer these events, says,

'Henceforth, it must be remembered, though it does not always appear on the surface, that Mr. Egerton was never alone in his work. From first to last Mrs. Egerton was entirely one with him in all he did. If sympathy and encouragement were needed, she was there to supply it; if a woman's influence could be helpful, hers was always at his service; if means were wanted, he was always welcome to what she had — for it must not be forgotten that while Mr. Egerton gave liberally of his energy and ability, she gave equally generously of her substance to the work they both had at heart. Mr. Egerton himself said on one occasion, "I could not have gone through the work of the last seven years without the loving help and support of my wife"'.

Egerton's worries were by no means over, and he sometimes revealed them to others — to bishop Wilberforce in the spring of the next year when he was considering the need to enlarge the school, and in that summer to a parent, Mrs. Davis of Abingdon, he wrote, 'I began with every conceivable thing against me, but with a bold heart (which has however begun to fail me)'. But there do not survive any more of those self-critical and doubting letters, such as those with which he had bombarded Liddon earlier, and now his anxieties were more for his school than for himself. It must be supposed that Harriet Egerton gave him the strength he needed, and soon they had the interest and joy of the birth of a daughter, Ellen, on 23 September 1863. Unfortunately, Harriet Egerton was slow

Harriet Egerton, about 1870.

to recover from childbirth and was still unwell twelve months later, and there were no further children.

The extent of Mrs Egerton's influence has probably been underestimated. As has been said, the Founder faced many difficulties which on occasions severely depressed him. In the early years these worries concerned the wisdom of his action in taking on the school and anxiety for its success. Later, he had recurrent fears for its future. Throughout, the finances of the school were insecure. His wife undoubtedly was a source of comfort and inspiration, and for about twenty years took a direct personal interest in the boys, some of whom later testified to her kindness. Others who came later, scarcely knew her, and it seems that as the school grew larger she had less contact with individual boys. An indication of her modesty is revealed in a letter to C. J. Wilson in 1887 on the presentation of her portrait, which now hangs in the dining hall. 'I never as yet have asked for a holiday of any sort for the school I believe — and this seems a fitting occasion, at the end of a quarter of a century in connection with the School — and I am sure the Warden will not object to grant a half holiday at my request'. Equally unobtrusive was her generosity and that of her sisters in contributing large sums of money towards the cost of the school buildings. Egerton expressed the wish that their names jointly should be remembered as founders and benefactors.

Despite her close interest, Mrs Egerton did not preside over the domestic affairs of the school. By November 1860 Mrs Bliss of Deddington had been replaced by Miss Arkell as housekeeper and matron at a salary of about £20 a year, with responsibility for the household and the two servant girls. The servants, advised H. Stevens, the Bloxham butler, should be strangers and not from the village, to avoid gossip. Elizabeth Arkell, known to the boys as "Mother", was the first of a series of outstanding school matrons. When after fourteen years at the school she died in 1875 Egerton recalled her devotion and ability in caring for a family which grew from seven to 180 boarders. Her obituary in the *Church Times* recorded furthermore that 'her influence was not merely that of a Matron, but she strained every nerve to assist in the promotion of the object for which the School was founded'.

When she came to Bloxham the household was small indeed — the headmaster, seven boys as boarders and, as the numbers slowly grew, the first servants and assistant masters. Egerton was inexperienced in choosing staff as in other matters of running a school and received both advice and practical help in interviewing from his friend Lomax. Much of the advice was sound — to choose men younger than himself and not to appoint someone however well qualified unless they impressed him personally at interview — and Egerton was becoming self-confident enough to ignore some of Lomax's views. Do not have a French or German master, he warned, 'They are such complete cads in general'. But in the 1863 prospectus there appears the name of Herr Stuhlmann, the first of a line of native German and French masters appointed by Egerton, an enlightened policy not continued by his successors. The other staff recorded in that prospectus were the Revd W. J. Panckridge, a Cambridge graduate described somewhat forbiddingly in the *History* as 'a fine specimen of muscular Christianity, who taught Euclid *vi et armis,* but was the most genial of men'; Samuel Blacker, who had trained as a teacher at Culham Training College, and F. H. Capner, the music master. Despite remarks in the *History,* the evidence suggests that some of Egerton's early inexperienced selections of staff were not too successful. A large proportion stayed for only a very short time, perhaps because the advertisements attracted young men preparing to be ordained, and there were other difficulties. Lomax sympathised over the inefficiency of assistant masters.

By early 1863 Egerton was ready to look ahead. Newly married, his own life was more settled, and with 50 boys the school seemed safely established, so that although financially it was not yet self-supporting the risk was almost over. It had, however, reached the limit of its growth in the existing buildings, and there was the double problem of how to finance an extension, and how to secure its permanence in the event of his own withdrawal or death. Accordingly he sought the advice of bishop Wilberforce.

The urgent need was more accommodation and Egerton listed as 'Immediately necessary priorities', a new block containing a schoolroom for 150 boys, with master's room, bathrooms and dormitories above for 120 boarders, thus trebling the size of the school and greatly improving the living conditions. An indication of overcrowding that some parents may have feared is revealed in the 1863 prospectus, which boasted 'Every boy has a separate bed', but the justification for improvements was underlined by two scarlatina epidemics in the autumns of 1862 and 1863 — one of the commonest but most feared school diseases usually attributed to poor sanitation. In the second priority of 'Necessary at some future time' was a dining hall and smaller dormitory, a chapel, and a house for the headmaster. The latter was too small for its purpose and was due to be demolished to complete Street's original plan, but has nevertheless survived a century of alterations and development around it.

Hewett's grandiose scheme was abandoned by Egerton, but Street produced an alternative design for the schoolroom block, estimated to cost roughly £2,000. With £1,800 already owed on mortgage and to friends Egerton was unwilling to increase his debt for this would mean borrowing up to £5,000 on buildings which were only of value as a school, and therefore unsafe as a security. Either he could try to raise the sum by subscription or hand the school over to diocesan trustees. Despite the obvious advantages of such a trust, which would relieve him of sole responsibility and liability, he was not prepared to surrender control. He was enjoying his freedom and thought that a trust would be less efficient. It was also a point of pride that he did not want to give up personal control until the school was proved to be both self-supporting and useful, writing to the bishop, 'I trust I shall not through anxiety, & a kind of weariness give up all into other hands before I am quite satisfied that it will be for some real permanent good'.

At this vital moment when the future of the school depended entirely on raising money for its growth, the influence and support of bishop Wilberforce was decisive. He arranged for a loan of £1,500 without interest or time limit for repayment as long as Bloxham remained a church school, the money being lent by wealthy county landowners, C. Langston of Sarsden House near Chipping Norton, J. G. Hubbard, later 1st Lord Addington, of Addington near Buckingham and the Duke of Marlborough. In fact, most of the money came from two large promises of £600 from the Langston estate, Mr Langston himself dying before the business was completed, and £750 from Lord Overstone. Of this amount £1,100 was required to buy the field (originally subdivided into three, with farm buildings) which was to become the main playing field together with a smaller plot of land and two cottages, but the balance of £400 was reckoned enough for the building to be started.

The new block, the first to be built by Egerton, was designed by Street to run at right angles at the east end of the original building, which had been left with a blank wall for such a purpose — for Hewett's proposed gateway and chapel extension. In style it was similar to the first part, of local Hornton stone with Victorian Gothic features of steep-pitched roof with crest tiles, gables and Decorated-style windows. The only architectural relief to the plain design was provided by the oriel window of the master's room and the severe buttresses on all sides. On the west was the staircase projection and a lean-to passage running to the headmaster's house, overlooked by a pair of windows in the schoolroom, a long, bleak eighteen-foot high room warmed by large fireplaces at each end. Old photographs show that in the old-fashioned early-nineteenth century way three

No. I or Crake senior dormitory, about 1890.

classes could be taught there at the same time, and a scholarly Old Bloxhamist recalled the time about 1870 'how when school commenced at 9 o'clock, the cane was placed remindingly on the master's desk: how all the boys did their lessons while toeing a chalk line on the floor', presumably when they brought their exercises up to the master, adding that the one invaluable thing that he learnt was how to work in the midst of a terrific row. The original desks remained in use until 1908 when the new floor was also laid down and lockers added, and although the south end was shortened when the chapel vestry was contrived, the schoolroom remained the communal living room for the junior school and was used for junior and middle school prep until the 1960s.

On the first floor were the master's rooms at the south end, first occupied by Panckridge (1863-65), and a new bathroom at the Banbury road end, with a temporary chapel between them. After the school chapel was built and with the school still growing in size, the temporary chapel became no. III dormitory, later known as Crake junior dormitory; an assistant master had a small bedroom at one end of the dormitory and the marks of the partition may still be made out on the beams. Above and running the full length of the block was the large 40-bed no. I dormitory, later Crake senior, with a long trestle of wash bowls down the centre and lit by little half-hour candles. Before going up to bed all the boys shook hands with the masters assembled below in the schoolroom. In the angle between the two blocks, where the porter's lodge had been situated, the main entrance of the school was given a porch with a steeply pitched roof, visible on a few late nineteenth-century photographs.

It is a matter for some speculation how at this stage Egerton and Street envisaged further development. The Hewett scheme had been cast aside in favour of more cautious and piecemeal expansion, and there is nothing in Egerton's correspondence and papers to indicate whether he was working towards an overall plan. His list of priorities suggests that he already had in mind to extend the dining hall wing from the west end of the original block, which had been designed to allow for it. The demolition of the old farmhouse was also among Egerton's ideas, and it is likely that in 1864 he thought that eventually the chapel would be built on its site in order to complete the inner quadrangle. Certainly the architect cannot have intended to build the chapel where it now stands, for he would not have given the master's oriel window such a gloomy outlook nor put south windows in the upper dormitory, one of which had to be blocked when the chapel was built; nor indeed would the laundry and other outbuildings have been built to cluster in ugly constraint at the east end of the chapel.

The new building went ahead rapidly during 1864 so that by September the invitation list for the official opening at All Saintstide could be prepared. Egerton again sought the opinion of Lowe of Hurstpierpoint and the character of the ceremony had a typical Woodard flavour. It was to be a prestigious occasion and an opportunity for publicity, with the Founder's eldest brother, J. C. Egerton, suggesting that if the bishop could be prevailed upon to write to the editor of *The Times* the day's proceedings would be reported, as indeed they were. Invitations were issued not only to the leading churchmen and laymen of

Oxfordshire — Liddon, Father Benson of Cowley, the rural dean, the Revd E. Payne, Lord Saye and Sele of Broughton, Lord North of Wroxton Abbey, Lord Macclesfield, but Egerton also invited his former headmaster, Dr Moberly of Winchester, the architect G. E. Street and the former chancellor of the exchequer, then in opposition, Benjamin Disraeli.

The bishop of Oxford preached at the service in the parish church on the importance of the middle classes for Britain's greatness, and then took a short service of dedication in one of the upper rooms of the new building, presumably in the later Crake junior dormitory which was in use the following term as the school chapel. Downstairs in the new big schoolroom lunch was laid for the 260 guests, presided over by the Duke of Marlborough, flanked by Lord Saye and Sele and the Hon. J. Fiennes, Viscount Dillon, Colonel North, M.P., the bishop and archdeacon. The bishop congratulated 'his friend Mr. Egerton', and in response to the warm tributes about his work Egerton — still relatively inexperienced as both priest and schoolmaster at the age of 32 — seized the opportunity to broadcast his aims for Bloxham.

CHAPTER III

P. R. EGERTON
THE YEARS OF SUCCESS, 1864-86

The completion of the schoolroom range was an important landmark in the history of the school. Its continuing growth and independence were assured under Egerton's direction without recourse either to a diocesan trust or to the Woodard Corporation. There was a good local support, finances were improving, and there were healthy signs that the school was both fulfilling a need and starting to achieve academic and sporting recognition. The year 1865 was a new beginning in both these fields. Egerton was 33, married to a wealthy wife and, having overcome the risks and crises of the first five years, could look forward to several years of steady development. Not until his late 40s, after 20 years' ownership of the school, did he again seriously worry about what was to happen to Bloxham after his retirement or death. In the meantime there was much to do, and these fifteen years were a golden age of new building, growing numbers, examination successes and sporting victories. Much was due to the personality of the Founder and his wife.

For twenty years building work was almost continuous. The first step was to level the ridge and furrow of the field north of the school to make it into a playing field for the 1865 cricket season. Village opinion thought it a shocking waste of good land, 'for a pack of boys to play on' and the tenant farmer delayed giving up possession as long as he could. For the school it was an important and excellent acquisition, though not without its problems, for there was a proposal to build the Banbury to Chipping Norton railway across it and it was divided from the school buildings by Water Lane. Egerton was advised to whip up influential support against the railway on the opening day of the schoolroom block, and the scheme came to nothing, but he had no success with attempts to stop up Water Lane. The village has always consistently opposed the closure of this narrow and winding right of way which cuts through the heart of the school property.

Flanking Water Lane and standing on the newly acquired field were an old cottage and farm buildings, the site being marked by the pump which remained for many years. These were demolished and the materials used by the village builder, W. Adkins, to build the laundry, a single-story Hornton stone house with attics apparently similar in appearance to the demolished cottage. The builders were careful to preserve its 1624 datestone; when in turn the laundry was demolished in 1936 the datestone was again saved to be set into the wall along Water Lane very close to its original position. Two years later Adkins completed the adjoining Botany Bay building. Of similar proportions to the laundry it is more pretentious, of locally dug Hornton stone with Bath and Painswick stone dressings and a York stone staircase, costing £436 0s. 11½d. compared with £189 11s. 11½d. for the laundry. It has been put to so many uses that its original

The school in 1865, showing the schoolroom wing completed and laundry under construction. The masters wearing caps and gowns are Egerton and, on his right, Crake.

purpose and reason for its name are now lost, and the estimates and bills for the two buildings do nothing to resolve the confusion. The laundry apparently also housed the school bakery, while Botany Bay was designed with a wash-house downstairs and a boys' 'playhouse' or covered playground with three broad arches facing the school. These survive inside the building, now concealed by the lean-to added when it was converted to a laboratory in 1898. There was also a fives court — in the open air — and upstairs the original single long room, with its oriel window overlooking the playing field and two fire-places, was used at first as a reading room and classroom for the seniors. The whole place seems to have been intended for recreation, and possibly it came by its nickname because of its comparative remoteness from the main building and dormitories.

The laundry and Botany Bay were minor projects, mere appendices to the main plan which was continued in 1869 with the dining hall wing along the village street to enclose the third side of the proposed quadrangle. Until then the school had fed in Hewett's schoolroom in the former barn with its rugged whitewashed beams and thatched roof. G.E. Street was again the architect with Thomas Barrett of Bloxham as builder, using Hornton stone quarried on the site to maintain a certain unity of appearance and style. There are, however, stylistic changes in the narrow four-story block which rises like a cliff above the village road, for Street abandoned the pointed Gothic windows of his earlier designs in favour of traceried square-headed ones. Each has wide dressings of Bath stone and their size and number break up the severe facade in a somewhat fussy manner.

By taking advantage of the slope of the ground Street was able to put the kitchens at road level, a convenience for deliveries until the heavy traffic of recent years made unloading direct from the carriageway a hazardous operation. The dining hall was therefore on the same level as the ground floor of the other buildings with the two stories above containing dormitories, masters' rooms and 'wardrobe room'. Within the 70-feet hall the tables were arranged at first in collegiate fashion, with the boys' tables running lengthwise down the hall. The building was opened at All Saintstide 1869 when nearly 100 guests visited the school for prizegiving and speeches in the schoolroom followed by 'a substantial and handsome luncheon, almost entirely prepared on the premises' in the new hall, which was 'prettily and tastefully decorated with evergreens and flowers.' Egerton again used this occasion for publicity to explain his aims, but although there was a good crowd of clergy the aristocracy did not attend to see the building opened by J. G. Hubbard or listen to the long succession of toasts and speeches. One of the lightest and shortest was that of the rural dean, the Revd E. Payne, quoting the morning's lesson from Ecclesiasticus, 'Whoso is liberal of his meat, men shall speak well of him, and the report of his housekeeping will be believed'.

To complete the whole plan there now only remained to be built a new house for the headmaster and a chapel. In the early 1860s, before he built the schoolroom block, Egerton intended to demolish the old farmhouse, but the intention was never carried out because there were always more pressing needs. In 1869 the house received a further reprieve when more rooms became available

The first chapel in No. III or Crake junior dormitory, 1864-71.

with the opening of the new kitchens. The old school kitchen in the farmhouse then became the headmaster's study when it was given the large bay window. Then in 1870 the need for a more suitable chapel took precedence over any further improvement in his own quarters, although they must have been cramped for his family and the school servants. Contemporary photographs show the two-story house with low, badly lit attics and a pleasant glass verandah, its plain stonework softened by creeper and climbing roses.

The chapel therefore was to be the last piece in the overall design, the ten-year delay in its construction being justified only by the first priority for essential buildings to create the school. In the words of the first *History*,

'To anyone familiar with Mr. Egerton's character and the spirit by which he was animated all through his work, it was clear that he would not long be satisfied without a permanent Chapel, and moreover that when it was built, it would be, in his own words, "the crowning building of all", and, as far as he could make it, worthy of the object to which it was to be devoted'.

The small chapel above the schoolroom was used for daily services and some special occasions. For instance, the first confirmation service was held there by bishop Wilberforce in 1865, but apart from overcrowding the need for the school to have its own chapel for all purposes was emphasised by a letter from the vicar of Bloxham in 1869. The school attended the parish church for main services, which were Anglo-Catholic in character, and in thanksgiving gave a set of vestments, but the parishioners were opposed to choral eucharist and the school was evidently not able to worship fully and freely in its own way.

First, however, Egerton made a careful and entirely characteristic appraisal of his financial position, estimating that the chapel would cost the same as the dining hall wing, £3,500. In a little over ten years he would have spent £16,000 on the school buildings.[1] This was divided into £1,650 for the original purchase of the Hewett school and £750 for four smaller adjoining properties; £2,000 for the schoolroom wing, £3,500 for the dining hall and an estimated £3,500 for the chapel; £1,000 together for the laundry, bakehouse and outbuildings, with a further £800 for stables and miscellaneous expenditure on the headmaster's house; £1,500 for furniture; £1,100 for the playing field on which an additional £200 had been spent.

Of this expenditure about 40% came from mortgages and loans, a similar proportion from his own private income and gifts, and about 20% from profits. The actual figures vary in the different calculations made during the winter of 1869-70. The profits amounted to £2,900 and Egerton reckoned that the school was yielding 4% on the capital expended as well as giving the headmaster his keep and probably about £600 a year, a considerable sum and reasonable rate of interest for the period. His London accountant was, in the manner of accountants, rather less optimistic three years later, pointing out that if the school were a company it could have paid investors only 5% interest and would only have given the headmaster a salary of £115 as well as his house and keep. It could also be said that Egerton had sunk a large part of his private income in the school, a sum given variously as £4,100 and £6,000 (but probably nearer the latter), including the cost of the whole dining hall wing which he met personally. Since his marriage and the death of his mother in 1862 he was no longer a poor curate, and in the late 1860s his income rose annually, being £1,029 in 1869. There was, therefore, a sound base to proceed with building the chapel. The school mortgage was capable of increase from £3,400 to £5,500, there were reasonable profits and private resources, including a generous gift (probably the £1,000 private donation listed in his account book) from his wife and her two sisters, Caroline and Frances Gould.

The chapel was designed by Street, following in general appearance the building he had proposed for Hewett nearly twenty years earlier. That had been planned as an eastward extension of the original building, but the schoolroom wing now stopped that. The decision to keep the farmhouse as a residence prevented any idea of placing the chapel on the fourth side of the quadrangle, and the only remaining possibility was to fit it with the least disturbance to the existing buildings into the space between the schoolroom block and the laundry and Botany Bay.

Work started in January 1870 with five or six masons and twenty labourers beginning to excavate for stone on the site. At a depth of ten to thirty feet below the surface is a good building stone, soft and easy to work but hardening rapidly

---

[1] It is virtually impossible to translate Victorian prices and values into modern terms, and no attempt has been made to do so. In 1864 Egerton was paying his second master £80 a year, and other qualified masters £40; the matron was paid £32 and the cook £25 a year. Skilled craftsmen, like the masons working on the chapel, received £1 or a little more a week, and the labourers about 14s. (70p). Boarding fees were about £35 a year.

on exposure to the air. It lies in beds of one to three feet thick, varying in colour from greenish blue to brown according to the proportion of iron in the stone, and the chapel was built in bands of the two colours. Egerton enjoyed working with his hands and took a personal interest in the quarrying, supervising the operation without employing a contractor, although the actual direction of Street's design was carried out by Egerton's cousin, William Oswald Milne, a London architect. The foundation stone, a fine grey-green block, was quarried by Egerton himself,[2] and he also used to point out the large quoin immediately above the string course some fifteen feet up on the south-east corner which he quarried from the deepest bed beneath the chapel.

Much of the stone for each successive school building was quarried on its site and although the chapel cellars are the most extensive, there are others beneath at least part of the original school and schoolroom blocks, while the dining hall wing was built into the slope of the ground. Construction of the chapel was in progress during the summer of 1870 when 27 masons and 27 labourers were at work. It is remarkable that the whole job from beginning the quarry to completion took only thirteen months with the men working a ten-hour day even in winter, and twelve or thirteen hours in the summer — and that for a weekly wage of £1 or a little more for a mason and 14s. for a labourer. Among the youngest on the task was 16-year old Joe Stevens who later recalled how the quarried stone was sawn in the gravelled quadrangle and that it was his father who carried all but one of the massive York stone chapel steps to their position.

The chapel was opened on Shrove Tuesday, 21 February 1871, the total cost being about £4,000. The chapel itself is at first-floor level to give it the necessary height and proportions without wasting space. Beneath were three classrooms, an architectural answer to contemporary educational reforms and a welcome change from the clamour of the big schoolroom, but like that room their windows are high; the Victorians did not believe in giving boys the distraction of window-gazing! The cellars beneath occasionally flooded badly as in 1875, 1975 and 1913, when the water was four feet deep. They were used at first for stores and for brewing and keeping beer sold by the mugful by the steward, William Treadwell. The lean-to chapel passage gave access both to the chapel by way of the new stairway and a ground-floor vestry (later no. 9 study and Crake house-room).

Inside, the chapel was bare and plain, lit by green-tinted glass in the Decorated-style windows, the only ornamentation being the Box stone window dressings and string course, the sedilia with their Devon marble pillars given by the masons and workmen, the Hereford glazed paving tiles at the east end and the thirteenth-century style carved bosses. There was an organ loft, but no screen, the organ being a gift from friends of the school and parents, who had already been contributing from fees towards the chapel building. The furnishings were as simple as the building — a plain altar raised on steps with a cross from Miss Scott-Murray and Miss Nixon (who acted as Egerton's secretary), and a pair of

---

[2] It is now almost entirely obscured by the central buttress added to the east end in 1950, in which was incorporated a stone of similar size with the same wording.

The chapel, 1871-82.

candlesticks given by the rural dean, the Revd E. Payne; prominently placed in the centre of the aisle was the brass lectern given by the Misses Gould; the seating, plain ladder-back chairs with rush seats, was arranged church-like to face the altar, not in collegiate fashion. Its plainness is perhaps unexpected for an Oxford Movement chapel and is a reminder of Egerton's lack of interest in ritual and ceremonial as well as the practical need for economy. The opening service, however, was a typically splendid occasion, beginning with choral communion at 8 a.m. and followed by a crowded morning service at 11, the choir singing at both services and organ music under F. H. Capner being particularly commended. The bishop of Oxford, John Mackarness, was celebrant in the morning and preached at 11 on the importance of the time of school life, using the text, 'And he came to Nazareth where he was brought up'. After lunch in hall, with the traditional bombardment of speeches, evening prayer was held at 6 p.m. for the chapel workmen and villagers.

The chapel completed the main school buildings, but as the school continued to grow there were new needs which effectively postponed any hopes for rebuilding the headmaster's house. Among these projects was the conversion in 1872 of the thatched farm buildings facing the playing field, the largest and easternmost into a pavilion. The present school pavilion stands on the same site, at one end of which was the first tuck shop presided over by Mrs. Spencer until 1880. This had been started in Botany Bay a few years earlier by Samuel Blacker, an assistant master, because a measles epidemic in the village put the shops out-of-bounds, and its profits, largely due to Wilson's management, went towards expenditure on the cricket ground and the wages of the professional coach. Between the tuck shop and Botany Bay stood a thatched cottage, so that a whole small village of low stone houses and out-buildings sheltered beneath the tall facade of the schoolroom and chapel. Another proposal, especially desired by Egerton, was a proper library, for which the reading room in Botany Bay was inadequate. A suggestion in 1875 to add another story to that building as part of the Arkell memorial, when the first editor of *The Bloxhamist,* H. E. Platt, put in a plea for an office, was not carried out.

More pressing was the need for a sanatorium and better accommodation for assistant masters. Recurrent epidemics, particularly a severe outbreak of scarlet fever in November 1872 from which one boy died, led to an appeal for an isolation hospital at an estimated cost of £1,500 to £2,000, to be placed at the eastern extremity of the school grounds 200 yards from the rest of the buildings. It was the first Bloxham building for which W. O. Milne was solely responsible as architect, and he achieved some success with it. The plans were exhibited at the Royal Academy and it is the only school building to receive a commendation in the Pevsner *Buildings of England* volume on Oxfordshire. Built in 1874 it is of restrained design, except for a projecting oriel window with a pleasant view of the playing field and school, and faced, like all Egerton's buildings, in Hornton stone. Inside were rooms for housekeeper and nurse, as well as wards for patients and suspected cases in a well considered plan. According to *The Globe,* 'Any lad presenting the slightest indication of sickness of a doubtful character is at once

Hospital, 1874, later Palmer House.

removed here, where every possible convenience for nursing has been provided and that in a style which might almost be characterized as luxurious'.

As the school grew in size assistant masters were lodged from 1868 at 'Spencer's', presumably one of the school cottages where Mrs. Spencer lived and probably on the site of the present Egerton House. In 1875 Spencer's was closed and the masters transferred temporarily to Bloxham Park Farm (better known now as Park Close, the former manor house of Bloxham Beauchamp), which the Founder's brother, Hubert,[3] had bought that year, together with land across Courtington Lane wanted for a second playing field. A new masters' house was then built on the corner of Water Lane and Rose Bank during 1876, a comfortable three-story house with quarters for a married man in the eastern part, occupied for a time by F.S.Boissier, and five sets of bachelors' rooms on the corner of the lane. The latter remained in use until about 1955, long after the rest of the house had been given over to other purposes. A range of miscellaneous outbuildings along Water Lane, henceforth known to the school as Masters'

[3]Hubert Decimus Egerton, tenth and youngest of the Revd John Egerton's children, was bursar of the school from 1872 to 1896, after which a tenuous but pleasant link with Park Close was maintained until the 1930s. It was traditional for the boys to have walnuts at All Saintstide and, after the school's own walnut tree was felled, Hubert Egerton supplied nuts from Park Close, a custom continued by later owners.

Site of Masters' House, showing arched doorway and Ivy Cottage, about 1870.

Lane, included one used as a classroom for the classical side, begun in 1877, and in another of the buildings at the back of the house is Bloxham's oldest architectural feature. This is the fourteenth-century arched doorway with dripmould that was re-erected here from its former position facing Rose Bank lane.

In the remaining ten years' of Egerton's headmastership there were no more building works, but every year the boys could expect to see changes in a continued programme of minor improvements. The chief of these were to the chapel, where the *Te Deum* east window by Clayton & Bell was installed in 1875 in memory of bishop Samuel Wilberforce who had died in 1873. Altar furnishings were given in the late 1870s but the biggest change was in 1882 when the organ loft screen, choir stalls, pews and pavement were added. Street is reputed to have designed the screen, but Milne was responsible for the rest and for their fitting during that summer. Elsewhere, the open-air fives court was made in 1878 at the east end of the pavilion in memory of Miss Arkell, who also has a memorial window in the chapel, and in the same year Botany Bay was improved to make the reading room and classroom better. In 1881 a carpentry workshop was built and a lathe room opened in the thatched building by the tuck shop under the supervision of the Jacksons, father and son, Egerton himself being an amateur woodworker and cabinet-maker of considerable skill; there is a fine sideboard made by him in the present masters' common room. Out of doors, the second field was levelled, drained and brought into use for football in 1882 and the gravelled playground covered with asphalt the next year.

40

The extension of the buildings was in response to the continued increase in the number of boys at the school. When the schoolroom wing was opened in 1864 there had been 50 boys in the school. There followed a rapid expansion to 170 in 1873-4 and 198 in 1876-7; a decline in the late 1870s and early 1880s was arrested so that by the time of Egerton's retirement from the headmastership there were about 180 boys in the school. After the early years, when some parents treated it as a sort of preparatory school for the public schools, few boys went on elsewhere but stayed their full time at Bloxham, so that by 1886, when he retired, Egerton said that of the 1,400 boys who had been at Bloxham, only 180 went on to other schools.

The staff had increased correspondingly. An advertisement for a temporary master in 1879 summarises the qualifications sought: 'A good churchman wanted, ready to fall into the ways of the place, — the chapel services & generally — to set a good example to the boys'. This particular post was for a classics teacher up to Cambridge locals level with some English, history and geography; the salary was £90 a year (lower than the big public schools) and residence. Competition was lively, with 43 applications for one post in 1871, and Egerton was able to select some outstanding men.

They included some notable Old Bloxhamists. Of these, C. J. Wilson was the most remarkable, being third on the school roll, head prefect and, staying on as a young man, even taking his Oxford degree in 1879 while still remaining partly in residence at Bloxham. He was utterly devoted to the school, chiefly teaching his own subject of French but also taking middle forms in history, geography and mathematics. After 30 years he gave up teaching in 1896 to act as school bursar for another 21 years, and finally was resident secretary of the Old Bloxhamist Society for 19 years before leaving Bloxham in 1936, less than three years before his death. Despite his short stature he was a good footballer and fives player as well as being a steady batsman and 'a great stealer of runs'; his 74 not out as opening batsman against Adderbury in 1878 was one of his best innings. It was reported that his strong right arm as a cricketer and fives player was also effective with the cane. There was Frank Churchill, fifteenth on the roll, entering the school with his two brothers in January 1861 before going on to Eton. He taught classics for three years from 1873, was a keen cricketer and in 1874 responsible with W. A. Pemberton (1873-76) for the radical change of introducing Football Association rules as an improvement on the peculiar Winchester-Bloxham game played until then. C. Walters (1862-65), a keen photographer who took some of the earliest school photographs, was in a slightly different category, being an Old Bloxhamist of Hewett's school. The most eminent in the educational world was H. E. Platt (1867-70), head prefect and the first to go up to Cambridge; he taught classics as an assistant master from 1875, in which year, though not officially its editor, he was closely concerned with restyling the *School Chronicle* into *The Bloxhamist*. He left in 1879 to become headmaster of Wellingborough, raising it from a moribund country grammar school of seventeen boys to one of the most successful public schools, where he is judged to have been among the best headmasters that the school has ever had. And there was F. S. Boissier (1865-71), claimed as Egerton's cleverest pupil and head prefect, who became assistant master in 1879 and succeeded the Founder as headmaster in 1886.

The long list of other masters given as an appendix to the first *History* shows that many stayed only a very short time. Their careers later are mostly unrecorded in *The Bloxhamist* but since schoolmastering was often a step in a clerical career before ordination, it is likely that many, like Frank Churchill, were only teaching for a year or two before being ordained. W. W. Bird was one of these, coming to Bloxham in 1868 as second master and being chiefly responsible for the high academic standard of the following years before his appointment as headmaster of Framlingham in 1872. Among those who taught for a longer time were Samuel Blacker (1862-73), who also contributed to the growing academic reputation of the school at the time, and it was he who gave Mrs Egerton the flowering may, or Glastonbury thorn, in the headmaster's garden, and W. J. Bridger, master in the junior school (1869-71, 1881-94), who lived with his family at Ivy Cottage and taught dozens of boys to swim in the muddy and chilly waters of the Sor brook. The junior school had its own team of masters under a separate head, who from 1872 to 1878 was the Revd E. V. Collins (whose namesake E. Collins taught for ten years between 1874 and 1890); Collins also served as curate of Hempton, which earlier had been Reginald Egerton's care. For several years after starting the school Egerton had continued to drive over to Hempton on Sundays to take services, and similarly Collins spent Saturday nights and Sundays in the little village, where he developed Anglo-Catholic services. With such an emphasis on its religious teaching and Egerton's interest and ability in choral music, he was fortunate in the long attachment of the two organists, F. H. Capner (1862-75) and W. H. Williamson (1879-86), as well as with his chaplains, who of course played a most important part in the life of the school.

The first was the Revd A. D. Crake (1865-78). He had a tremendous influence on the everyday religious life of the school, being possessed of a strong personal religious fervour, perhaps due to his conversion to Anglo-Catholic practices from a strict Calvinist Baptist upbringing. He was a powerful foil to Egerton, having asked to come to Bloxham from a previous teaching post in Chipping Norton, sharing with him a love of music, and starting together the regular habit of saying mattins which the boys could attend if they wished. He was wholly committed to the Anglo-Catholic teaching of a thorough preparation for communion, including reading the exhortation from the prayer book, and confession, and favoured ritual though as a non-essential adjunct to worship. He was an exceptionally good extempore preacher — after his first sermon in the parish church, the vicar advised him never to write his sermons — because he was a born story-teller and it is this which earns him a place in the *Dictionary of National Biography*.

After dinner on his very first Sunday at Bloxham he told 'an hour's tale from Church history to the boys in the classroom', and Crake's weekly stories became a popular feature of school life. In the winter the boys gathered for this treat in the big schoolroom, in summer beneath a tall elm tree outside the tuck shop, a famous school landmark which fell in 1882. Some of these boys' historical stories, for example *Alfgar the Dane* and *The Last Abbot of Glastonbury,* were published and became widely popular in Victorian times, when they brought Bloxham useful publicity, remaining in print even to modern decades. *The Rival Heirs* was serialised in *The Bloxhamist,* and though its style and perhaps its history are now unfashionable as a way of telling stories to an assembly of boys (even if the average age of the school was younger then than now) its quality as a story is undeniable; the reader is unerringly lured on to the next instalment. As a historian he was elected a fellow of the Royal Historical Society, but he would probably have preferred to be remembered for his devotional works, particularly the *Book of Private Devotion for Boys,* originally published as *Simple Prayers for Schoolboys* (1868), the first school book of prayers to be published, and for his contribution to *The Priest's Book of Private Devotion,* still in print a century later. He would probably also have been pleased that his name is perpetuated at Bloxham in the name of the house where his own rooms were, for he occupied the master's rooms above the schoolroom during his thirteen years at the school.

The emphasis on religion in the life of the school must be recognised — and accepted. Egerton, his masters and his boys worked hard, played hard and enjoyed themselves in a wide range of activities — the debating society, photography, long bicycle excursions on 'penny-farthings', on one of which Wilson lost control on a steep hill and was lucky only to be hurled into the hedge, an occasional more distant adventure when Crake took some boys to Switzerland. They also worshipped hard. For a century successive chaplains instilled into generations of boys the religious basis of the school, and despite the revolt of individuals the school as a whole has always admitted that this deliberate emphasis has been one of its identifying characteristics to distinguish it from other schools, even from those of the Woodard Corporation with their similar ideals. This characteristic was, of course, particularly strong in Egerton's own headmastership.

Religion at Bloxham has always been taught as a matter for enjoyment, cheerfulness and colour, as well as self-discipline. It was in order to relieve the drabness of Victorian Sundays that Crake started his story-telling, because unofficial games by the boys were checked. The custom was singled out for attack in 1869 by an anti-catholic critic who claimed that the stories were disloyal to the reformed Church of England. The same critic predictably attacked confession, the custom of silence at meals on Fridays and accused Crake of playing draughts with the boys on Sundays — a harmless enough pastime, one would have thought, but one which was vigorously denied. On Sundays the boys did not play games of any sort nor were they allowed to read novels, the day being occupied with morning service at the parish church, which for those taking communion was preceded by preparation and meditation the night before, an hour's singing practice under Egerton, walks, approved reading and story-telling, and evensong in chapel with the new *Hymns Ancient and Modern* (1860) and Gregorian chants. On weekdays there was a daily service in chapel (but not a daily celebration) and a timetable which incorporated four hours of divinity periods a week. This regime, started by Egerton and Crake, essentially survived for over a century, with modifications only by reducing the periods of divinity and length of services, and relaxing the Sunday no-games rule. The example and teaching of Egerton and Crake inspired the school as a whole. Crake recalled preaching one Maundy Thursday, asking the boys to be silent and think on Christ's agony. 'Their obedience was wonderful. I do not think there was a syllable uttered among the boys afterwards through the evening and night. The silence was death like. The chapel was full of boys at 9 o'clock'.

Like other thoughtful Anglo-Catholics, Crake considered becoming a Roman Catholic, and this inner debate, combined with depression following his mother's death in 1871, affected his health. In 1878 he was again ill and decided to close 'the most important epoch of my life's work' in favour of a younger man and friend, the Revd A. L. C. Heigham (1878-81, 1883-85), who was also vice-principal, a good teacher and in 1895 the donor of the school bell which was hung at the foot of the Crake staircase.

The teaching ability of Bloxham's masters in the 1860s and 1870s was reflected in the examination results which Egerton recorded as meticulously as his accounts. In 1865 boys for the first time entered the new examinations known as 'Cambridge locals', which were held in the dining hall about Christmas time. Of the six junior entries, five passed. In the next year there were sixteen junior and three senior candidates, one for Cambridge locals, two for the Oxford examination including C. J. Wilson. The first major success was in 1868 when F. S. "Freddie" Boissier won first class honours at junior level, repeating this achievement as a senior three years later when there were 63 candidates, of whom 36 passed; eleven were seniors. It was a triumph for various masters, among whom W. W. Bird deserves mention as master in charge of the top forms, that a school only ten years old should have the second best results in the whole country in competition with some 300 others like Manchester, Wolverhampton and Bradford grammar schools, Mill Hill, Framlingham, Trent College and Liverpool College.

This high standard was maintained during the 1870s with the whole school competing in Cambridge locals and giving up the alternative diocesan board examinations in 1875. For some years 1873 was the best for results, but year after year Bloxham was among the top five from the 400 schools which took the examination, claiming first position in 1877 and 1879 and thereby repudiating a somewhat tart remark in *The Globe* in 1875 which stated that no science was taught, the classrooms were poor and the school took all boys who applied — and then called them 'middle'! Even in 1881, when much disappointment was expressed at the lack of honours, the school came fifth, and following that criticism the school was second in 1882 out of about 600 others, and easily first among comparable 'county' schools. Results continued to be good for a further few years and in 1884 there was a record number of certificates won. Individual boys did exceptionally well, like Boissier, whose brilliance Egerton was quick to recognise and encourage, or J. W. Mackenzie who in 1875 was first out of 318 candidates in applied mathematics and fourth out of 1,815 in pure mathematics. And although Egerton would remind parents that it was not his aim to educate boys for the universities, he was pleased with those who did go up to Oxford or Cambridge. It was certainly gratifying that with a school of boys aged between nine and seventeen there were eight Old Bloxhamists divided equally between the two ancient universities.

At that time the school was graded in five divisions, which about 1875 were extended to eight forms. The two lowest were very small, each middle school class being about twenty boys, and forms 1 and 2 containing 40 and 29 respectively; one-quarter of the school was in the top form. The morning timetable was three one-hour periods from 9 a.m. to noon, followed by a half-hour period which was always free for division 1 and always dictation for division 5. Three periods or preparations filled the afternoons on Monday, Wednesday and Friday, the other days being half-holidays. Within the week the lowest forms had seven hours' Latin, five hours' arithmetic, four of divinity, three each of dictation, drawing and writing, two of French and one hour of geography. In the top form the emphasis was on mathematics, with nine hours devoted to the subject including Euclid, or geometry, and the delight of land-measuring which was carried out on hot summer afternoons conveniently close to the Sor brook bathing place; Latin, French and drawing were given three hours each, and history and geography three hours between them; there were two hours of English and the usual four hours of divinity.

In imitation of Arnold's system at Rugby eight senior boys were chosen as prefects and Egerton laid down their administrative and disciplinary duties. All were responsible for general order, taking roll-call and supervising the bathrooms and dining tables. One had special responsibility for the conduct and tidiness of the whole school, another looked after the library and schoolroom, one the dining hall, two the playground and similar areas, and three the cricket field.

The emphasis on this last duty illustrates the importance of sport and games in the daily timetable, for this was the period when games were first becoming an increasingly vital feature of boarding school life. Masters at public schools were beginning to organise and take part in games, which hitherto had been played on a haphazard basis with such little organisation as existed being provided by the boys themselves. Admittedly and as befitted a country school, the boys also had considerable freedom to amuse themselves, not always approved officially, and probably rather more freedom than in the excessively games-conscious large public schools — birds'-nesting, rat-hunting by Sor brook, cutting down the willows to make canoes or, for the seniors, Saturday visits to Banbury. An Old Bloxhamist excused the enthusiasm for the traditional country games of catapult-shooting and 'chestnut-conquerors' in the early 1860s because of the lack of organised games, especially in winter, although from the early days Egerton, himself a keen and competitive games-player, led the boys in organised games. In those days the staff turned out with the boys for matches against club sides which made up most of the fixtures, at cricket the clergy playing in grey shirts and black trousers held up with wide, red, knitted silk braces. At football Egerton was said to have been able to kick the ball over the high elm treee in the playing field, and he was an effective round-arm bowler, fast in his younger days, and a vigorous fast-scoring batsman at cricket. He would challenge the school XI single-handed — and win! He was still playing football in 1883 (habitually full-back with Wilson) and cricket in 1885, both when he was over 50.

A surviving exercise book of the head prefect in 1862 reveals that there was a cricket XI that year, but the first matches were played the following season, and the team of young-looking boys is pictured in the earlier *History*. The first recorded match was at Upton House on 5 August against Ratley village under Captain Fitzgerald, when the school scored 86 and 103 for 5 wickets (Mr C. Walters 34, Revd P. R. Egerton 25), and Ratley 97 and 92 runs. A week later the *Banbury Guardian* reported the first match on the school ground, apparently playing on the field roughly where the great hall and classroom block stands now, when the school XII, reinforced by Egerton, Walters and Blacker, defeated a Deddington XII by six wickets, the scores being Bloxham 55 and 40 for 5 wickets in reply to Deddington's 53 and 41 runs.

The fixture list slowly expanded as other village sides were challenged and in 1865 the first match against St Paul's, Stony Stratford, middle-class school was held, an annual needle match which came to be regarded as the most important one of the season. Boys who played in that match won their colours. Bloxham won twelve of the eighteen years' matches played before Stony Stratford school closed. On that first occasion the result was inconclusive, but rather than call a draw when a second innings was not finished the winner of the first was given the victory. Therefore, with scores of Stony Stratford 46 and 41 for 3 wickets and Bloxham 42 and 111, the former won. Also on that occasion masters were playing, and the first time that the boys alone fielded a team seems to have been the following year when the school routed a Banbury Junior XI on 1 August 1866 at the school by 60 and 103 to 19 and 82, R. Mooney taking seven wickets. In that season the school also played two Oxford colleges and in 1867 the press reported the first match against the village when a boys' XI won easily by an innings and 30 runs. This match became a regular fixture, though not without occasional disputes from the close rivalry and in 1885 it was decided to abandon it for a year. A happier event was the match on the school ground in August 1870 between two sides of the men working on the chapel; Bloxham Builders Labourers, who had cannily gone to the trouble of getting in a good deal of practice, beat the craftsmen Stone Masons by 53 runs.

One of the most curious results, reflecting either the uncertainty of cricket rules at the time or the lack of umpiring knowledge in interpreting them, was the match against the Cotswold Waifs and Strays in 1874. The *Banbury Guardian* recorded the scores as All Saints 150 (W. H. Lockey 59), Waifs and Strays 149, but noted, 'It is a question whether it resulted in a tie or was won by the School by one run, as three byes were scored for a ball which touched the boundary, but for which only two were run, and the umpire could not give a decision thereon'. The newspaper also avoided giving what would seem to be a straightforward verdict!

The 1874 season was talked of for many years as only one match was lost of the 22 played, largely due to the batting of W. H. Lockey and a record last wicket stand of 105 — of which the last man, S. A. Upton, was the hero — against the habitually strong Upton House side fielding a first-class Cambridge Blue fast bowler. It was also the year in which the committee of games was formed, composed of captains of teams and their officers, to lay down the regulations for fixtures and for competitions within the school. A few years earlier the first match against the Old Boys was played in 1868, only five years after the school's first cricket fixture, when the Present won easily by 126 to the Past's 57 and 67; playing for the Past were Pearce (either William, no. 1 on the school roll, or George, no. 6), C. J. Wilson (no. 3 on the roll) and George Warriner (no. 43 on the roll). In 1879 the school lost its first match against another school side for six years, but it would be tedious to recall the feats and disasters of cricket matches a century ago except to indicate the importance of the game in school life. Cricket was always the premier sport. It was compulsory, and the names of those who played in the XI were displayed on boards in the old thatched pavilion. Dormitory matches (there were no 'houses' then) were played from the 1870s, being replaced for a season or two in 1884 by 'house' matches. Egerton engaged a professional coach in the 1870s and 1880s until the need for economy prevented it, and year after year the school could compete on equal terms with local club sides.

No other game enjoyed the same interest and prestige. *The Bloxhamist* was wont to complain at the lack of interest in football. Played originally under Winchester rules modified by Bloxham customs and common-sense it was a game in which the ball was handled, though less than at Rugby, and handling continued to be tolerated even after the school adopted Association rules in 1874. By then they were playing several Oxford colleges, usually fielding teams of fifteen, including some masters, rather than eleven players. The lack of standard rules caused much difficulty. In 1876 the school XV beat Trinity College, Stratford on Avon, who 'had the disadvantage of not being accustomed to Association rules' and with many clubs still following their own rules a writer in *The Bloxhamist* that winter advocated either a local variation of Association rules or a change to Rugby rules for the 1876-77 season. At the same time there were demands for everyone to change for football, the lower school being accustomed to playing in their ordinary clothes and boots, but Egerton replied that lack of changing room space prevented it. However, it was from about then that regulation knickerbockers were worn in favour of trousers with what is described as the usual school colours of black and dark blue jerseys, stockings and ties; football caps of the same colours were worn from 1881. Another difficulty was the shortage of fixtures, since even by 1877 most nearby schools were playing Rugby rules. At cricket over twenty matches could be arranged, but even after an Oxfordshire Football Association was formed in 1884, with Wilson as its first chairman, only half a dozen matches could be fixed and no school within easy distance played the game.

The alternative winter games were steeplechases, hare and hounds or paperchases, scattering 'scent' regardless of the litter. A run of thirteen miles was not thought excessive and seems to have been reasonably popular, but far less than skating on the moat at Broughton Castle or at Bradshaw's mill on the Sor brook, which apparently was common in those harder winters of the late nineteenth century. Sor brook was also the primitive bathing place where Bridger so perseveringly taught generations of young boys to swim in conditions which caused one master to comment that 'it grieved him sorely to see the youngsters go into the water white and come out black'. The more competent swimmers could venture away from the muddy shallows with its 'pea-soupers', and despite all the difficulties races were swum in good summers; in 1881, for example, 130 out of 159 boys were swimming, a very good proportion considering the handicaps.

There was also poor provision for athletics, which aroused little enthusiasm. In the early 1870s races were run on a measured length of the South Newington road, later being moved to the less well surfaced Bloxham Grove lane with some races taking place on the Banbury road. Traffic was sparse, and the occasional pony and trap or horse and cart had to run the gauntlet of cheering spectators. It was hoped that there would be some improvement when in 1881 a course was laid out on the cricket field, but running conditions on the grass were poor and they reverted to the road until the second field was available in 1884 and the cinder track constructed the next year.

Various other games were suggested or tried, all under the control of the committee of games started in 1874. Tennis was begun in 1877 but failed to attract players, hockey was played in odd free moments in the early 1880s and in 1890 someone suggested the introduction of baseball. The only minority game with a regular following was fives, played under various rules so that not until 1888 had 'hand fives' at last completely ousted 'bat fives'. The first court was at the back of Botany Bay until the Arkell memorial court was opened at the east end of the pavilion in 1879, and from 1882 both fives and football were played on a dormitory competition basis.

Non-sporting diversions were limited. The reading room was restricted to about 75 senior members, though a growing library contained a good proportion of popular boys' books for lending. The debating club, formed in 1875, was the first senior social society and reflected boys' opinion of the times — in favour of a Channel tunnel and fagging, for example — but like most school societies collapsing and reviving according to the interest of a handful of boys. The fortunes of the photographers with their complex and primitive equipment, the essay club, the natural history society, the museum and the lathe shop fluctuated similarly.

Although Egerton kept firm to his aim of giving a public school education to boys who would go straight into business he found that his modest fees attracted parents with higher aspirations for their sons. Of the 164 boys in the school in 1870 the fathers of 42 were in business, 50 were farmers and the remainder were the sons of clergymen, lawyers, doctors, army or naval officers and other professions. Inevitably among these there were some, university men themselves perhaps, who hoped that their sons would follow them to the universities, either direct from Bloxham or after a period with a tutor or in a larger and more expensive public school. Some also were of outstanding ability, like F. S.

Boissier, whose academic successes were forecast by Egerton when he was only fourteen. According to the *History* eight of the first twenty boys in the school went to the universities. Platt was the first to go up to Cambridge in 1871 but within a few years there were four each at both Oxford and Cambridge, including T. Hands who got a first in mathematics at Oxford in 1878, the year after Boissier had done equally well in the same subject at Cambridge. Egerton also took pride in the success of Reginald Cave-Browne-Cave, eldest son of his old friend, Ambrose, winning first place in the naval cadets' list in 1872.

The *History* also lists the names of early Bloxhamists who achieved distinction without giving the details which in 1910 were still well known. It is a list which reveals the calibre of boys whom Egerton educated — men like F. C. Caffin (1870-74), assistant engineer of the Tay bridge; R. J. G. Read (1866-70), engineer to the Blackpool Tower, then the highest building in the country, and many railway and public schemes here and abroad; a group of artists and academicians, A. Chevallier Tayler (1871-77), the portrait painter who painted the school and Mrs Egerton's portrait as well as those of Earl Haig and Earl Beatty, and whose "Viaticum" hung for years in the *Church Times* office before F. B. Palmer gave it to the school; G. W. Ostrehan (1883-85), the stained glass designer and L. A. Shuffrey (1865-67), the architect responsible for the school's 1914-18 war memorial. Among those ordained were Father Tiverton Preedy of Pentonville (1874-77) and Tsan Baw (1875-79), the first Burmese to be ordained a Christian priest. Major-General B. M. Skinner, C. B., C.M.G. (1872-74) was founder and second editor of the short-lived *School Chronicle* at the end of the summer term of 1874, his collaborator and the first editor being Hubert Palmer (1870-74), whose younger brother, F. B. Palmer (1872-79), edited its successor, *The Bloxhamist* for his last two years; he then joined the family paper, the *Church Times,* where he succeeded his father as sole manager for 30 years before his retirement in 1941.

The publication of a school paper was a sign of the school's growing maturity. It had begun as a double-page news-sheet produced by Skinner, Hubert Palmer and Caffin with the encouragement of H. E. Platt. The *School Chronicle* ran for two issues (some reports say five issues), the first in August 1874 being sold out on the day of publication, but no copy of any of them is known to have survived. It was said to have been little more than a record of cricket matches and of an inconvenient shape, giving way to *The Bloxhamist* in 1875. This was published monthly in term-time with ten issues a year at 4d. each and an index. Despite recurrent crises from lack of finance and copy the magazine maintained this rate of production until the Great War, although by then the price had risen a little to 5s. a year. From the beginning the quarto-sized magazine contained a variety of general school news, detailed sporting reports and articles. It ran a lively and not always uncritical correspondence column, which Egerton regarded as frivolous. He himself used it to lay down policy or make appeals, but was scrupulous not to influence its editors directly except to rebuke them that it was not the proper place to attack the school authorities anonymously. He did, however, give them the salutary reminder that the prime function of a school magazine is to be a chronicle of school events. On its title page from 1876 was printed the Egerton family coat of arms and this was the first public use of these as the school arms, adopted, said the editors, because there was no symbol to embody the idea of 'all the saints'.

The school has never obtained a grant of arms from the College of Arms and has no legal right to use those of the Egerton family. Egerton was a member of an armigerous family, and by extension could use the family arms for his private school, but according to the strict rules of heraldry the school should perhaps have dropped their use when it joined the Woodard Corporation. The Egerton crest, *a stag's head erased or*, is far less familiar to Bloxhamists than the shield *sable a chevron between three pheons argent*, but may be seen carved on the headmaster's house built for Egerton in 1886. The motto was not that of the Egerton family, but, it will be recalled, the one chosen for the school by Hewett.

The Bloxhamist from 1880 also regularly contained news of old boys, and a further sign of maturity was the formation of an old boys' society. The first step was the annual Present *v.* Past cricket match on the last Saturday of the summer term from 1868. Another was the proposal in the *School Chronicle* of 1874 for an old boys' dinner. It was organised by R. J. G. Read and T. F. Holt and held on 7 January 1875 at the Holborn Restaurant in London; 32 were present with Egerton in the chair. Among the many speeches two were notable. In proposing the toast of 'The Old Boys' Egerton coupled the toast with the name of Wilson, already marked out as *'the* Old Boy', the oldest Old Bloxhamist and 'one whom he was proud to reckon among his greatest friends'. Later in the evening John Read forecast that 'this meeting would only be the beginning of a more important institution, and that by and by a Bloxhamists' club would be formed' and he hoped that something might be settled that evening. He was moving too fast for Egerton. The latter replied that for the moment they must be content with an annual dinner and suggested that Read was the best candidate to arrange a second one, which was held at the Criterion Restaurant in Piccadilly.

The caution was justified, for although about 1,000 boys had passed through the school even the annual dinner lacked support. In 1878 the date was moved to the summer to coincide with the Oxford *v.* Cambridge cricket match, but the change was disastrous and no dinner was held at all in 1879. From then the annual meetings were renewed with differing fortune; in 1881 only 19 attended, in 1883 there were 64. The evening's entertainment was by that time falling into a traditional pattern. A typical Criterion meal for 5*s.* comprised hors d' oeuvres and nine courses of soup, fish, *pâté*, main meat course (say, saddle of mutton), poultry, fruit salad, sweet or pastry, and dessert. This was followed by a long series of toasts and speeches which eventually drew the fire of a correspondent in *The Bloxhamist* complaining at 'the short time... for renewing old acquaintances wasted by a long toast list, and still longer speeches'. The last toast was drunk with relief, and the evening ended with songs and repeated demands for Egerton to sing his favourites.

Egerton was aware that the pleasant occasion of the annual dinner was merely an excuse for nostalgic conviviality and more than once reminded the gathering that it was Bloxham's religious aims that set it apart from other schools. Recalling also his original ideas for a fellowship of men in a collegiate society it was natural that his ideas for an old boys' society should rather take the form of a guild 'to bring out not merely the attachment to the School but the reason for that attachment. This was, an intelligent love of the principles of the Church as taught there'. A guild was started in 1882 and rapidly acquired a membership of 34 senior (Old Bloxhamists) and 29 junior members, including the faithful F. B. Palmer and John Read. Its declared object was 'to unite together in a spiritual bond those who have taught or been taught in the School; and to deepen and cement the loyalty and affection of Past and Present Bloxhamists towards the religious work of the School'. This aim was to be achieved by continuing the habits instilled at school — daily prayers, careful preparation for communion and attendance at guild meetings held three times a term at school. The roll ceases in 1884 when there were 77 members and no later activities were reported in *The Bloxhamist*.

Equally unsuccessful was the attempt to form an Old Bloxhamist Football Club. This had been proposed in 1876, but was not followed up until F. B. Palmer, captain of the football XI in his last year, left the school in 1879. He formed a club in London in 1882, playing matches every Saturday with a home ground at Wandsworth. They ended the first season with six wins and a draw out of eighteen matches, and did rather better the following winter with five wins and five draws out of seventeen games, but it was always difficult to field a team and the club collapsed for lack of support in 1885 when even the annual Past *v.* Present match at Bloxham had to be cancelled.

Palmer had better luck in his appeal in 1885 for a permanent committee to organise the annual dinner and with the support of two other active Old Bloxhamists, John Read and A. V. Clarke, such a committee was appointed two years later. Another step had been taken towards forming an Old Bloxhamist Society. For the rest, Egerton had been proved right. Bloxham was not yet ready for the full range of activities of an old boys' society, even though the school had been open for twenty years and there was a potential membership of 1,200.

There were other more urgent problems for the headmaster. The school was successful and thanks to the generosity of his wife's sisters the mortgage could be paid off at any time. But it was still his private property and entirely dependent upon his health and interest for its continuance, and at the age of 46 he was feeling the strain. He had overcome his early fears and doubts, carried many risks and responsibilities and worked incessantly for twenty years. He was headmaster for longer than any of his successors, none of whom has had both to direct the school and be solely responsible for its financial survival. He had no Council to advise and support him. He was alone except for his wife and her sisters and his younger brother Hubert, who was bursar from 1872, living at Park Close until 1893. It is not surprising, therefore, that he was getting tired, writing 'I do long now for some rest — some time that I can give to myself — & to escape from the ties of school work'.

Accordingly in the spring of 1879 he started to explore the possibility of affiliation with Keble College, the newly founded Oxford college built in memory of John Keble in 1870. With the financial backing of Caroline and Frances Gould, who expressed a preference to settle affairs then with a gift of £7,500 rather than leave the money in their wills, Egerton was able to offer the school as a gift free of debts and mortgages. Undoubtedly he was attracted to the idea by the Wykehamist example of Winchester and New College, Oxford, for he repeatedly referred to this in his speeches at Old Bloxhamist dinners. Keble should appoint a warden for Bloxham who would be responsible for the management of the school and appointment of staff, but not for teaching which would be directed by the headmaster. He himself was to retain absolute control during his own lifetime and be empowered to nominate his successor. The college's legal advisers strongly opposed the idea on the grounds that the terms of its charter prevented it from holding land of the annual value of more than £5,000 or property for educational purposes outside Oxford. Individually the college council had been sympathetic, especially Earl Beauchamp of Madresfield who promised Canon Liddon that he would pay no attention to the views of the lawyers. In the winter, therefore, with pressure from Earl Beauchamp, Liddon and Pusey, the proposal was reconsidered, but with the same disappointing result as the college council did not feel able to take on the responsibility. In conveying the news from Keble, J. A. Shaw-Stewart, then bursar of the college, reiterated his earlier advice that Egerton should either form a trust or affiliate with Woodard's society.

The second alternative was the obvious next possibility and the approach was made on 23 January 1880. Canon Woodard's response on 27 January was prompt and hopeful.

'My dear Egerton,

I have never forgotten your zeal in purchasing, and in sacrificing yourself to Bloxham. It was a noble enterprise, and on all sides I have heard of your success — In my mind there is not the same prejudice against Bloxham which existed years ago — you have remade it and consecrated it. I think now it is quite worth considering whether it might not be incorporated into my system, which is more and more tending to develop into a Systemised Department in the Church for giving all classes a public school education in church principles . . .'

He went on more cautiously about Bloxham's defects, its lack of space compared with Lancing's 260 acres and the 60 acres of the schools in the Midland division, and its lack of endowments to help it survive bad periods. As the negotiations proceeded with Woodard and Dr Lowe, now headmaster of Denstone in whose Midland division it was proposed that Bloxham would be placed, they suggested ways of appealing for funds to obtain an endowment and held out to Egerton the prospect of a fellowship of the Corporation.

As twenty years earlier, Lowe was more favourably disposed than Woodard and had a better understanding, commenting that 'Egerton lacks decision in "affairs" just as he is full of it on "principles". In business he seems to have no resistancy power, but succumbs to a difficulty or overcomes it by a heavy fine from his pocket'. Lowe tried to persist with the negotiations, writing on 29 February, 'I am unwilling to daunt Egerton who is easily depressed, and the most guileless of men; yet as such, likely from apprehension of not dealing justly by himself, to break off negotiations, that another might bring to a successful issue'. But a week later, despite a unanimous decision by the Midland division to accept Bloxham, he had heard nothing from Egerton. The latter, as Lowe recognised, was uneasy about it all. He disliked asking for favours by appealing for funds, having avoided until then the need for general public appeals, in case he had to compromise his beliefs. More fundamentally, he was not confident that the Woodard Corporation would remain firm to Anglo-Catholic principles. The negotiations faded out after a couple of months' correspondence.

A year later another possibility was briefly canvassed. One of Keble College's legal advisers, W. Ford, wrote unexpectedly to suggest affiliation with Selwyn College, Cambridge, then being built. Its charter was in the course of preparation and as the college's solicitor he could see that the technicality which had prevented affiliation to Keble might be avoided with Selwyn. Egerton's reply is unknown, but he is unlikely to have been attracted by the uncertain character of a college not yet in existence and no more was heard of the idea.

Instead he followed up the earlier advice of the Keble council to form a trust, writing first in 1881 to the sympathetic Earl Beauchamp to explain that he was prepared to hand over to the church the £25,000 investment that he and the Gould family had put into the school, that he would complete the chapel interior and would start a private preparatory school to be sold to Bloxham later. In return, the church must be ready to subsidise the low fees charged in order to compete with schools used by the farmers and yet provide a headmaster with a reasonable livelihood.

The problem was not easy to resolve. Egerton wanted to obtain security for his school without surrendering its independence, and to give up his own responsibility without losing control. He was acutely aware, from the precedent of New College, Oxford, how a founder's ideals became changed over the passage of centuries and how completely they could be altered by legislation, as for instance at the Reformation. His strong and inflexible purpose for Bloxham is revealed in his letter of 16 April 1879 to Keble College:

'I do very much hope that something may be done towards the permanent foundation of this School.

The one single idea that I have about the matter is — that — as I appeal to no one for funds — as I have in no way to consult 'the Public' — as there is no necessity for 'trimming' — in order to get support — I want *one thing* only in return for my very willing gift to the Church — that one thing is that the property may be really secured for the Church — in whatever way it may be made most useful to Her.

For any half & half measure — for any school, *merely as a school for secular teaching,* or for the *popular* form of Christianity — I am in *no way* disposed to give the property or any part of it'.

In the 1880s there was talk of disestablishing the Church of England and even fears of the state seizing the church's endowments. Bloxham had been dedicated to the service of the church and had to be protected from falling into the hands of the state. The likelihood of such an event seems much more real in the 1980s than a century ago, but this is to forget the secular character and pace of reform in Victorian times. Then as now the state, nominally the guardian of the Church of England, seemed to threaten the Anglican schools more than Roman Catholic ones. He told the story of how he had conversed at a dinner in London with one of the assistant Charity Commissioners.

"I have been scheming for the last ten years how to keep out of your hands."
"What do you mean?", said he. "I want to found a school which I wish to keep out of the clutches of the Charity Commissioners". He answered, "You can't help it". That was very unpleasant to hear, but he asked, "How do the Roman Catholics keep their institutions out of your hands?" "By telling a lie", was the answer. "They convey property to trustees as if it were really their own property; and so by a quibble they get out of it".

Where others could find a legal loophole, so could Bloxham and a scheme was eventually worked out by which the school was conveyed to trustees without any conditions whatever except that the trustees should agree from time to time on the way of disposing of the property for such purposes as were in law considered charitable. By giving the trustees such freedom without forming a trust for any specific purpose Egerton was able to avoid the ultimate approval, and therefore control, of the Charity Commission.

Advance news of the trust was given to the Old Bloxhamists at the dinner in London in January 1884 and the deed was signed on 1 March. The school was conveyed to eight trustees by Egerton, who remained the senior with a right of veto at meetings. His co-trustees were Canon Liddon, Earl Beauchamp, Shaw-Stewart, the Hon. C. L. Wood (later Lord Halifax), Dr (later Sir) W. G. F. Phillimore, Q. C., his brother Hubert Egerton and the vice-principal and chaplain, the Revd A. L. C. Heigham. The last was shortly replaced by an old friend, E. Wingfield, C.B., with whom Reginald Egerton had talked over his original purchase of Bloxham long before in 1859.

With the legal business completed the headmaster departed on a three-month tour of North America, but on his return there were further arrangements to be made. His portrait was painted, a good likeness by W. Wontner which was hung in the Academy before its presentation by Earl Beauchamp early in 1887. There was the choice of a new headmaster. Egerton planned to hand this post over to a successor, retaining for himself the title of Warden and the right to continue to live at the school. The choice presented few problems. His former pupil, the Revd F. S. Boissier, had been on the teaching staff since 1879 and was the obvious man. More difficult was the problem of living accommodation, and the building of a new headmaster's house could no longer be delayed. The school architect, W. O. Milne, designed the house to stand between the farmhouse and the road, again requiring much excavation of rock by the village builder, W. Adkins, who carried out the work in 1886-87. The house fits awkwardly into its position and a later inhabitant commented that it was an extraordinarily pretentious home compared with the school buildings, with its imposing entrance and front doorway, vast kitchens, beautiful cedar-panelled dining room and great bedrooms. There was no bathroom — just hip and round baths and huge cans of hot water for each bedroom. At the same time an old cottage on the site of the garage was demolished, opening up a view of the chapel from the village street.

For some years Egerton had been referred to as 'The Founder', a title which he refused to accept. The word for him, mindful again of his Wykehamist education, 'meant not merely the beginning of an institution, but one who placed it on a firm and lasting foundation'. Now at last he could rightly claim the title, Founder.

CHAPTER IV

F. S. BOISSIER
1886-1898

F. S. Boissier was faced with exceptional difficulties throughout the twelve years of his headmastership. Despite his absolute loyalty to both Egerton and Bloxham he suffered the unique disadvantage for his first few years of sharing direction of the school with the Warden in residence, and although the *History* is discreet there is a hint of occasional friction as a result. Even after the Egertons left Bloxham the Founder and his co-trustees restricted their headmaster's freedom to adapt the school to changing circumstances. These included growing competition from the reformed grammar schools and higher-grade schools of the state-supported school boards, which from 1870 began to provide a cheap education for some of the same kind of boys for whom Bloxham had been founded. A new top standard was introduced in many elementary schools in 1882 and by the late 1890s there were in addition about 70 higher-grade schools offering a secondary type of technical, scientific or commercial education.

At the same time the long period of agricultural depression was seriously affecting the farmers and market town businessmen, who could no longer afford even Bloxham's modest fees. The numbers in the school were already dropping when Boissier took over. From a peak of almost 200 in 1876-77 they had fallen to under 150 in 1879-80 and it is also noticeable from the school registers that whereas in the 1870s most boys had stayed up to six years at the school, in the 1880s it was only for four years or less. In 1886 there were 180 boys, but year by year the numbers fell to only 62 when Boissier resigned, imposing a severe financial strain on the school and a constant worry to its headmaster, as well as leading to questions about its government, curriculum and purpose. Although Egerton had carried out his promise to the trustees to open a preparatory school, that also had failed. It had started in the autumn of 1882 in the former girl's school at St Mary's Lodge, opposite the parish church, to take boys under twelve years old, but it was running at a loss in 1891 and by 1894 had been closed for some time. Furthermore, most of the main school buildings were fifteen to thirty years old with growing maintenance costs. Faced with a crisis of such magnitude Boissier remained business-like and clear-headed, repeatedly identifying for the trustees both the problems and the solutions for the school's decline and recovery. It was his achievement that eventually Egerton and the trustees submitted to the force of his arguments and accepted the need for change. He should have been given the opportunity of introducing his own reforms earlier.

Frederick Scobell Boissier, born in 1854, was the son of the Revd P. H. Boissier. He was educated with his two brothers at Bloxham, entering the school in 1865. He soon showed evidence of academic ability, obtaining a first-class in both junior and senior Cambridge locals, being placed fourth in all England in

Masters, 1888. Seated (l. to r.) are Revd F. S. Boissier (headmaster 1886-98), Revd P. R. Egerton (Warden) and Revd W. A. Marshall (Chaplain). Among those standing are Dr H. Hain (second from l.) and C. J. Wilson (third from r.).

mathematics. He won a scholarship in that subject to Queens' College, Cambridge, in 1871 and graduated as 20th wrangler in 1877. After ordination the next year he returned to Bloxham as an assistant master, also serving as curate of Deddington until 1882. He was a useful cricketer and a keen mountaineer. His headmastership falls into three periods, the first from his appointment until the Founder and Mrs Egerton left Bloxham at the end of 1890.

At that stage the approaching crisis was not fully apparent, although the signs were causing Egerton deep depression. From the average of 182 boys in the years 1883-86 the numbers started falling to 163 in 1887, 157 in 1888, 140 in 1889 and 125 in 1890. Financially this meant that a profit of £1,130 in 1885 was converted to a loss of £328 in 1889. As yet the reasons for the slump had not been identified and Boissier could not be blamed, for Bloxham, with the Founder still in residence, remained very much Egerton's school. These were not the only causes for anxiety. The scourge of Victorian headmasters was disease. There was a series of epidemics of which three cases of measles in 1887 were so serious that the parents stayed at the school and one boy died. In the autumn of that year there was a chronic shortage of water in the main school well beneath the cellars, and there could be no regular baths except by using the better supply at the hospital.

Breaches of discipline led to the unusual steps of a public birching and expulsion, and there were also staffing worries. The saddest for Boissier was the health of the chaplain from 1885, the Revd W. A. Marshall, who was his wife's brother; in 1888 he had to have his arm amputated because of a diseased bone and he died in 1889; his successor stayed for only one year.

On the other hand the school was still doing well in other ways. The staff of ten masters was adequate for the size of the school and examination results continued to be satisfactory, with 1886 and 1887 exceptionally good years. Six masters were graduates and the two junior school men, Bridger and Collins, had great experience; the others were the organist, W. H. Williamson (1879-86) and his successor, W. E. Thomas, Mus. D. (1887-94) and Dr H. M. Hain, Ph.D., F.R.S.L., M.C.P., J.S.M. This Bavarian-born master was both a talented linguist, fluent in five languages and knowledgeable in others, and an outstanding musician with a high reputation outside Bloxham. He enjoyed the unusual distinction of being a volunteer officer in both the German army and the Oxfordshire Light Infantry. His association with Bloxham started in 1886, when he asked Egerton for an unsalaried post for the sake of experience, and continued until 1927.

Dr Hain formed a string band and there was a new profusion of other school activities with the formation of a choral society and natural history society and the revival of the museum and debating society, Egerton having ordered the winding-up of the first society because he strongly disapproved of masters and boys debating on equal terms. By far the most popular activities were bicycling and photography, and in the school photograph albums there are groups of boys casually posed in the quadrangle with a variety of machines, penny-farthings and solid smaller bone-shakers of formidable weight while Egerton himself habitually rode a large tricycle or after 1880 one of the strange-looking Otto dicycles. About 30 boys could ride in 1886 when a bicycle club was proposed, and such was their stamina and enthusiasm that four cycled on Ascension Day to Woodstock — about 28 miles over rough and muddy roads on machines for which brakes were not made compulsory until 1896! Amateur photography had been encouraged by the provision of a camera and dark room in 1888 and became a craze throughout the 1890s. Understandably, magic lantern shows were immensely popular, and the library now contained about 2,000 books, including those of the universally favoured boys' writer, G. A. Henty — and were they the same copies still there half a century later? The reading room took the stalwart newspapers and journals like the *Morning Post, Daily Telegraph, Field, Punch* and *Illustrated London News* (as it continued to do for decades) and some less likely ones such as *Exchange & Mart, Moonshine, Fun* and *Sportsman,* but a move to a less accessible position in Botany Bay in 1885 was not favoured.

There were also significant improvements in sport. The 1888 cricket XI was a good one, winning thirteen and tying one of its sixteen matches, with E. A. Ostrehan already showing himself to be a useful bowler. Two years later as captain he was acclaimed the best bowler that the school had known, ending the 1890 season with 95 wickets for 543 runs taken with his leg breaks. Down at Sor brook a primitive dressing shed was erected for the swimmers in 1885, but the biggest improvement for sport was the construction of the cinder running track that same year. It was a marked improvement on either the road or the games fields, which were usually too wet. Bloxham was one the first schools to have a cinder track, and although its narrow width and odd 543-yard length have recently put it out of use, when it was well maintained it provided a fast course for the smaller school before the 1960s. The track, much favoured also by the bicyclists, revived interest in athletics and yearly new records were achieved. The first match against Magdalen College School was arranged (but not held) in 1887.

There was also growing success at football with a longer fixture list made possible by the opening of the Banbury to Kingham railway in 1887; Dean Close, for example, was played for the first time in 1892. Before then, in 1889, new football colours had been appointed, a dark shirt with white knickerbockers, and presumably everyone changed for football and hare and hounds, although only division I changed for cricket in 1888. *The Bloxhamist* appealed for the rest to do so 'as it is much cooler and looks so much better to passers by'. The winter of 1888 had produced one of the heaviest snowfalls of the century with an eighteen-inch fall and drifts up to sixteen feet deep. Two young new boys, J. C. Todd and E. G. A. Van Holst (neither of whom were otherwise notable at the school) started a snowball which they rolled to a giant size, and others rapidly joined in amassing a collection of these snow swiss rolls to build a tower. The rage caught on and the 'Tower of Babel' steadily rose, a steep cone of snow 23 feet high with a winding spiral stairway leading to its summit. The *Banbury Guardian* reported it and it is recorded in a faded photograph in one of the school albums.

The year 1890 started badly. In January the Warden felt obliged to speak out strongly about parents' complaints of bad language, something unheard in the 1860s, there was a 'flu epidemic and on 13 January the Revd A. D. Crake died at Cholsey, Berkshire. A little later the Cambridge locals results were less good than the previous year and Bloxham slipped down the league table to tenth position. With the fall in the number of boys it was clearly going to be necessary to reduce expenditure and reorganise the staff. In the face of all these difficult and depressing circumstances Egerton decided that it was time for him to leave Bloxham altogether, though it must have been intensely disappointing to do so when all his earlier achievements seemed to be crumbling away.

The Egertons' last term at Bloxham was eventful. Their daughter Ellen married Dr Frank Hinde, son of Major-General G. L. Hinde, C.B., on 28 October when the village decorated the street and packed the parish church.[1] A few days later it was All Saintstide, which Egerton always regarded as the main school festival. Indeed, although the school concert and prize-giving were at the end of the academic year in the summer, traditionally held on his birthday on 14 July, he wrote to Wilson in 1896, 'My birthday is the 14th of July but I hope and

[1]Mrs Hinde took a close interest in the school all her life. Shortly after her father's death in 1911 she bought Bennetts in Rose Bank, coming over to Bloxham frequently from her home at Shipton under Wychwood. She made Bennetts her home before 1922, dying there in 1943.

Headmaster's house, 1886, and Egerton memorial library, 1894.

trust that whatever memory is kept of me may be connected with All Saints' Day'. At the end of term the Warden gave each boy his photograph and was himself presented with illuminated addresses from the village and clergy of the deanery. He had lived in Bloxham for 31 years and been in Deddington for a few years before that, so that although his main interest was his school rather than local affairs the sense of loss at his departure extended beyond the school. Old Bloxhamists at their dinner the following January regarded with gloom the Warden's absence from Bloxham, but it spurred them into raising funds for the Egerton memorial library, first proposed in 1886, particularly as there was an added incentive in the bequest of £200 by Canon Liddon for buying books.

By 1894 enough money had been raised to go ahead with the plans by W. O. Milne and J. C. Hall for the two-room library ingeniously inserted on the site of the barn between the old farmhouse and chapel. Shaw-Stewart laid the foundation stone and W. Adkins of Bloxham carried out the work by 1895, the completed building being photographed to make the first illustration in *The Bloxhamist* that year. From the beginning the lower room was the lending library and the upper a reference room, approached from the chapel stairs where formerly there had been a window. This became known as the Liddon room because at first it held little more than the Liddon bequest, though the editors of *The Bloxhamist* were dismayed at the ranks of empty shelves and small array of Liddon books. By limiting the bequest for the purchase of books of the ancient Christian writers and the Anglo-Catholic leaders, Keble and Pusey, Canon Liddon showed a lack of understanding of the juvenile mind and condemned his books to little more than decorative value. Even that has now been lost, since for years the leather-bound volumes have lain in obscure storage, and few boys can even have handled them. On the other hand, right from the beginning Boissier established the purpose of the room, 'One thing I wish to make *quite* clear, and that is — it is not intended as a pleasant lounging room, where boys can go at odd times to pull the books about and play; but it *is* intended as a quiet retreat where masters and boys can retire for study'.

In the autumn term 1890 all the staff had received a term's notice from the Warden 'in consequence of his leaving at the end of the term & a reduction & reorganisation of the staff being necessary'. E. Collins, who had taught for nine years, and W. C. Wisby both had to leave because of the reduction in staff, and the chaplain, the Revd R. A. Ransom (1889-90), also resigned together with Miss Martin, matron for fifteen years but now suffering from poor health. At the beginning of the new era the staff comprised Boissier and six other graduates, W. J. Bridger, experienced but not a graduate, and a foreign master, P. Egli, who replaced Dr Hain for three years. There were also changes among the trustees, for Liddon had died in 1890 and Earl Beauchamp in 1891.

Boissier was now no longer directly overshadowed by the Founder's presence and in small ways started to impose his own personality on the school. He moved into the headmaster's house in the spring of 1891 where he began the custom of having prefects in for late evening readings once a fortnight, a practice reminiscent of undergraduate reading parties. He appointed a chaplain, the

Revd. H. Wigan (1891-99), who was the first not to be a dormitory master also concerned with disciplinary matters. The boys preferred the new scheme and later when T. G. Blofeld was both chaplain and Crake housemaster (1917-25) it was the general opinion among them that the duties of the two posts did not mix.

As a scholar himself the headmaster attempted to revive the academic standards which were declining in step with the size of the school, pursuing this policy by offering entrance scholarships from 1894, to which Egerton contributed generously, by giving more school prizes and by lengthening afternoon school. In 1891 a new examination set by the College of Preceptors, founded and controlled by the teaching profession, was introduced for all those in the upper school not taking Cambridge locals, and better results in both examinations were reported in subsequent years. Indeed, the aim to pass through locals over 25% of all boys in the school was surpassed in 1896 when a 33% pass rate was obtained and in the next year the first entrant for the Oxford and Cambridge higher examination (giving exemption from Oxford university responsions), R. W. Sutcliffe, was successful. The school still did not aim to prepare boys for the universities, but at the 1893 prize-giving Boissier expressed regrets that some eminently well qualified boys had not been given the chance for financial or family business reasons. Neverthless, there were usually a few old boys at both Oxford and Cambridge, three taking their degrees in 1899, for instance.

The standard of music was particularly good under Dr Hain and the organist, Dr W. E. Thomas, who in 1893 set to music the first school song written by J. H. T. Goodwin (1887-98). Much of the music was choral in chapel, of course, and the choir sometimes had heavy duties. Easter at school had always been an important feature of the year, for example, when numerous services were held throughout Holy Week culminating in a two-hour service of the stations of the cross on Good Friday. The chapel itself was slowly becoming less bleak and bare as stained glass memorial windows were inserted, for the chaplains Crake and Marshall, and for Panckridge and Coxeter in 1890, for Canon Liddon in 1891; and with the gift by Mrs Egerton of the ante-chapel window in 1893. The chapel bell, which had been cracked and silent for some years, was recast in commemoration of Queen Victoria's jubilee in 1897.

That was the year of the first school play, directed by Goodwin. In an over-optimistic mood he started rehearsing *Julius Caesar,* but decided to be content with a two-act comedy, *The Test of Truth,* which was produced at All Saints' and well reviewed in the local press. At the next All Saintstide a farce was produced and scenes from *Merchant of Venice,* to begin a new tradition in school life. In the winter terms there also developed a keener interest in football, reflected in the provision of team boards in the pavilion to balance those of the cricketers. There were seventeen fixtures in 1894-95; in 1896 the tough Britannia Works side from Banbury was beaten, and the school reached the semi-final of the Oxfordshire cup in the 1896-7 season with three boys playing later in the Oxfordshire 2nd XI.

Cricket, however, remained the main game, with masters still playing with the boys against club sides — Boissier scoring 83 runs in six innings in 1893, Wilson

84 and J. F. Turner 179, both in seven innings. A new batting record was made in 1891 when in reply to a score of 82 runs by the village the school scored 323 for 3 wickets, of which R. C. Wilkinson made 164 before being caught by his fellow opening batsman who was playing substitute for the village. In the school side was the Founder's nephew, J. R. Egerton, who has claimed that he was the only lob bowler ever played by the school XI. In the 1890 match against the Old Bloxhamists the latter put on 50 runs without loss against the school's 116, when in desperation E. A. Ostrehan brought on Egerton. 'I had a tremendous leg-break', he recalled many years later, 'a slight off-break, when I thought such would be advantageous, and sometimes no break at all — generally the ball was sent up rather high and very slow, and occasionally a fast one. Whilst as to pitch almost every kind was used according to circumstances. In fact, the *head* had to be used all the time, not only just the *hand*'. In eight overs he ran through the O. B. side with seven wickets for fourteen runs, and they were all out for 95!

The end of a cricket era occurred in 1893 with the last match against the Upton House C.C., a country house side brought together by Mr W. H. P. Jenkins, who left the district that year. The school's first match in 1863 had been at Upton House, near Edge Hill, and for at least 25 years it had been played annually. The Upton House sides were always notoriously strong and the school rarely won; in 1893, despite good innings by both Wilson and Turner, they were well beaten. One of the 1893 Upton House players, Major H. C. Maul, brought together strong teams in subsequent years, including four Warwickshire players in his 1895 team, just triumphant from defeating Gloucestershire under Dr W. Grace, and three county players in 1898. To replace the Upton House fixture another country house side, Lord North's Wroxton Abbey XI, was played, against whom Mr D. L. Evans and A. H. Horner put on a third wicket stand of 189 in 1897 with Horner going on to score 145 runs not out. A greater variety of school matches was also arranged, the old rivals of Magdalen College School being joined by St Edward's, Dean Close and Leamington College.

The Bloxhamist duly reported all these events but a school magazine gives a very incomplete picture. Fortunately for this period there also survives Boissier's annual reports to the trustees and his own massive log-book. These show, for instance, how concerned he was about the prevalence of sore throats and 'flu, combined with water shortages — matters of little interest to the editors of *The Bloxhamist,* but essential for the health of the school. After 1890 he immediately set about improvements. The wells were analyzed and though the main one in the cellar, worked by a pumping engine, was pure, there were doubts about the subsidiary well between pavilion and workshop. The school's sanitation was modernised, the schoolroom redecorated, the little-used lathe-room converted into a larger tuck shop in 1891 and a new doctor was appointed.

These matters rightly continued to worry Boissier throughout his headmastership, and emphasise the great change in living conditions in the countryside that followed the provision of main services. Incandescent gas lighting was proposed in 1896 but it was years before there could be much improvement in the water supplies. Even those who can remember the unpleasant earth closets that survived until the 1930s did not suffer from the water shortages such as those in the frost of 1890-91 or the autumns of 1892 and 1893, with the added risk that the supply was polluted. The school relied on various wells, of which the best was the inaccessible one on the cricket field outside the hospital. In the summer of 1896 the old cottage well in the cricket field near Botany Bay was enlarged and piped to the kitchen gas engine. It was in October of the same year, while he was dusting this engine, that the young Fred Mallett had his arm caught and crushed in the machine. He was raced to the sick room where the school doctor amputated his arm. This is the only record of any such emergency operation being carried out at the the school, and its success was a tribute to the speed and skill of the Victorian doctor. "Jumbo" (later shortened to "Bo") Mallett served the school until 1958, a stocky man of fearsome integrity, great kindness and exceptional strength. His one-armed dexterity was extraordinary, shrugging on his jacket, handling loaded trunks as though they were empty, riding his bicycle to the post or unerringly flicking welcome letters from home across the breakfast tables.

The main problem which faced Boissier and the trustees was the continuing decline of numbers in the school, which in turn led to the loss of income and a fall in academic standards. Boissier confided his worries to his private log-book, shared them with the trustees in his reports and voiced them publicly at prize-giving. He commented in his 1892 speech about the competiton from the greatly improved education offered by the board schools and high schools, and correctly forecast that all secondary and grammar schools would become controlled by the government. Ten years later his forecast was largely proved true when the Education Act 1902 established the modern secondary school system. Bloxham and similar schools were distinctive only in their religious education and better sporting facilities, and the religious foundation was in fact one of the school's greatest handicaps.

Bloxham was not the only public school to suffer such a handicap in the late nineteenth century and another local Oxford Movement foundation, St Edward's, Oxford, went through a similar crisis in the 1890s. An over-ambitious building programme caused financial collapse there and at Bradfield, which almost closed because of the size of its debts in 1880. The middle-class demand for public school education was so satisfied by then that few new schools were founded after 1880. Even the expansion of the Woodard Corporation, which opened new schools at Denstone (1868), Ellesmere (1884) and Worksop (1895) was illusory for there was a shortage of funds to exploit early growth and Lancing itself went through a severe financial crisis about 1900.

The religious handicap took differing forms. Much of the zeal for the provision of church education had been spent, and educational reformers looked in preference to the state with its larger resources. From 1889 Technical Instruction committees could give financial assistance from the rates raised by the newly formed county councils for technical and secondary education, but when Boissier enquired of Oxforshire county council in 1891-2 he was asked if Bloxham had a "conscience clause". Schools other than the 1870 board schools were entitled to aid from the local rates provided that among other conditions they operated a "conscience clause" allowing parents to withdraw their children from religious instruction of which they did not approve. Bloxham, of course, did not. At the same time, prejudice against High Church practices remained strong, reducing the number of parents likely to send their boys to Bloxham. At Lancing the chaplain exercised too much influence until a reforming headmaster reasserted his authority in the early 1900s, and although there is no evidence of a similar position at Bloxham Boissier did advise Egerton in 1892 that too much time was spent on religious matters to the detriment of other teaching, repeating the warning to the trustees in 1895. The upper school was still spending more time on divinity than any other school subject except mathematics and Euclid together, and there was no science teaching of any sort in 1888 when Boissier had appealed for greater use of the carpentry and engineering workshops. He suggested then that boys might take up studies in mechanical engineering and electricity in place of Latin but his far-sighted proposal was rejected by parents intent on the academic curriculum of grammar schools and universities.

Since Egerton had attributed his earlier success to the religious principles upon which he had started Bloxham and never admitted that they later were a handicap, it took some courage for Boissier to point out the changed circumstances to the trustees. He diagnosed and exposed the difficulties facing the school and suggested remedies for overcoming them, but the trustees were reluctant to recognise that he was right. On the one hand the board and high schools with their free ladder of education from primary stages to university were attracting Bloxham's entrants, as on the other were the scholarships offered at the better endowed public schools. Even after he introduced scholarships in 1894 Boissier complained that it was hard to keep clever younger boys, who left to go on to other schools. This was because of Bloxham's low academic standard as other schools improved. The public schools were at last beginning to take some interest in the teaching of science, but although the Oxfordshire county council deputation had been impressed in 1892 that Bloxham was 'the only school in Oxfordshire that had attempted to supply any technical education at all', it did not amount to much more than the provision of the under-used workshops (one of which, it will be remembered, was converted into a tuck shop about that time!) and when a keen master wanted to start botany the opportunity was not followed up. This was not so much Boissier's fault, since he was clearly forward-looking, as the inability of the trustees to invest money in this sort of teaching and the unwillingness of parents and boys to take advantage of what opportunities there were. He felt that too many subjects were taught, and that even on the classics side they were not taught well enough, urging the appointment of a good classics master at the high salary of £110 to £120 a year. 'CJW and the chaplain both get £120 (& are *worth* it) but neither represents any *scholarship* such as the top boys want', he wrote to the Warden in 1892; the usual starting salary for university graduates was £70 to £80.

His report to the trustees at the end of that year suggested wisely that they should seek an inspection and advice on the academic side, and he put forward a case for increasing the size of the school — even then the headmaster reckoned that for educational purposes he needed 300 to 500 boys, though for domestic and religious reasons the single household of 150 to 170 was best — investing in new laboratories, library, swimming bath and gym. Already it was evident that a small school could not afford the staff to teach up to university and army and navy entrance requirements and Boissier, feeling that Bloxham in any case did things in a style that justified higher fees, advocated the aim of becoming a first-class school by carrying out these improvements and raising the fees. Later headmasters used the same gambit of an independent inspection to expose deficiencies and back their case for academic and building improvement, but Boissier's trustees were not persuaded.

Bloxham, therefore, continued to weaken and the headmaster to suggest alternative remedies. The school should be advertised in those parts of the country where it already had support, and it is of interest that he specifically mentioned the Liverpool area, Wolverhampton and Salisbury, but without explaining whether many boys came from those parts. Furthermore it should be made known that Bloxham was the only church school of its grade in the south Midlands and diocese of Oxford. More controversially, patrons should be able to purchase nominations for places, a scheme borrowed from nineteenth-century charitable institutions. Finally, in 1894 and after a request from the Headmasters' Association[2] for information about the trust in connection with government proposals for reorganising secondary education, Boissier underlined the need for the church schools to stand together. He advised the trustees to consider affiliation with other schools. Either that year or the next he repeated the same advice in an undated letter to Egerton. 'I believe', he said, 'our best policy would be to try to affiliate with the Woodard Schools', reminding the Warden of Bloxham's lack of endowments once the Egerton fortune was removed. It was sound and courageous advice, as was his offer to resign the headmastership of the school which had been his whole life and love, because he felt too personally involved to carry out the necessary reforms.

The trustees did not accept his resignation, but for the third time negotiations were opened with the Woodard Corporation, in circumstances far less propitious than in 1880. They would also have been prompted by their concern for the Founder's health. Mrs Egerton was ill in 1893 and suffered a long and distressing mental illness from at least 1894. This put a great strain on Reginald Egerton, in addition to his worries over the school. Certainly he was now more often wondering whether Bloxham would survive. Its 184 places were only half filled and it was losing money nearly every year, totalling about £1,100 over the period 1891-95. On 11 October 1895, therefore, a meeting was held in London between Egerton, his brother Hubert, still the bursar, and three of the trustees with the provost of the Woodard Corporation (his old friend Canon Lowe), W. B. Woodard and some of the Woodard trustees in order to continue formal discussions on the offer that Egerton had made to give Bloxham to the

---

[2] An association of secondary school headmasters who were not members of the Headmasters' Conference.

Corporation.

A few days later the bursar of Lancing, the Revd E. Blackmore, the custos, W. B. Woodard, and the headmaster of Hurstpierpoint came to inspect Bloxham. With uncharacteristic parsimony Egerton instructed Boissier that 'a plain piece of cold boiled beef or a veal and ham pie would be sufficient' for their lunch. For their part the Corporation remained hesitant, since they were already committed to new schools in the Midlands and faced with financial troubles at Lancing. They insisted, therefore, on a guarantee fund against further losses for two or three years, which the bishop of Reading quickly raised within Oxford diocese, and pressed Egerton to include the playing field and the cottage next to the school in his gift although neither belonged to the trustees. Eventually after the chapter agreed the terms on 6 March the provost wrote,

'We decided yesterday to accept your munificent offer of Bloxham School to the Provost & Fellows of S. Nicolas College. Your gift lays upon us a special responsibility to strive under God's blessing that the School shall under our direction never fail to keep in view your high purpose in its Foundation, & above all maintain in our teaching within it the full Catholic doctrine of the Church of England'.

He suggested that Egerton should be elected a fellow of Lancing, an offer which was apparently declined by the Founder and, recognising Egerton's sad disappointment at the failure of the school and his fears for its future even with the Corporation's support, made the proposal that should they ever wish to dispose of it, they would give him the first offer of the property. Egerton was still reluctant to make the break, but at last headmaster, staff and parents were informed and the negotiations were completed in the summer. Their successful conclusion must have owed much to Canon Lowe, who understood Egerton so well and who would, if not over-ruled by Woodard, have gladly accepted Egerton and Bloxham into the Corporation nearly 40 years earlier. The school was officially transferred to the provost and fellows of the Corporation of SS. Mary and Nicolas, Lancing, on 8 August 1896, the Bloxham trustees formally confirming the transfer and winding up their affairs on 20 February 1897.

According to the *History,* written only a few years after the event,

'By its incorporation the School gained much and lost nothing; for while it has benefited by the long experience of those now responsible for it, and by the security derived from belonging to a large foundation, on the other hand it has lost none of its distinctive character, and is not likely to do so'.

Some of the practical benefits followed immediately. During 1897 the wells in the cricket field were enlarged and piped to the kitchens, new bathrooms were built and central heating installed in schoolroom and chapel. The dais was built in the dining hall, which had recently been redecorated — from blue and chocolate to light green and dark red! Of greater significance, the boot room was moved to the schoolroom cellars from Botany Bay, so that the latter could be altered and enlarged for conversion as a laboratory, opened by the Earl of Jersey in 1898. Plans were announced for building a gym at the east end of the chapel.

The change was not made without expressions of regret by the Old

Bloxhamists, and it was probably more than coincidence that Egerton's former pupils at last formed an Old Boys' society in 1896. Although the idea had been rejected earlier, there had always been a small group keen on it. Some had met for the first provincial dinner at Liverpool in 1892 and the former secretary, F. G. Clarke, and two others dined formally in Calcutta on the same night as the 1893 London dinner. There had been talk of compiling an Old Bloxhamist directory, of reviving the football club, and in 1888 was recorded the entry to the school of A. N. Rye, first 'second-generation' Bloxhamist, son of H. A. Rye (1860-64). In 1889 A. H. Johnston called for the foundation of an Old Boys' society without success and it was eventually formed on a proposal at the 1896 dinner by R. N. Lyne. Whereas earlier the Founder had discouraged such a society as being premature, now he was enthusiastic, writing to Lyne, 'The movement has my warmest support. I shall be delighted to join in it, and to send my subscription as soon as you let me know to whom it should be paid'. The Bloxhamist Society was formally constituted at a meeting on 23 April 1896 at Anderton's Hotel, Fleet Street, with the dual objects of promoting the interests of the school and keeping Old Bloxhamists in touch with each other.[3] Its rules were based on the Cheltonian and Marlburian societies, and an annual subscription of five shillings was levied.

The first secretary was C. L. Clarke and the committee members included Lyne, F. B. Palmer and Wilson. R. J. G. Read and F. S. Boissier were vice-presidents, and Egerton the first president. For the Founder the loyalty and appreciation of his old boys, expressed in the presentation of an illuminated address, were some compensation for his sense of loss at handing over his school to the Woodard Corporation. In thanking the Old Bloxhamists for their gift he replied,

'I am thankful that its permanence as a Church institution is now secured, though I have had to sacrifice much of my own private strong convictions as to the constitution of the school, for which I worked independently all these years, and I feel, as I cannot help saying, most intensely, the being no longer Warden of this School'.

The other casualty was the headmaster. It was Boissier who made Bloxham a Woodard school. Egerton and the trustees had to take the decision and conclude the negotiations, but it must be doubtful whether they would have done so without Boissier's persistent advice. Having accomplished the handover it was sensible for him to give way to another headmaster appointed by the Corporation, so after seeing the changes safely carried through he resigned at the end of 1898 after 26 years at the school as boy, second master and headmaster. He returned to Derbyshire, where he had been a curate between Cambridge and his appointment as a master at Bloxham, and for 30 years was vicar of Denby, rural dean for much of that time and a canon of Derby cathedral in 1930. His retirement was divided between Derbyshire and his son Paul (O.B.) who was headmaster of Harrow, and he died at the great age of 96 in 1951. Bloxham remained his first interest all his long life, and four generations of his family have been educated at the school in a century, a record for Bloxham.

---

[3] Two years earlier the Founder had ruled that the correct name, again following the Winchester example, was Bloxhamist, not Bloxhamite.

CHAPTER V

G. H. WARD
1899-1914

The first Bloxham engagement of the new headmaster, even before the beginning of his first term, was to attend the annual dinner of the Old Bloxhamists at the Holborn Restaurant. The Founder was present and naturally his old boys gathered round him to enjoy his company and recall past years, some regretting that Bloxham had joined the Woodard Corporation. The new headmaster, however, immediately proved his character, by his presence at the meeting, his praise for Egerton and the declaration of his own intentions for the future.

The Revd George Herbert Ward, a scholar of Hertford College, Oxford, where his father was fellow and senior tutor, came to Bloxham at the age of 37 after being an assistant master at St Paul's in London for eleven years. His young family all revelled in the freedom that Bloxham offered after a flat in Earl's Court, enjoying country walks and bicycle rides, croquet and tennis on the school lawns, indoor holiday games in the fives court and gym, and entertaining in the spacious headmaster's house. The somewhat stern photographic portraits of Ward may suggest his clear and incisive thought but not the energetic and broad-minded headmaster who led the senior boys on a 25-mile choir outing to Blenheim Palace by bicycle, outpacing the drag filled with trebles sufficiently to give his party time for refreshment at the Falkland Arms in Great Tew and at Hopcroft's Holt; and who, having arrived, smuggled his forbidden camera into the precincts of the ducal mansion. Photography was his main hobby and he took many school photographs, also experimenting with early colour photography in the dark room rigged up in the cellar of his house. He possessed a lively sense of humour and a patient tolerance towards his colleagues, whose weaknesses he sometimes privately found rather trying, confiding on one occasion in his diary, 'Had a rather warm interview with the Chaplain over Good Friday but did not actually come to blows! We compromised in the end'. He was a firm High Churchman who liked to emphasise the attractive and cheerful character of Christianity and disapproved of gloomy or long-winded sermons, hymns and services. His sensitivity and tact earned him Egerton's friendship, of which one small but significant example will suffice. In his first year he replaced the mixture of school colours — originally blue and white, then dark blue and gold for cricket and blue and black for football — with the black and white theme taken from the Egerton coat of arms and used ever since.

He was the first headmaster chosen for Bloxham by the Woodard Corporation, who, having taken on the struggling school, fulfilled their promise to invest capital in it and looked to their headmaster for reform. The priority was to check the decline in the size and profitability of the school, for which the

Revd G. H. Ward, headmaster 1899-1914.

necessary first step was the introduction of better control and administration by the Corporation, together with modernisation of the buildings and an improvement of academic standards. A Bloxham Committee was appointed in 1901 consisting of the provost (the bishop of Southampton), the bishop of Reading, the warden of Keble (Dr W. Lock), the bursar of Lancing (the Revd E. Blackmore) and the custos of Lancing (W. B. Woodard). The headmaster was in attendance and they made Wilson as secretary and school bursar responsible through the headmaster to the Committee and to the Lancing bursar. Wilson carried out this job until 1917, when he was 70, although as he got older he seems to have found it difficult to master the load of work in running the domestic affairs of the school, and was understandably testy when criticised for housekeeping economies imposed by the Committee. They met each term and kept a strict financial control over expenditure, with the result that every year until the jubilee in 1910 a profit was made, sometimes very small as in 1902 when it was only £21, but between £225 and £445 in good years like 1904 to 1907, even allowing for the sums spent on the buildings.

The improvement was partly due to the rising numbers of boys in the school with 104 in 1907. This total fell shortly afterwards and by the outbreak of the war in 1914 there were only 70 owing, it was said, to the success at that time of Magdalen College School at Brackley. Over a quarter lived locally, and of the 88 in the school in 1911, 27 were local, 22 from London, 37 from other parts of the country including Oxford, and 2 from overseas. It seemed, therefore, at first as though joining the Woodard Corporation with their policy of advertisement and entrance scholarships was achieving recovery, despite the appearance of the state in secondary education after the passing of the Education Act 1902. That act for the first time enabled a clear distinction to be made between state-aided schools and 'public' schools, while Bloxham's membership of the Woodard Corporation removed any lingering doubts that from its origin as a privately owned middle-class school it had joined the company of the public schools. Ward seems to have gently advanced this change of character by his selection of boys entering the school, and although he could hardly afford to refuse any parent willing to pay the fees he did little to encourage those whose sons he thought would be unsuitable, either those who were farmers or of strong evangelical principles.

The change of character was more evident in the building improvements undertaken to equip Bloxham with some of the facilities expected of a public school, and the Woodard Corporation rapidly invested as much money as the trustees had been able to afford over the previous fifteen years. They built the new chemistry laboratory in Botany Bay and Ward had at once opened a building fund for a gym which had been proposed in 1898. The first site considered near the chapel was rejected in favour of one on the far side of the gardens near Water Lane and the foundation stone was laid in 1901 by Lt. General the Hon. N. G. Lyttleton, then on leave from active service in the Boer War. The lofty Hornton stone building with mansard roof was designed by T. Tyrwhitt. Contemporaries were critical of its appearance, but since the architect planned a three-stage scheme, with flanking fives courts and swimming baths, which was never fully carried out, it is perhaps unfair to judge it too critically. Like the earlier school buildings the stone was quarried on the site and the search for a good water supply for the swimming baths added considerably to the cost of the gym. The masons dug twenty feet to find a spring, which rapidly filled up the vast hole to give the gym a peculiar resonance and later generations of boys a hide-out known as "Fingal's Cave". The gym was opened in 1903, the original fitted equipment coming from Leamington College. No sooner was it finished than an appeal was made for the fives courts, the unlovely extension containing two excellent courts, whose slow construction in 1907-09 was a cause for editorial comment in *The Bloxhamist*. Later editors successively derived much merriment from the progress of the swimming baths. The headmaster launched the appeal in 1909 and four years later, when in fact the custos of the Corporation viewed the proposed site by the gym, *The Bloxhamist* unwisely reported 'there seems every chance of the construction of the much-needed swimming bath being taken in hand at no very distant date'.

The other building improvements ordered by the Committee were less striking

School from the cricket field, about 1900, showing Arkell memorial fives court, pavilion, carpentry shop and tuck shop.

and controversial than the new gym, but in total equally important. It was in those first years of the twentieth century that the big schoolroom was refurnished with the desks and lockers that most living Old Bloxhamists remember, some of the original desks being used to make the chapel pulpit, designed in 1933 by T. M. Walker in memory of John Grove (1927-30). The direct result of a fire in the headmaster's house was the fitting of fire escapes, then as now the route from the Crake dormitories being by an unsightly metal ladder which in those days led down to the main school entrance porch. In the same period the passages were retiled, the hall, prefects' study and Egerton reading room in the library refurnished, and various domestic alterations carried out, including the linking stairway between headmaster's house and dining hall and a novel 'speaking tube' from his dining room to the kitchen. One desirable work was not approved, a corridor extension to link the outdoor latrines beyond the east end of the chapel with the main buildings, because 'The Custos . . . found that it would involve the destruction of the foundation stone of the Buildings, he had therefore abandoned it'.

The Committee and headmaster were also active in attempts to raise academic standards. Soon after taking up his post Ward announced that the entrance scholarships, to which Egerton continued to contribute generously, were attracting eleven new boys, and there were fifteen exhibitioners in 1902, eleven being awarded by Egerton or Old Bloxhamists; later, on at least one occasion Mrs Hinde paid the fees of a boy at the school. Ward also succeeded — where Boissier's similar proposal had failed — in obtaining Bloxham's first inspection in 1901, which in the way of inspections identified and reinforced the case for improvements. The Committee introduced some novel schemes — an increase in salaries, an incentive payment of three guineas a year to any master responsible for the admission of a new boy, and a bonus of £10 to the master chiefly responsible for a boy winning a university scholarship. They also spent a lot of money advertising, which they could do since Bloxham was not a member of the Headmaster's Conference, and in 1904 they again considered opening a preparatory school at St Mary's Lodge.

Ward, who obtained first class honours in mathematics at Oxford, had considerable success in his desire to raise the level of school work and much was due to his personal lead. Soon after his arrival he had introduced early morning school from 7.0 to 7.40 — he was an early riser himself, and in the summer was up at any time from 4 a.m. — and had cut the number of half holidays from three to two. On special occasions, of course, extra half-holidays would be given, and it is a sign of his understanding of boys that he recognised that exceptional circumstances demanded exceptional remedies. In February 1913 he let the whole school off an early morning period when a military biplane force-landed in one of the fields by the Bloxham Grove road, noting in his diary,

'A plane flew past about 8.45 this morning & came down in one of Salmon's fields. Captn. Dawes from Moreton-in-Marsh. Brought down by the strong N.E. wind. Let the boys off 1st hour to go & see the machine. Crowds trooped out all day long from Bloxham & Banbury to inspect it'.

He also started the hated card system by which each boy's progress was marked at the end of every lesson and scrutinised weekly by the headmaster.

Following the inspection the school changed to the Oxford examining board, and in the first year in 1901 obtained 21 certificates; that was also the year that H. W. A. Wadley won a mathematical scholarship to Selwyn College, Cambridge, and there were fourteen boys at the universities. By 1904 36 certificates were obtained and five boys were entering Oxford or Cambridge, and this trend was maintained. Friendly criticism from a parent was used by Ward to justify the immediate appointment of an additional classics master, music was encouraged to the extent that 21 out of the 104 boys were learning it in 1907, and botany was introduced as a new subject in 1910, though it must be admitted that in common with many other public and grammar schools there was little interest in science teaching. By 1913 Bloxham had better examination results than any of the other Woodard schools except Lancing, gaining more honours and distinctions from the 40 boys out of 80 who took Oxford locals than double or treble that number of candidates from the other larger schools.

The Committee's sympathy towards the needs of the teaching staff was less evident in their dealings with the school servants. They refused the carpenter, Richard Bartlett, an increase in his salary and generations of Old Bloxhamists may be startled to learn that Bo Mallett was given six months' notice to find a new job in February 1901; he was later retained 'provisionally' but warned that he would get no increase in his salary, although they relented a year later and raised it to £15! This may be compared with £35 a year for the matron and the 25s. to 30s. a week received by the newly appointed gym instructor and the school butler (to replace the veteran Luke Bartlett, who had held the post since 1870). A farm labourer's wage of that period was only 10s. a week, and the masters' salaries ranged between £90 and £120 a year, depending on their service and experience; the new chaplain received £100.

The most senior in this respect remained Wilson, universally known as "Pym" although the origin of the nickname has not been explained. In addition to his work as bursar he was still teaching some French despite his age, growing deafness and an attempt to retire and leave in 1914. The conversion of Botany Bay had driven him from his rooms there to quarters high above the dining hall wing from which he could control the domestic affairs of the school. He managed to introduce some innovations in the school meals, providing porridge every morning for breakfast, meat for breakfast if parents wanted it for their boys, and laying on cocoa and biscuits for supper. Formerly this last privilege had been restricted to those in the headmaster's house, where Ward admitted boys at slightly higher fees. About twenty boys were taken, and the headmaster's daughter can remember how every night an extra leaf was put in the dining table, a white cloth spread, bread, butter, cheese, jam and cocoa set out and the boys filed in and silently ate their supper. One summer day a new boy was dared that he would not walk into supper, go straight to the window opposite the door and jump out. He did, ignorant of the fact that owing to the fall of the land it was a long drop — and had to be rushed into Banbury to have a tooth replaced!

The other long-serving members of the staff were Dr "Hansy" Hain who gave up his full-time teaching in 1912, F. W. Attwood, the organist (1902-11), who may be credited with being the first master to possess a motor bike, and J. F. Turner, who left in 1909 to be ordained, having taught mathematics to the lower school with one break since 1892. He played cricket and football throughout his career, and as a sportsman and dormitory master was popular. Masters were still playing with the boys against club sides, so a batsman was likely to be popular who could produce these scores in one season for the school — 0, 131 not out, 76 not out, 66, 2, 19 not out, 65, 33, 11, 64, 20, 4, 28, 6, and take a crop of wickets. The year was 1906 and not exceptional, the school winning ten and losing four of its seventeen matches, the best players among the boys being R. S. Campbell and L. B. Ostrehan. In the second XI J. G. Whiting secured fame by taking seven Magdalen College School wickets for one run.

The outstanding cricketer a few seasons earlier had been H. B. Tordiffe. In 1898 he was a successful division II bowler, but the next year was already showing himself as an all-rounder and in 1901 he broke all previous records with three match centuries in one season, 100 not out against Hook Norton, 147 not out against Leamington College and 181 not out against Magdalen College School, the last being the highest since records were kept in 1874. His total of 1,157 runs in one season for the XI has not been beaten. His highest score was a shattering 211 in a dormitory match, played with all the partisan struggles of later house matches, and was of the stuff of a *Boys' Own* story. In the first innings of dormitories I and III (the later Crake house) Tordiffe opened the batting and was out for 7 runs; the rest of the side collapsed for 35 and his was the highest score! In the second innings they scored 310, thanks to Tordiffe's 211, but dormitories II and V still won by 5 wickets. In the following year he scored a new record of 218 in a first division game and two more centuries in school matches.

A cricket professional was engaged all this time and A. Sheppard of Faringdon served as a football coach in 1899-1900 with a marked effect on the results, for the school won more matches than it lost for the first time for several years. F. Y. Horner, the best goalkeeper that anyone could remember, conceded 44 goals in seven defeats against the 83 scored in nine victories with three matches drawn, and he played for Oxfordshire and Watford F. C. on leaving school. An elder brother, A. H. Horner (1890-98), killed on active service in 1916, had been amateur heavyweight boxing champion, a sport not recorded at the school in his time. The first occasion that Bloxham entered the Public Schools Gym competition was 1904, a year after the school's own gym was opened, but not until 1909 did Bloxham boys box in the Public Schools Boxing competition at Aldershot.

These last two events indicated widening horizons, at least partly brought about by contact with the ways of other schools through the Woodard Corporation as well as by having a headmaster with experience of schools other than just Bloxham. Another indication was the move to form an Officers' Training Corps. The Boer War encouraged the spread of the idea that military leadership was expected of public schoolboys and like the rest of the country the school followed the war news with enthusiasm. Two Old Bloxhamists had joined Jameson's Raid of 1896 and even so small a school had 47 old boys serving in the war, five of whom lost their lives. However, only eight were officers, clearly revealing the character of a small school with no pretensions of producing a military officer class, unlike Cheltenham, Haileybury or Wellington. Ward called for the formation of a cadet corps and to rally interest allowed the Banbury Volunteers to hold an exercise on the cricket field in 1900. However, peace — heralded by a master 'speeding from his class room with his coat tails flying in the breeze' — postponed further plans for a corps for some years although the headmaster kept the idea alive. The country had been severely shaken by its miserable inability to win the war and the poor physical condition of its soldiers, with the result that the government forced physical education upon the new secondary schools and the military heroes and leaders of the war, notably Lord Roberts, toured the public schools calling for their leadership and patriotism. Ward was in tune with the times, therefore, in building the gym and appointing a gym instructor, Colour-Sergeant W. S. Grinter, using drill as a punishment and inviting Admiral Sir Gerard Noel, K.C.B., an old boy of Hewett's school, to give a rousing speech at the 1907 prize-giving. Grinter even tried giving holiday drill classes to the headmaster's children and their friends, among whom Osbert Sitwell was briefly recruited, remembered as a clumsy and awkward boy who stayed with his father's cousins at Park Close.[1]

School opinion was mostly unfavourable. Long before, in 1879, it had

---

[1]He described Park Close in detail in *Left hand, right hand. The scarlet tree* (1946), 199-215.

haughtily dismissed a visit from the Banbury and Deddington Volunteers as 'eccentric manoeuvres in the way of mimic warfare', and if the minutes of the debating society accurately reflect the views of the school it was overwhelmingly believed in 1904 that war with Germany was unlikely within ten years and a master pronounced confidently in 1908 that 'civilisation had done away with the necessity for fighting'. Even after the O.T.C. had been formed and with the evidence of European rearmament, the debating society recorded a strong dislike of conscription. By then the military rivalry within Europe had brought a renewed interest in the idea of a cadet corps and in November 1910 an Officers' Training Corps was started under the new science master, A. Child. Although later recalled as the most important single event of Ward's headmastership, at the time it was completely overshadowed by other happenings in the school's jubilee year.

The main celebrations were held on 14 July with school and village decorated overall to welcome some 500 guests, a great procession to the thanksgiving service in the parish church, with lunch and speeches in hall afterwards, a two-day cricket match and evening entertainment. The schools of the Southern division of the Woodard Corporation were represented by their headmasters and boys and among a galaxy of clergy, both masters, Old Bloxhamists and neighbouring incumbents, were the bishops of Chichester and Reading, the archdeacon of Oxford (the bishop being ill and unable to attend), the warden of Keble College and the provost of Lancing, Canon Southwell. His after-lunch speech was short and witty, introducing the bishop of Chichester as the first occasion that the Visitor had visited the school. "Am I right in this statement? I pause for reply". Mr Boissier, "The Bishop of Oxford visited the School". The Provost, "But that was under the old regime, not under the present regime". Continuing his speech he said, "Really, I feel quite like Mr Lloyd George in the House of Commons; by dint of shifting my ground, I emerge triumphant'".

Inevitably a history of the school was proposed for publication. E. W. Maud aroused interest in 1908 by suggesting that an Old Bloxhamist register might be compiled — something which greater public schools had already done — a proposal particularly welcomed by Wilson who already maintained the records. He had for years been the main link between Old Bloxhamists and the school and was a meticulous keeper of registers, address lists and other records, all in his neat, small handwriting. J. S. Chatterton then suggested that the register should include a history of the school, and when it was soon found that the size and expense of making a register and keeping it up-to-date were prohibitive, the more modest proposal for a history was preferred.

The *History* was published in 1910 and although the identity of the author does not seem to have been deliberately concealed, his anonymity was preserved so effectively that no one in more recent times could name him. Authorship was attributed to Wilson, although the style was not his, and certainly he must have contributed much of the information as well as being responsible for the actual publishing and distribution. He was, of course, also celebrating his own jubilee. The headmaster also contributed, and it was said in 1922 that he had actually written it. Ward however revealed at the jubilee Old Bloxhamist dinner that the history was being written by the Revd Sidney Boulter (1865-69), who was later made an honorary member of the Old Bloxhamist Society, presumably in recognition of this work, still not acknowledged in his obituary notice in *The Bloxhamist* in 1932.[2] His *History* was relatively short with only about 45 pages of text and an invaluable list of masters as an appendix, but it is remarkable among school histories up to that time for the number of illustrations. Perhaps the headmaster with his interest in photography was responsible for this, and the 85 photographs — of which the advertisement in *The Bloxhamist* remarked somewhat ingenuously, 'The reproductions are all *good* and nearly all are *very good*' — are now highly prized as evidence of the old buildings and former well-known personalities.

The *History* is largely a tribute to Egerton and in the sermon and speeches on jubilee day and at the Old Bloxhamist dinner at the Trocadero Restaurant on 12 January, the bishop of Chichester and the provost praised Egerton again and again. The provost reminded his jubilee audience of Egerton's friendship with Liddon and Gladstone's remark 'that England owed as much to him as to any man in religious education'.[3] Bloxham and the Woodard Corporation had taken a long time to come together, but the Corporation was warm and generous in its appreciation of Egerton's foundation and gift. The Founder was too overcome with emotion to speak at the Old Bloxhamist dinner and ill-health prevented him from attending the jubilee at school, when his younger brother, Hubert, answered for him.

There can be few founders who live to see the jubilee of their schools, and Egerton was now failing. He had suffered the distress of his wife's long illness and death in 1907, and his own health had been poor for some time. He continued to live at Vale Mascal at North Cray, Kent, where the Old Bloxhamists occasionally gathered and the Ward family regularly visited him. The children were enchanted by the formal style of the household, dressing for dinner taken under the watchful eye of the butler, driving out in the open landau in the afternoon, and were captivated by Egerton's own humour and kindness together with that of his long-serving housekeeper, Miss Mabel Tyler. His last illness was short and he died at Vale Mascal on 28 April 1911 at the age of 79. He was buried at North Cray on 3 May, with the headmaster taking part of the funeral service with the provost and parish clergy. Among the hymns was the school All Saintstide favourite "Who are these like stars appearing?" sung unaccompanied at the graveside. The Egerton grave is marked by a dark stone Irish cross, with a simple inscription

---

[2]Like the present writer his main qualification seems to have been that of an Old Bloxhamist who had not frequently visited the school and was therefore regarded as reasonably dis-interested and objective!

[3]As a High Churchman Egerton had a high regard for Gladstone, though he distrusted Liberal policies towards Church education. One of Hubert Egerton's spaniels, "Duchess", was trained to sit up with a biscuit placed on her nose which she was not allowed to eat until she had voted for her favourite statesman. The Founder would call out the names of various politicians, but Duchess remained motionless until Gladstone was named, when the biscuit was at once tossed up, caught and swallowed.

recording only the names of Philip Reginald and Harriet Egerton with the dates of their births and deaths. His daughter gave the school many of the Founder's possessions from Vale Mascal, including his sideboard, the illuminated address when he left Bloxham and Chevallier Tayler's painting of the school from Hobb Hill, books and personal relics, and made two requests: that his birthday of 14 July should be observed as Founder's Day and that in all commemoration of the Founder his name should be coupled with that of his wife Harriet. He himself had asked that he should be particularly remembered on All Saints' Day.

Wilson was sent dozens of letters from his own contemporaries and others who had been Egerton's old boys. They all repeated similar sentiments, worth quoting here to illustrate the extraordinary influence that "the Guvnor" had on his boys. Cecil Kidson commented, 'The nine years and a half I spent at Bloxham under his guidance and kindly discipline have left an impression which can never be eradicated and although separated so long from the old school I have frequently thought of him & often told my own children that I looked upon him as the finest specimen of an honourable & just man that I had ever met'.

'We shall not soon look upon his like', wrote the Revd Arthur Guest, 'How one's memory goes back to the old days. Though never a good teacher. yet his manliness & love of all that was good & true had a wonderful influence upon us. He could never do a mean or an ungentlemanly thing. He inspired a high tone of honour & truthfulness both in & out of school, in short we respected & loved him. He was our beau ideal of a true man'.

And finally, the school historian, the Revd Sidney Boulter,

'The more I think over what the investigations I made last year brought to my memory & to my knowledge, the more impressed I am with his high aims, his saintly character, his manliness, & in addition to it all the real & special blessing that God bestowed upon his work. . . There was something about him which gripped us, & has held us, as witness those who were at the funeral.'

The Bloxhamist for April/May 1911 is filled with other tributes from his friends and pupils familiar with his exceptional character. His talents and achievements are little recognised outside the Bloxham fellowship for his school has always been small and relatively little known, but a recent book on *The Victorian Public School* (1975) has claimed that he 'was one of the most interesting headmasters of the whole Victorian era'.

The recent expenses of the jubilee led John Read, one of the most loyal of Old Bloxhamists and again serving as their secretary in place of his son who had gone abroad, to suggest that no special memorial appeal should be made. Experience had shown that recent appeals among Old Bloxhamists for the Egerton library, gym and swimming bath were decidedly sluggish, but fortunately the chaplain, the Revd H. R. Willimott, thought otherwise. Immediately after the funeral he was explaining his ideas to some of the old boys — to place a reredos behind the altar in the chapel, lowering the altar steps to avoid obscuring the east window, to insert a north sanctuary window to light the altar and to panel the chancel. Willimott's plan was carried out in 1912, not without the justifiable criticism that the reredos is glorified at the expense of the altar and that it detracts from the appearance of the Wilberforce memorial east window. It was dedicated on 21 September, the headmaster noting in his diary,

'Consecration service at 9, very fine, Bp and Provost in copes, servers in white albs for the first time, over soon after 10. Communicants had breakfast in dining hall afterwards ... Mrs Hinde also Dr. B [oissier] are very cool about the memorial, the boys think it gaudy!'

So it was, especially after the plain stonework and dark aspect of the east end beforehand. The scale of the reredos, carved in Cambridgeshire clunch stone with the crucifixion scene and eight flanking saints designed by W. Bucknall, a pupil and partner of Sir Ninian Comper, immediately attracts the eye and together with the new marble pavement, oak panelling and north window gave the sanctuary a fresh sense of richness, space and light. A new two-ton altar of Bath stone was raised in place, with frontals designed by G. F. Bodley, and the former altar and furnishings were given to Deddington parish church. Over half the cost of the whole memorial was paid by Willimott.

Revd H. R. Willimott, chaplain 1904-09, 1910-17, 1926-27.

Hugh Willimott had come to Bloxham as chaplain in 1904 and with a short break in 1909 remained until 1917. His arrival heralded changes of which the refurnishing and elevation of the chapel sanctuary was only one permanent sign, for he brought to Bloxham the growing elaboration of services and ceremonial which were the common practice of Anglo-Catholic priests of his time. Although the regular use of vestments, not approved by the Woodard Corporation before 1897, was actually introduced by his short-term predecessor in 1903, the Revd

E. J. Crombie, it was Willimott who made the great change in the style of worship for the next half-century by holding a daily communion service and starting the Sunday mid-morning choral eucharist. Some of the Old Bloxhamists were critical about this last move and F. B. Palmer, for instance, recalled the old 8 a.m. sung eucharist. 'I don't feel myself that a 10.30 Choral Eucharist is a step forward ... A late Choral Eucharist without communicants which is becoming so common is not surely the mind of the primitive Church at least'. Some of the boys also were uncomfortable about the new practices and Gregorian chants and there was an undercurrent of feeling that there was too much chapel, a feeling which Ward, who seems to have liked ceremonial, shared at least to the extent of wishing that the services were livelier.

In addition to the Egerton memorial many minor improvements were made to the chapel at this time — the sanctuary gong from Willimott's brother's parish in Leeds; the new ciborium from the confirmation candidates of 1904-08; memorial windows to B. S. Ashworth (who had died soon after leaving in 1904, his father being a generous benefactor who also gave the processional cross), Mrs Egerton in 1909 and Miss M. E. Mallinson, the matron, in 1914; new vestments and chest in 1912; banner and altar cloth embroidered by the headmaster's sister, May Ward; and the oak panelling in the nave given by F. Haden Crawford (O.B.) in 1913. On Willimott's leaving in 1917 *The Bloxhamist* reminded its readers that, 'A Chaplain's influence depends, in the long run, not upon what he says but upon what he is', and Willimott's influence extended to a wide range of school activities. He was a keen gardener, and "Gillies' Garden" at the front of the school was named after him; more spectacular was his organisation of the 1910 jubilee and more appreciated his long editorship of *The Bloxhamist,* and for some years he also edited the *Kalendar* of the Woodard Corporation; perhaps most important in the long run was his revival of the defunct Old Bloxhamist Society.

The society had been growing steadily weaker for some time. The strong personal loyalty to Egerton was broken by his retirement and incorporation with the Woodard schools, and the decline in the numbers and age of the school in the 1890s must have affected recruitment. The Old Bloxhamists found it difficult to raise a cricket team against the school in the opening years of the century and the Society restricted its activity to the London dinner. The jubilee reawakened interest and at the 1911 dinner both Ward and J. S. Chatterton urged that the Society be revived. A new committee was promptly formed and Willimott sent out invitations for membership. By the date of the next dinner he had obtained 76 members, half of whom attended, and it was they who in 1912 chose the present Old Bloxhamist Society colours, a blend of the various school colours worn in Egerton's time. They also restarted the football match against the school in 1913 after a lapse of thirteen years and arranged the first hockey fixture in 1914 before plans for a further revival were checked by the war.

It was in the jubilee year that the Officers' Training Corps was formed. In November 1910 22 boys enrolled as soon as the corps was announced and the membership rapidly doubled, the only bars to recruitment being a small extra fee and parents' consent; by the outbreak of war over half the school was enrolled in the corps. Much of this success was due to the enthsiasm of the first commanding officer, Arthur Child, strongly supported both by the War Office and the headmaster, who valued Child sufficiently to increase his salary when he showed signs of wanting to leave. Drill classes under Grinter and excruciatingly noisy bugle lessons in the Michaelmas term of 1910 were followed by the provision of a miniature rifle range, semaphore signalling, uniforms and an armoury over the laboratory in Botany Bay. In January 1911 the O.T.C. had its first muster in uniform and a month later its first march-out round the four-mile grind. One wonders whether the popularity of soldiering was partly due to the alternative: the corps paraded on Thursdays when the remainder of the upper school and third form were condemned to run round the six-mile grind. A first privately-run winter camp at Shere in Surrey in January 1911 was followed in July by Bloxham sending a contingent of sixteen cadets under Child and Grinter to the coronation royal review at Windsor. The first annual inspection of the corps came a few days later when the inspecting officer was 'on the whole quite complimentary' and at the end of term sixteen cadets went to their first annual camp at Tidworth where they learnt some of the things that their successors discovered for themselves every year afterwards — the importance of not arriving last, the lumpiness of badly filled straw palliasses and the advisability of cat-napping whenever an opportunity occurs. They took themselves seriously from the beginning, storming Bradshaw's bridge over the Sor brook in a night exercise in December and joining in field days with other schools. The first was with Radley, then in February 1913 with large contingents from Uppingham and Rugby at Chipping Norton and later they combined with even more distant public schools.

Even at that first Tidworth camp in 1911 the assembled O.T.C.s were warned of the imminence of war and *The Bloxhamist* devoted increasing space to reports not only of the school corps but also of offers for reserve officers' commissions on leaving school. When hostilities with Germany did break out in 1914 the advantage of O.T.C. experience and the possession of certificates A and B was immediately seen in the army's appointments to commissions. The war had an immediate direct effect on the school as masters joined up and staff were reduced. By the time the October *Bloxhamist* came out two masters had already left, one of whom, James Pastfield, was the first man connected with Bloxham to be killed in action in December 1914. The two men in charge of the corps, Child and Charles Allen, both joined the army in 1915, the former being disappointed in his ambitions for the headmastership but one of the few who forecast a long war, in which he won the Military Cross. The corps itself was mobilised on Sundays in 1915 to help pack and load ordnance stores at Didcot, the *Church Times* reporting the incongruous sight of uniformed preacher and schoolboys in chapel before they marched to Banbury station 'to do their bit'.

The headmaster was himself out of the country when war was declared, having just sailed from Liverpool for British Columbia. He had long been interested in and was a leading member of the British Columbia Church Aid Society and at their request was making the visit to enquire into the needs of the churches there.

He and his wife had decided some years before that they should leave Bloxham when the opportunity occurred, and the arrangements for his Canadian trip more or less coincided with the offer of the benefice of Hilgay in Norfolk. As this was the parish he had long desired, he accepted without hesitation, and although he was back at school soon after the start of the Michaelmas term he left at its end.[4] The final entries in his diary at Bloxham summarise much of the life of the school under his headmastership.

'Saturday, Dec. 12th. Very busy all day with examn. papers & letters . . . C. J. W. had a go at me about extra remuneration for the Chaplain & Golding [the organist].

Sunday, Dec. 13th. Preached my farewell sermon at Mass. Made up my new Mass book in the afternoon & then went for a short walk with Walt. [His son, just home on leave from the Royal Marines]. The prefects came into tea. Talked to the boys a bit after supper.

Monday, Dec. 14th. Finished up my 28 years of school-mastering today. Sang Requiem at 10 for those lost in war. . . Turned out my kneehole table in the afternoon & started on my negs & the big cupboard. Mr. Bartlett came in & presented us with a silver mounted biscuit barrel from the servants. M [his wife, Mary] had some little boys to tea. Excellent sing song at 7.30 & we were presented with a rose bowl & four silver candle sticks at the end. . .

Tuesday, Dec. 15th. Boys all went off about 9.30 — much goodbye saying. All gone but C.J.W. . . .'

---

[4]His ability was recognised by his appointment as archdeacon of Wisbech in 1924. He died in 1946.

CHAPTER VI

A.R.M. GRIER, 1915—1919
F. H. GEORGE, 1919—1925

In reporting the announcement of Ward's resignation *The Bloxhamist* forecast gloomily, 'Changes are not pleasant; at any rate, prospective changes are not'. In 55 years Bloxham had only three headmasters and the school had been fortunate in this continuity of leadership, policy and control. It was unfortunate now that the fourth headmaster had only a four-year reign, for in four years a headmaster can achieve little. His senior boys are those accepted as juniors by his predecessor, his own new boys have only started to come to maturity, he is only just beginning to secure the rewards of his own innovations and earn the full loyalty of his colleagues and boys. In four wartime years there were, of course, additional handicaps.

Alexander Roy MacGregor Grier was a Woodard boy, being educated at Denstone before going up to Oxford where he read history, and at Bloxham he taught both history and English. After obtaining his degree he became an assistant master at Worksop in 1900, was ordained two years later and promoted headmaster of Worksop in 1905 at the young age of 28. In his time there he carried out a great building programme of chapel, laboratories, classrooms and gym, and Worksop flourished in all ways. When Ward showed him over Bloxham he was well impressed, noting in his diary, 'I was very taken with him and sincerely hope he will apply. They could not expect to get a better man'. He was equally complimentary about Mrs Grier who 'was very pleased with everything & seems distinctly tempted. She is very pretty & would make a charming H.M's wife'. His reaction when Grier wrote to him to say that he was applying for Bloxham was the short and heartfelt '*Deo Gratias*'. When the Woodard Corporation chose him for Bloxham he was still only 37 and the school could reasonably look forward to his headmastership for the next ten to twenty years, certainly stretching well beyond the anticipated end of the war. Tallish and goodlooking he was both popular and respected; as English master he had a liking for amateur dramatics and a love for Shakespearian plays; he was a slow right arm bowler at cricket; and a preacher of better sermons than the chaplain.

Despite the handicap of his four short wartime years Grier introduced some long-lasting changes. First, in 1916, was the inauguration of a scout troop under a new master, J.H. Stembridge, open to boys too young for the O.T.C. and holding its first camp that autumn at Aynho Park; two years later a wolf cub pack was formed for the youngest boys. This had come about with the establishment of a preparatory school in January 1915 after many years of abortive proposals. It was based in the hospital building with the boys sleeping in dormitory II, the hospital quarters being transferred to the eastern part of the masters' house in 1919.

Revd A. R. M. Grier, headmaster 1915-19.

This upset the traditional alliances of dormitories for matches and the opportunity was taken to form houses to challenge the existing Headmaster's house in sporting rivalry. The earliest suggestion for named houses to promote 'the public school spirit' had followed the scheme of the Committee of Games in 1884 to divide the dormitories for football matches — dormitories I and III became Mr Heigham's (the later Crake house), V and VI Mr Jones's (Wilberforce) and II, IV and VII Mr Wilson's (Wilson). A correspondent in *The Bloxhamist* soon suggested that masters' names should be replaced by something more permanent, such as Chapel house, School house and Hall house, but the whole idea was short-lived and the familiar dormitory numbers continued in use. No doubt one reason why the house system was so slow to be adopted at Bloxham was the fact that the whole school lived in the main buildings and it was difficult to distinguish or separate the houses. Since house prefects in their studies were mixed together and the later house day rooms all adjoined in the same part of the buildings it was in fact only the dormitories which provided any architectural distinction between the houses. The names in 1916 were well chosen. The original school building which the bishop had consecrated in 1855 was called Wilberforce (or 'Force, for short); the 1864 wing where the former chaplain had his rooms for so many years was named after Crake; the rooms in the old farmhouse and headmaster's residence remained Headmaster's house, and as numbers rose a fourth house was briefly added in Michaelmas term 1918, called Wilson's. The system became formalised about 1920 with the appointment of housemasters and choice of house colours — gold for Headmaster's, purple (? episcopal) for Wilberforce, scarlet for Crake, pink for Wilson's, blue for the preparatory school and green for the day boys. By 1922 only the first three survived.

Dormitory loyalties had long been an ingredient of school games, and these were now sharpened by the new house rivalry to such an extent that there was criticism of the support given to house matches, though compared with other public schools Bloxham, probably because of its size and centralised buildings, was always notable for the strength of loyalty to the school first and houses second. By this time it was becoming rare for a master to play with a school team, though in 1919 both the chaplain, the Revd. T.G. Blofeld, and B. Hoole did so, the practice completely dying out by 1926. More of the other formalities of traditional public school games were adopted. The team colours had been revised in 1913 and the correct dress was laid down three years later not only for cricket and football, but also for hockey, fives, athletics, gym and boxing; second eleven colours were introduced in 1917 and in 1918 the Games Committee authorised house colours. The cult of games, long established in the great public schools, had reached Bloxham in full strength.

The war indirectly aided the public schools in proving to parents that there were advantages in the education they provided, fitting their sons to become officers and leaders of their fellow countrymen, and by the end of the war every public school was full, indeed bursting, with boys for whom no additional buildings could be built. At Bloxham the preparatory school offered a new entry, and at last there was a recovery in numbers. When Grier was appointed there were 74 boarders and 9 day boys in the school, which expected a financial loss on the Lent term of £120, the sort of loss that the provost was prepared for in all the Woodard schools. By the end of the war the numbers had almost doubled to 142 boarders and 13 day boys.

The fees also had risen from 46 guineas a year but despite the increase in both numbers and fees the school was still struggling to balance expenditure, and its overdraft facilities were enlarged from £75 a term to £2,000. Early in the war an appeal had gone out to parents to give a guinea a term voluntarily 'during the war so that they might help to defray the extra cost of living owing to the general rise in prices', but the appeal had only a limited success and the Committee had recourse to more "extras" —for membership of the O.T.C., a medical capitation fee and a charge if a boy was in the sick room — until at last in 1919 fees and extras were consolidated at £75 a term. The Committee also took a firmer attitude towards parents who failed to pay the fees promptly. One of their difficulties was the contribution of £4,000 which Bloxham had made to the

Corporation's funds, of which in 1914 only £2,500 had been repaid despite the efforts of Ward and F.B. Palmer to obtain a more equitable share in the Corporation's finances and benefit funds; another was the untidy legal and financial base of the school property.

Ward and Palmer had consulted closely on Bloxham's business affairs, and although there is no evidence it would appear that Grier and Palmer also worked well together. Palmer was the first Old Bloxhamist to be elected a fellow of the Corporation in 1913 and was a member of the school committee. The first of his many large benefactions was made the next year when he gave £500 to purchase the freehold of the school estate, which, it will be remembered, was copyhold of the manors of Bloxham Fiennes and Bloxham Beauchamp owned by Lord Saye and Sele, and to reduce a mortgage of £1,000 raised in 1906 when the school had bought the second field and some cottages from Hubert Egerton of Park Close. In 1917, when Wilson retired as school bursar, the Committee bought Merton Cottage opposite the main buildings for extra accommodation and two years later decided to strengthen the management of the estate by disposing of all the outlying school property in the village.

They now had the opportunity to start thinking of expansion, although little could be done beyond the purchase of Merton and the opening of the fourth house dormitories called Wilson's at Michaelmas 1918. Building improvements were almost at a standstill. One minor piece of modernisation was the installation of that novelty the telephone to connect school and hospital, which the Post Office had told Ward in 1913 would be brought to the village if there were six subscribers; for years the school telephone number was Bloxham 6. The central heating had been improved in 1914 but there continued to be anxiety about the water supply since, despite Ward's insistence that to safeguard its supply the school should buy the Bloxham Water Company, their bid for it in 1912 was unsuccessful. The sanitation remained primitive and unpleasant, only slightly ameliorated by extending the passage beneath the chapel to a new door at the east end, thereby reducing the size of the third classroom there, in order to give easier access to the outside lavatories.

Living conditions, therefore, continued to be spartan. The dormitories were still bleak and austere with their wooden trestles for the wash basins and cold water jugs; hot water was an unknown luxury for morning washing and in winter the cold water froze in the jugs. There were no studies and no day rooms except in the Headmaster's house where some had been partitioned off on the top floor of the farm house, so that throughout the day the big schoolroom was the only noisy home for most of the boys. There, each one had a locker, just large enough to take school books and a few private possessions. Classrooms were only used for lessons, and the whole school did evening prep in the big schoolroom with a master in charge, an unnerving experience for a new man. An example of Roy Grier's personality and control is recalled on the occasion when the schoolroom was an uproar of noise from boys demonstrating against an unpopular master. The door burst open and Grier stood in the opening. The whole room froze and order was restored in seconds.

The big schoolroom after refurnishing in 1907-08.

As the war dragged on its indirect effects penetrated even the isolated world of a boarding school. *The Bloxhamist* changed its format for the first time in 1916, and because of the shortage of paper and rising costs appeared only once a term instead of the pre-war eight issues a year or once a month during term time. Indeed, by the end of the war it was coming out only twice a year. Its pages are still depressing to read. Within a few weeks of the beginning of the war 71 Old Bloxhamists were in uniform and by the end 400 had been serving in the armed forces, an impressively large number from a school containing less than 100 boys for the preceding twenty years. Of those 400 about half were casualties. There were 76 killed (the original count of 94 was later revised) and 106 wounded. The first Old Bloxhamists killed in action were F.H.M. Robertson in April and R.E. Cunliffe in May 1915. One of the very first men to die in battle in August 1914 was the Founder's nephew, Philip Egerton (not an O.B.), and Boissier's youngest son, W.A.M. Boissier, was killed in 1917. Robertson's brother, T.A.M. Robertson, was also killed, at the battle of Jutland, as were the two brothers, H.B. and R.V. Rylands, and C.H. and J.C. Smith. Term after term the pages of *The Bloxhamist* were filled with the obituary notices of young men universally acclaimed by their senior officers, most of whom had left school only shortly before.

Old Bloxhamists served in every theatre of the war and at every rank from private to general. They included six members of the Boissier family and three Whitings; H.F. Percival (1874-76) and his two sons all survived, and M.H. Webb Bowen had one of the strangest military careers, serving in the marines, English, French and Belgian armies and also seeing action against the Bolsheviks. Old Bloxhamists were awarded 170 honours, including 22 M.C.s, 13 D.S.O.s and 2 D.F.C.s. An outstanding record was that of V.H.S. Davenport, regimental sergeant-major of the 2nd Border Regiment, who was the first man to gain three honours in the war, the M.B.E., M.C., and D.C.M., all before October 1914.

During the war the Old Bloxhamist Society did not meet so that news of old schoolfellows could only filter through by chance encounters and the thin and irregular issues of the school magazine. Despite the space and prominence given by it to war news and the general assumption that the war would be won, the patriotic confidence of boys still at school was tempered by the presence of a nearby prisoner-of-war camp, whose inmates were equally convinced of an ultimate German victory, and the refreshingly critical attitude of the only master who tried to interest the boys in the progress of the war; "Gus" Hoole was prejudiced against all politicians and doubtful of the ability of most of the British High Command!

Even though the conduct of the war aroused little interest at school and the events seemed so remote that Ward made few entries about it in his personal diaries the effect on everyday life could not be entirely ignored. The food deteriorated and one Old Bloxhamist writes,

'Fruit, vegetables and eggs were lacking and nobody thought of putting defaulters on to planting the spacious gardens around the school buildings. I was always hungry. The tuck shop opened after our midday meal on certain days and then there would be a rush to buy chocolate with our 6*d*. a week pocket money. We had not even heard of queueing in those days'.

The Liddon library had to be curtained to avoid revealing lights, and in 1918 the O.T.C. was training on the one anti-aircraft gun in the neighbourhood before the school closed just after All Saintstide because of the notorious 'flu epidemic that raged across Europe and Britain, continuing to affect many in the following term.

The unexpected announcement of Roy Grier's intention to resign the headmastership was greeted with dismay. It was understandable that as an Old Denstonian the Corporation should invite him to become headmaster of his old school, and for him to accept. Bloxham, on the other hand, felt that it was losing a good headmaster who in post-war years was likely to become a great headmaster, a forecast proved by his record at Denstone in the twelve years up to his retirement in 1931. Afterwards he was British chaplain in Montreux and rural dean of Switzerland and provost (dean) of the episcopal cathedral of St Ninian's, Perth, dying at Edinburgh in 1940.

In appointing Grier to Denstone the Corporation were doubtless influenced by the knowledge that they could move another active and respected headmaster to Bloxham, a man, moreover, who already had experience in reforming and developing a backward school. Frank Henry George, a scholar of Jesus College, Cambridge, had taught at Berkhamsted under the Revd T.C. Fry at the period when the latter was converting that ancient small-town grammar school into a minor public school. From there, after ordination, he went as second master to Hurstpierpoint for seven years, the Woodard school most nearly Bloxham's twin, before the Corporation promoted him as headmaster of King's College, Taunton. There he revived a school suffering, like pre-war Bloxham, from dwindling numbers and financial crisis. By the time of his Bloxham appointment King's College had recovered and the Corporation must have looked forward to a similar success story here. However, the national post-war recovery was sluggish, hitting middle-class fee-paying parents and preventing appeals for building expansion.

George has left only shadowy memories among surviving Old Bloxhamists. Known by the boys as "Buggins" he is remembered as a golfer, first-class teacher and good classical scholar of the old-fashioned pedagogic type, book in one hand and cane in the other, who beat for the good of your soul! He delegated authority much less than Grier, resuming a stricter personal control over school affairs. A Low Churchman, despite his long connnection with the Woodard schools, he preached in chapel rarely, and then briefly. Much more vividly remembered is the colourful chaplain of the period, the Revd T.G. Blofeld, in cassock and biretta, pipe in mouth, 'the sort of man you could open your heart to' (though perhaps only if you were not in Crake, of which he was housemaster). Under Blofeld the chapel services became yet more elaborate and a high mass was occasionally sung, using vestments lent by All Saints', Margaret Street, London, where Blofeld had formerly worked. A figure of St George was placed in the antechapel in 1919, but lack of space prevented any

Revd F. H. George, headmaster 1919-25.

proliferation of images.

George was content to let Blofeld run the chapel in his own way, and indeed, since the provost appoints chaplains not the headmaster, he had little choice, the arrangement always being a potential source of friction. However, in the matter of the other staff where he did have control he was similarly content to carry on without making the changes that a more ruthless headmaster might have felt were justified with the return of peacetime conditions. Consequently the common room contained masters — all bachelors bar one — who had been taken during the war to replace the more active and younger men who had joined up, or those who were still suffering from the nerve-shattering after-effects of the 1914-18 warfare. Some were unfitted for the strain and challenge of teaching, but nevertheless the school's academic standards improved remarkably.

The school certificate examination with its emphasis on university entrance requirements and therefore on an academic rather than vocational syllabus had begun in 1917, and by 1923 the headmaster was comparing the Oxford board results with the excitement and successes of Cambridge locals in Egerton's early days. In his last year the 1925 results were the best since 1913 and there were thirteen boys at Oxford and Cambridge. Much of this improvement must be attributed to the influence of George himself, who was a good teacher of both classics and VIth-form English, and to Jasper Stembridge, an outstanding geography teacher and text book author.

At the same time he was widening the school's activities in various ways. *The Bloxhamist*, while retaining its wartime format, again took to including literary articles, and he invited Ward to spend a week at the school to write a *Supplement* to the *History* to bring it up-to-date to 1925. When published the author remained anonymous and from comment in *The Bloxhamist* it is evident that both Wilson and the editor, the Revd H.R. Willimott, contributed; the latter rightly expressed dissatisfaction at its meagre content. There were few leisure-time activities but school clubs and societies revived, languishing or recovering in the way of their kind — a philatelic society, field club, debating society, chess and draughts club and photographic society. Of greater significance, because of George's personal involvement as producer, was the 1922 Founder's Day performance of *As You Like It,* given in the open air on the headmaster's lawn. It was the first time that the school had attempted a full-length Shakespearian play and although the acting was somewhat hesitant on that first occasion a new pattern for Founder's Day was established, and in the following years the headmaster produced *The Tempest, Twelfth Night* and the *Merchant of Venice.* The programme for the two days' celebration was the familiar one of sung eucharist in chapel and prize-giving and play in the inner quad on the first day with the cricket match against the Old Bloxhamists on the second. Traditionalists will note that Mrs Hinde's wish that Founder's Day should always be held on Reginald Egerton's birthday had been abandoned in favour of the weekend nearest 14 July, partly for the convenience of the Old Bloxhamist cricket match. Founder's Day, because of both the season and the transfer of prize-giving to that weekend, was also becoming more important than the patronal festival of All Saints, increasingly treated as a domestic event for the school and Old Bloxhamists.

The Old Bloxhamist Society had been held together during the war by C.J. Wilson's correspondence and resumed its activities afterwards under the leadership of T. Rigby Taylor, bound more closely for a time by the common desire to commemorate worthily those killed in the war. Only 23 had attended the first post-war annual dinner, but in 1924 there were 64. The old Victorian musical character of the evening, recalling the days when the Founder would lead the singing of glee songs, was given up that year, which also marks the first Old Bloxhamist rugger match against the school.

Apart from Wilson, the most prominent Old Bloxhamist was F.B. Palmer. Throughout the inter-wars period he was the school's most generous benefactor, giving largely to every appeal. From time to time the school had flirted with the teaching of science, the Botany Bay laboratory dating from 1898. One of the few wartime expenditures authorised by the school Committee had been the purchase of physics apparatus in 1915, and in 1922 the Committee viewed plans by a Mr Carter for a new laboratory to be built on the fruit garden between Water Lane and the rifle range. The cost was partly met by F.B. Palmer, whose fate it was to spend thousands of pounds on the school, all for much-needed works like

The bathing place on the Sor brook near Wykeham mill.

new roofs and modern kitchens, none of which showed off his generosity or were fitting to be given his name. He was a genuinely modest man, brought up in the Egerton tradition of service and not one to seek publicity. No one would wish to be remembered by the ugly and utilitarian laboratory that was completed in 1923, the first of the school buildings not to be built in Hornton stone though mercifully it was masked by trees for about 40 years. Amid all the many extensions and new buildings in a variety of twentieth-century styles the laboratory remained the least beautiful.

Its ugliness was almost matched by the equally utilitarian open-air swimming bath, but even George did not see the completion of that project, already described as 'much-talked-of, and long-wished-for' when an appeal was first made by Ward in 1901. At least, however, he saw the hole excavated, the baths constructed and almost finished. The appallingly slow progress of the appeal fund, to which the tuck shop profits under Jumbo Mallett were a considerable help, the repetitive increase in prices always tantalisingly out of reach again as soon as each new target was achieved, the search for a site where the water supply would not immediately tap the underground springs and deprive the main buildings of their sources — all these difficulties and delays were well known to successive headmasters and the Committee, and enlivened Old Bloxhamist dinner speeches for years. It was especially sad that the original ambitious plans for a covered and heated pool adjoining the gymnasium, linked with a two-story pavilion by a bridge over Water Lane, had to be abandoned on the grounds of cost. Had an open-air pool been chosen at the beginning there would have been sufficient funds and the school would have missed twenty years' bicycling down to Sor brook to swim in its chilly and muddy shallows.

Perhaps because George came from Taunton with the reputation as a 'building headmaster' the Committee soon after his arrival had resolved, 'No new building or drainage work to be undertaken except as necessary for the health of the School', and apart from the laboratory and swimming bath, both aided by subscriptions and gifts, work was restricted to maintenance and modernisation. The removal of the laboratory from Botany Bay made it possible to convert that much-altered building once again, this time as a changing room. The main buildings were considerably altered in the same year (1923) by the removal of the ivy on the front and by much reroofing done at Palmer's expense, while another Old Bloxhamist, L.C. Vaughan, gave money towards restoring the cricket pavilion.

Inside the main buildings the Committee felt unable to go beyond such modest improvements as in 1921 installing more wash basins, rearranging the prefects' study or bureaux (pronounced 'burrows') and masters' common room to give an extra classroom in their place, the masters moving temporarily to the Liddon room. The school remained crudely insanitary and poorly lit to an extent that is unimaginable today. Since George attributed the boys' good health to the new changing rooms it is extraordinary that the old lavatories were tolerated and a marvel that no serious epidemics occurred like the scarlatina and throat infections of the nineteenth century. Inadequate water supplies still bedevilled the school for only the Headmaster's house was connected to the mains supply of the Bloxham Water Company. For all other purposes the school relied on its own wells, for drinking, cooking, baths and washing linen and clothes. In the old laundry building with its four large coppers fired with wood and coal and belching great clouds of steam out of the door, seven or eight elderly village women could be discerned in the fog-like atmosphere. There they boiled and ironed the school's clothes, using primitive flat irons heated by the fire, before despatching them to the matrons for mending and storage in the locker rooms. Lighting mostly still came from the village gas works in Cumberford Lane, feeble gas lamps casting shadows across the classrooms, although there was an engine behind the masters' house providing unreliable electric lighting in some parts of the school, little better than the gas. Although the Committee discussed the installation of electricity they decided in 1925 to defer the decision as 'at present it was not considered practicable owing to the state of the finances of the Chapter'.

This same prudence was reflected in other decisions, such as the cost-benefits of the gardens in 1920 and a reduction in wages of 5s. of the school servants in 1923. This was no small cut as at the time the head gardener and carpenter were each being paid £3.5s.0d. a week and their assistants £2.10s.0d.; William Payne, the boot and furnace man, had a corner of the cellar boothole and a great bath of cheap polish for the endless job of cleaning off mud and blacking outdoor and house shoes and for this uninspiring task was paid 1s. an hour, though he used to earn a little extra on the side by acting as a bookie's runner. Lower down the scale again, the two pantry boys received £20 a year.

The Committee had less opportunity to economise with staff salaries having decided to adopt the newly introduced Burnham scales in 1921 as well as paying superannuation benefits, but some perquisites were cut and a reduction in staff considered in 1924. Throughout most of George's headmastership the public schools were flourishing despite the uncertain state of the national economy and at Bloxham a termly profit was made, but the school was operating on a very narrow margin and the smallest fall in numbers or non-payment of fees would have been sufficient to convert a small profit into loss. It took seven years, for instance, to pay off the £710 for the purchase of Merton and an overdraft was still required every holidays until the payment of fees at the beginning of term. It was against this background of the troubled national economy, the need for careful domestic management, the absence of endowments and the lack of wealthy Old Bloxhamists that the school had to be run.

The austere conditions made school life a tough survival test and by comparing the recollections of Old Bloxhamists with Egerton's letters and notes one has the impression that Bloxham was more uncomfortable in the 1920s than in the 1870s. For example, Egerton used the cane sparingly himself and discouraged its use by his staff, and also disapproved of boys fighting. George was a disciplinarian who beat frequently, sometimes though rarely in public in the schoolroom, as did the housemasters (including Blofeld the chaplain who was Crake housemaster) and the prefects. It has not been possible to establish the date when prefects first obtained the powers of beating, house prefects with a slipper, school prefects with slipper or cane, but by the 1920s some boys suffered frequent punishment, though possibly less than middle-aged memories suggest. It was conventional for the victim to be allowed a moment or two for recovery between strokes though prestige would be won from the waiting queue lined up outside the study by taking the strokes without pause, and honour really required it. Those who would still argue over the merits of corporal punishment should first recall that boys are (or were) conformist by nature and will accept the common code of behaviour, whether it be compulsory chapel or corporal punishment, and Bloxhamists regarded a beating as an effective, just and swift punishment. Some beatings were taken light-heartedly because the prefect (or master) was ineffective or only token taps were administered for the sake of appearances. In a minority of cases there was an element of legalised bullying but in fact bullying is chiefly remembered as a feature of the middle and lower school suppressed by the authorities rather than carried out by the prefects.

On the other hand, there was developing a complex code of conduct, fortunately less petty than in some public schools, every infringement of which brought down punishment upon the offender. New boys were provided with a copy of the school *History* before their arrival, by which time they were expected to answer an initiation test. Hands, hair, clothes and shoes had to be presentably clean and tidy in the 'line-ups' before chapel and meals. Until about 1920 trouser pockets were sewn up and later it was an offence to put hands in pockets; regulation dark suits were worn, black on Sundays, and caps had to be worn outside the school grounds. Certain parts of the school grounds, like the prefects' lawn and the headmaster's garden were out-of-bounds, together with parts of the buildings not in use during different times of the day, like the dormitories in the daytime Bounds were tightly drawn compared with Egerton's time when senior boys had been allowed to go into Banbury on Saturdays. The village was firmly out-of-bounds except on Sundays when a walk down the main street was permitted; any wandering into the side lanes or contact with the villagers was expressly forbidden, and the same rule applied to neighbouring villages and Banbury where entry was completely banned. Pocket money was therefore almost unecessary except for the 6d a week — as in Egerton's day — doled out by the chaplain from the cash hole at the end of the dining hall passage for spending in the tuck shop. There Bo Mallett resolutely refused credit however special the pleading, though he did serve as an unofficial link with the village. The monastic isolation of the school could be broken in other ingenious ways for Bo's brother, Will, a familiar figure lame from the war, could be persuaded to teach the arts of poaching Lord Saye and Sele's pheasants or how to skin and gut a rabbit.

Such skills were useful. School food is traditionally said to be inadequate and unappetising and Bloxham's at this time was no exception. The midday meal was the main one; breakfast was not very sustaining and tea at 3.45 of one slice of bread and treacle with a mug of tea was followed only by a similar meal at 6.0 p.m. of tea and bread with jam or cake from tuck boxes. Supplementary game was therefore welcome, cooked precariously on pen nibs over the gas jets. Fags were also expected to cook for their fagmasters, but fagging at Bloxham was not onerous since only school prefects could fag and, as any junior was liable, the chores of cooking at tea-time on half holidays, cleaning studies or boots were well shared. Like corporal punishment the date when fagging was introduced is unknown, but it was probably more or less coincidental with affiliation to the Woodard Corporation as Egerton's personal influence was replaced by the desire for recognition and conformity as a public school.[1] The cult of games came first together with the narrow outlook and restraints imposed by a full timetable and isolation from the local community; the O.T.C., corporal punishment, fagging and house rivalry developed later. By the mid 1920s Bloxham was conforming to the public school pattern in all ways but one — the continued emphasis on its Anglo-Catholic instruction.

This conformity was fostered by increasing contacts with other schools, notably through the O.T.C. The public schools' corps camp was revived in 1920 at Strensall near York and in 1923 the school was host to a combined field day of some 1,200 cadets from Cheltenham, Rugby and Radley, defending Hobb Hill with Cheltenham against the other two public schools. By that time a resident sergeant-instructor, S.M. Sykes of the Oxford & Bucks Light Infantry, had just replaced the visiting instructors who had been coming since 1916 and he rapidly improved the standard of shooting. This had previously been restricted to a competition for the house shooting cup, but in his first year the school entered two teams for the *Country Life* competition in 1922, won a match against the 4th

---

[1]Although Debating Society speakers were in favour, Egerton discouraged fagging in any form.

Oxford & Bucks Light Infantry and in the following year was placed 5th in the *Country Life* 'B' competition for smaller O.T.C. contingents.

In football rugby was the game played by most public schools, though in the Woodard Southern division all then played soccer. For years Bloxham had found difficulty in obtaining soccer fixtures with other schools and the increasing professionalism of the game was disliked. In 1920 seven matches were arranged but only one opponent was a school, Magdalen College School. It had been a good season with five victories, but after Christmas the school tried rugger seriously for the first time. Warwick offered to put an 'A' team in the field and although they won easily the school team under D.K. Evans (who actually missed this first match through illness) had enjoyed itself and the experiment was repeated the following year — again with a hefty defeat by Stratford Grammar School, against whom a sort of rugby game was reputed to have been played long before.

The school may have enjoyed their rugger and started to think seriously of giving up soccer altogether, but such a proposal was strongly criticised by Old Bloxhamists. It is the common reaction of old boys to expect their school to remain as they remember it and a vigorously worded letter in *The Bloxhamist* after the first term's rugger from an anonymous Old Bloxhamist illustrates this abhorrence of change.

'Dear Sir —

News has just reached me to the effect that the School is playing football this term under the Rugby Union Rules. I am informed that this is only an experiment and that it is not intended, at any rate at present, to adopt "Rugger" as the School game.

However, I venture to write to you, Sir, to express the hope that Bloxham will remain true and loyal to their great "Soccer" tradition and will not eventually follow the example of some other Public Schools, and give up "Soccer" in favour of "Rugger". The powerful "Soccer" tradition of Bloxham should not be lightly thrown aside.'

And so on, for 'A Lover of Amateur "Soccer"' pleaded his case at length.[2].

The school, however, wanted rugger. There were masters to coach the game and senior boys led by Dennis Hibbert wished to play it. Accordingly in the 1922-23 season soccer was dropped entirely and at all levels rugger was played. There were, of course, some regrets — there were fewer opportunities for conversation on the field — and the tactics were unfamiliar: in the loose, the forwards tended to scatter rather than bunch, and tackling was weak. House matches were played and proved remarkably equal with Wilberforce taking the old football cup off Crake, and of the three school matches two were lost heavily against Warwick and St Edward's, but Stratford was defeated, Bloxham's first rugger victory.

Compared with the long cricket fixture lists of Victorian times, when there had been two summer 'quarters', the seasons of the early 1920s were short and disappointing with relatively few matches, the school ones being restricted to

---

[2] The writer may have been Palmer, who later admitted to regretting the change, but it seems unlikely that as a member of the school Committee he would have entered the controversy.

Magdalen College School, Warwick, Stratford and St Edward's. In both 1922 and 1924 infectious epidemics caused the cancellation of matches, particularly unfortunate in 1924 which otherwise was the best season for 50 years when only two of the eleven matches were lost. Against club sides masters still turned out for the school, E.T. Hirons, B. Hoole, and the chaplain, for Blofeld was a useful bowler, and *The Bloxhamist* that year published the total of match results since the surviving score books began in 1874. Against the Old Bloxhamists, now regarded as the chief match of the term, the school had not been too successful, having won 15 and lost 36, but against other schools the record was good; of the 128 school matches played Bloxham had won 84, lost 37, tied 1 and drawn 6.

It was still rare to compete against schools in other sports. Athletics had never been very popular, partly because of the discouraging weather conditions of Lent term and partly because it had to share time in that short term with hockey, rugger, steeplechases and skating. Some fresh interest had been aroused in 1917 when the keenest athletes were observed training before breakfast and Lady Cartwright of Aynho Park gave the cup for the house relay race. School records were reported in *The Bloxhamist* and frequently broken. It would be tedious to chronicle them again, but to take the example of the mile, a record of 5 minutes 5.4 seconds was set up in 1912 by P. Hill, reduced to 5 minutes 4 seconds by P. Mier in 1918 before A.L. Christopher broke the 5-minute barrier with 4 minutes 54 seconds the next year, this being equalled by H.J.S. Walkley in 1921 when he also put up a new half-mile record of 2 minutes 15.6 seconds. But all this publicity of records had little effect. One unenthusiastic steeplechase against Warwick is recorded in 1920, but not again until 1925.

By that year George could look back at Founder's Day on the modest scale of achievements since the end of the war, recorded briefly in the Supplement to the *History*. There was at last a purpose-built laboratory and new changing rooms, and both the main buildings and the pavilion had been put into a good state of repair. The school was profitable, although numbers were again falling and the general financial outlook was discouraging, not through any fault of either Bloxham or its headmaster. The school had changed in character since the end of the war and was unmistakably a public school of the commonly accepted pattern with its house system, corps and Shakespearian plays. It was still handicapped by its size, lack of endowments, prejudice against its Anglo-Catholic practices and unremarkable staff. Neither George nor the Committee were ambitious for the school but his resignation coincided with that of other staff, Lloyd Jacob, bursar and officer in command of the corps, E.T. Hirons and S.L. Ware. The new headmaster had an unusual opportunity to appoint his own men from the beginning and later acknowledged that his own more spectacular achievements in the next ten years had owed much to George's groundwork.

CHAPTER VII

V. L. ARMITAGE
1925 — 1940

The same issue of *The Bloxhamist* which welcomed V.L. Armitage as the new headmaster in the autumn of 1925 also recorded the appointment of W.F. Jackson Knight and K.T. Dewey as assistant masters, a formidable triumvirate of complementary characters who revitalised Bloxham.

Valentine Leathley Armitage was Bloxham's first lay headmaster, a welcome breakdown of the tradition of clerical headmasters which restricted the Corporation unduly in their choice, though it must be recognised that in 1925 Bloxham was probably not an attractive post for an ambitious and able schoolmaster. In a further break from tradition he was a modern linguist who after King's, Canterbury, and Balliol had spent two years at Rennes University from which he held a *diplôme des lettres;* he had spent some of his war service in the Provost Corps in France and Germany, an experience which not only flavoured his attitudes as a schoolmaster but which later influenced his actions as World War II approached. By coincidence he started his teaching career at the Grange, Folkestone, where George had also taught. This was followed by Rossall in 1914 and St Bees in 1922, where in both schools he was a housemaster for three-year periods. He had, therefore, worked exclusively in minor public schools, each of which was to have a struggle to survive the depression of the 1930s. Armitage has generally been given a poor reputation at Bloxham, chiefly because of the financial strain imposed by his great building programme at a time of economic crisis, his abrupt departure in 1939, which his successor never entirely forgave, and his hectoring discipline frequently described as Prussian. This ignores his very real successes in the first ten years of his headmastership, which falls into three periods — the early years when with a new young staff he was imposing his character on Bloxham, the building expansion of the mid 1930s and the last two or three years when his interest in Bloxham was diminishing.

One of Armitage's good qualities was the ability to choose and retain good staff, although extraordinarily his first appointments of a classics master to replace George and a chemistry master for the new laboratories were both made by friends on his behalf while he was still in the north of England. Both choices were inspired. W.F. Jackson Knight, "JK", and "Val" Armitage had much in common — an interest in acting and histrionic ability, nostalgia for their military experiences and interest in archaeology[1]. For years they were friends and partners, the 37-years old headmaster being treated like a father by the talented but inexperienced classics master, seven years his junior and in his first post.

K.T. Dewey, just down from Lincoln College, Oxford, was even less

---

[1] By coincidence, one of England's notable Roman archaeologists, M. R. Hull, taught at Bloxham under George for a year in 1924-5.

experienced and in later years also paid tribute to Armitage's guidance and training. At 23 he was a large fair-haired young man of ruddy features and soft, urbane voice, fashionably dressed in well-cut jacket and Oxford bags. He was always benign and easy-going and as a junior master teaching chemistry without any special skill, a subject still hardly taken seriously, he created little impression except for his consistently warm and welcoming friendliness. His rise in the school was gradual, becoming Junior housemaster in 1927, succeeding L.H. Sutton as housemaster of Crake in 1932 and JK as commanding officer of the corps in 1931, when he was also using his very notable organising powers in starting the Friends of Bloxham society.

Another colleague, arriving a few years later on his first day at the dark and dimly-lit village railway station, recalls the almost comical contrast between JK, short, shrill and immaculate, and "KT", "Katie" or "Kate" (or, again, "the Clamp" to some generations from his frequent instruction in the laboratory of 'Boy, fetch a clamp'). He had emerged hesitantly from the little branch-line train to the sounds of an excited and high-pitched monologue interspersed by an occasional soft rumble, which continued in ever-rising shrills until the train pulled out of sight for Chipping Norton. Kate had just given JK a lift to the station and was seeing him safely away. Then, seeing the bewildered young man, Dewey introduced himself, 'and you must be coming to the school' and swept him off with benevolent ease.

The other staff changes were the departure of Hoole for Canada and the chaplain Blofeld to Nassau at the request of his friend, the bishop. He was replaced for a short term by Willimott, just returned from Africa. Others with long connections with the school were also replaced. The three Smiths went; L.E. Smith, master and bursar for various periods from 1916 resigned shortly before his death in 1927, E.C. Smith, the gentle Crake housemaster after Blofeld left in 1926 and H.A. Smith, a great teacher of mathematics, in 1929. Armitage encouraged some of these moves, although he was (not surprisingly) unpopular in the common room for his ruthless weeding-out, and Willimott resigned in protest in 1927. 'Few who saw it', recalls one Old Bloxhamist, 'will forget the moving sight of his last chapel service, which he left walking down the aisle, weeping silently'. He loved Bloxham and its chapel dearly, suggesting the reredos and completing the panelling, striving for the war memorial and giving vestments over many years right up to 1955. He continued Old Bloxhamist Society activities and happily returned to the school on occasions to preach; he died in 1964. But, however unpopular Armitage's actions may have made him as a new headmaster, they were necessary for the school and gave him the opportunity to choose his own younger men.

Among those whose influence is still remembered were B.O. "Bogie" Wheel (1926-33), L.H. "Shiny" Sutton, Crake's new housemaster (1928-32), F.G.L. Crawshay, the Norfolk and Oxfordshire county cricketer and later Wilson housemaster (1928-38), M.R. Craze (1930-36) and J.C. Pallister (1930-38). These were the men, together with C.N. Lawrence, the senior master with experience of Bloxham since his release from prisoner-of-war camp in 1919, upon whom Armitage chiefly relied to transform Bloxham, a transformation tempered by the continuing presence of Wilson, gently but persistently linking the roots of the school with its new growth, the one man known universally to every Old Bloxhamist of every generation. One of Armitage's earliest and happiest inspirations was to rename Head's house in his honour as Wilson house.

The new team of masters started to achieve practical results so remarkably quickly that some tribute must be made also to George and his staff. The first higher school certificate was obtained in 1925 by A.C. Hordern after which a few boys took the examination each year. The 1928 results were the best since 1913 and seven boys went up to Oxford that year. In 1929 the first Oxford scholarship for 30 years was won by J.E. Anthony and by 1930, only five years after his appointment but when he could justly claim all the credit, Armitage was proud to announce that 20% of the school was in the VIth form; two years later, having just won three open scholarships, there were 20 Old Bloxhamists at Oxford or Cambridge and four at Sandhurst. At last and for the first time for a long period, academic distinction was strongly encouraged, and Armitage received the recognition due to him by being elected to the Headmasters' Conference in 1929.

Soon after his appointment Armitage secured from the Committee the right to dispose of £150 in scholarships as he thought fit, a sum which was later increased; he insisted that all entrants must take the common entrance examination for public schools; and in 1929 he had honours boards fitted in the schoolroom — a small and overdue counterweight to the cricket and football team boards which had long hung in the pavilion. He deplored the lack of musical appreciation in the school and tried to redress this failing by nominating one scholarship for organ or music and by starting to hold concerts at the school. Attempts were made to train instrumentalists for a school orchestra and to introduce a house music competition, but although it was not until 1927 that Dr Hain finally gave up coming over to the school from his home at Leamington,the musical tradition of the school had been weak since his days in residence before the Great War, and the school's only musical successes were the Gilbert and Sullivan operas in 1930 and 1931. More unusual for Bloxham was the production of Sophocles' *Ajax* by Jackson Knight in 1927 and the beginning of house plays in 1929.

Much of Bloxham's academic success came from the headmaster himself for Armitage was a first-class modern languages teacher, but it was Jackson Knight who supplied a rare distinction to the common room. He was a born and dedicated scholar who, according to his brother and biographer, was far happier in his natural environment as a don at Exeter University than as a schoolmaster at Bloxham. At the time this did not appear to be the case. Although testy in the mornings as a result of poor nerves and shell-shock, he was a brilliant conversationalist, a most conscientious housemaster of Wilson house, and an exciting and inspiring teacher whether conversing in Ciceronian Latin with a visiting French professor lacking English or demonstrating his skill as a despatch rider by riding figures-of-eight round the quad with one foot on the saddle and the other in the air. Jackson Knight won Bloxham coveted university classics scholarships, P.A. Schofield, Michael Hewlett and Kenneth Jenkins, and in return Bloxham gave him self-confidence. One of the many stories about him, and one not recorded by his biographer, sums up the whole secret of keeping order and was related by two of his former colleagues. He was approached by a young master, whose discipline was not of the strongest, with the question, 'I say, JK, what would you do if a boy burst a paper bag in your form?' To which, with scarcely a moment's thought and his shrill voice rising, he replied, 'I should try to look as if I was the sort of man one couldn't burst a paper bag in the classroom of!' He paused. 'And if that didn't work,' his voice rising higher still, 'I should have shot my bolt!'

Bloxham also gave him the chance to begin his life work of classical Latin research, sitting up in the Wilson housemaster's rooms in the early hours of the morning after earlier discussing Latin prose or problems with his senior pupils until midnight. His apprentice articles on his excavation of the Romano-British settlement by the Tadmarton road appeared in *The Bloxhamist* before their publication in learned national journals, while his first book as the leading British expert on Vergil was published in 1932 while he was still at Bloxham. The good reviews and immediate success of *Vergil's Troy* opened up prospects of university posts for him even in the difficult and competitive times of the 1930s. From then on, Bloxham was unlikely to hold him.

In the meantime his exciting and excitable personality filled everything that he undertook. His brother regarded him as a natural soldier with battlefield experience and so did Armitage, seeking someone to tighten up slackness in both corps and school. The school, however, saw only an extraordinary genius, an eccentric and shrill-voiced little man in dapper clothes and ragged gown, and his choice to command the O.T.C. was greeted with ridicule. Such was his zest and power of leadership that with the professional aid of F.A. Stevens, M.M., of the Coldstream Guards and former regimental sergeant-major of the Queen's Westminsters and Earl Haig's sergeant-major at G.H.Q., he rapidly raised the small contingent of this obscure minor public school to one of the very best in the country. E.A.C. Lee recalled them both:

'On parade he always wore breeches and buskins and a very flat cap pulled down almost to his nose. From under that cap issued forth those high pitched prolonged words of command ending in an abruptly explosive monosyllable which I swear could be heard miles away, and which were in striking contrast to the deep-throated boom of S/M Stevens, who was reported to have had the fourth best commanding voice in the British army and who was, I believe, the S/M in charge of the reorganization of Sandhurst after the Great War. At any rate their respective performances were so impressive that it often seemed as if the whole village of Bloxham had turned out to witness them.

From under that cap, too, darted about those two eyes, hawk-like in their intensity, missing nothing of what went on and spotting the slightest error in turn-out or manoeuvre.

His rapidity of movement as he darted now here, now there in the pursuit of his duty, the fiercely imposing moustache, and that shrill denunciation which brought woe to the cadet at the receiving end and which invariably began "Get

The O.T.C., about 1930. In front, Jackson Knight, and on right flank, F. A. Stevens and K. T. Dewey. In the background, Palmer (then Junior) House, 1923 laboratory, and pavilion (1872).

along with you ma-a-an!", made him to me, as I'm sure it did to other boys of my age, an object of awe and a cause of relief that we were still young enough to be in the Scouts under a less tempestuous regime!'

It became the custom to expect 100% passes in the certificate A examinations and in 1932, just after Jackson Knight had relinquished command, the headmaster claimed that Bloxham's certificate A results placed the school second in all England. At camp where JK's high pitched orders attracted the ribaldry of other units, Bloxham defended their commanding officer vigorously, and after inspecting the O.T.C. in 1929 Brigadier R.M. Luckock, C.M.G., D.S.O., commented, 'In a long experience of O.T.C.s I have never seen a corps as good as this one is now'. He asked the War Office to extend JK's command for a second term of three years at the end of which he was given the rare promotion to brevet-major. At camp that year the band under D.D. Zvegintzov had earned such high praise in the competition that Zvegintzov was chosen to train and lead the massed school bands in the final display. That also was the era of spectacular field days with other public schools, such as the triumph of organisation in 1928 fully reported in the *Morning Post* when Bloxham, Radley, Rugby, Magdalen College School and Abingdon, supported by army aircraft, fought over the Bloxham countryside.

The shooting VIII was also JK's responsibility and again his inspiring leadership produced remarkable results. The first objective was Bisley and the school competed for the Ashburton shield for the first time in 1927 thanks to the

102

generosity of an Old Bloxhamist, Colonel L.A. Grimston, C.I.E. The headmaster commented on the creditable result,

'I have seen many Public Schools' Days at Bisley and many a young, inexperienced eight go to pieces when first faced with the ordeal of shooting shoulder-to-shoulder with 70 other schools. I may be slightly prejudiced, but I was immensely struck with the steadiness of the Bloxham VIII, and this was in no small measure due to the studied nonchalance of Captain Knight and the calm (almost blasé) attitude of Sergt. Harvey who coached excellently on the firing point. No one would dare to suffer from "nerves" with those two about'.

Two years later the Bloxham VIII under D.C.B. Harvey was placed 6th in the Ashburton, P.G. Hunt having the highest individual score and P.V. Lovett-Campbell being first equal in the Gale and Polden cup. In 1932 the scores were actually higher but standards had so improved generally that after an exciting morning shooting at 200 yards when the school VIII was 3rd, the final position was 32nd. Roger Armstrong, whose 500-yard score of 32 was the best school shot of the day, recalls how the headmaster drove four of them back from Bisley. 'Do we stop in Oxford for ice-cream or outside for something else?' queried Armitage. 'What a silly question!' replied Armstrong. 'I thought you'd say something like that', rejoined his headmaster and they duly stopped at a country pub for beer and darts. That, however, was the best Ashburton score for a long time. The next year the school was in quarantine and the high standard fell when JK gave up coaching the VIII.

Armitage shared JK's successes with special delight because of his own enjoyment of the army. He remained a reservist and would put on his old uniform to take the salute on field days. The corps and the shooting VIII satisfied some of his own ambitions for Bloxham and in a rare letter revealing his depression in 1932 he wrote to JK, 'Sometimes I feel that all we have tried to do at Bloxham has been fruitless, and then I get out the nice neat parcel of your six years in command of the Corps and find that we have a least one solid bit of achievement which nobody can take away'. Stevens had also contributed to the shooting successes, which led Armitage to appoint him bursar in 1931, a post for which he was less suited particularly under the financial pressures of the 1930s. Though efficient he lacked the imagination and flexibility of mind necessary for running the school's domestic side and the catering and housekeeping became rigid and spartan.

In calmer style Dewey looked after the recruits and old photographs show him leading the march past at general inspections, a man of impressive military bearing who sartorially rivalled Jackson Knight's sharply creased uniform and gleaming shoes and Sam Browne belt. He took over command from JK in 1931 until 1939 and it was during his time that the school won the guard-mounting competition at the Tidworth public schools' camp in 1932, the *Boys' Own Paper* shield for certificate A results in 1934 (coming second in 1935 and 1936) and was second in the camp band competition in 1936.

None of these achievements would have been possible or so fully exploited without Armitage's ambitions for the school and his flair for publicity. No

End of term, December 1932. In the background at the east end of the chapel is the laundry building.

headmaster since Egerton could match his ability in this, and he was years ahead of his time in recognising the power of the press for good publicity. He wooed the national newspapers by plying them with stories of newsworthy interest. The *Morning Post's* "Military Correspondent", who reported that 1928 field day, possessed a literary style curiously like that of the headmaster; he appealed in the *Daily Telegraph* for advice on how a seventeen-year old prefect might spend a £50 legacy in travel; and he fed the popular papers with an account of Wilson's long attachment to the school and allowed them to take photographs of Heath's cart loaded in the quadrangle with end-of-term trunks, a story which backfired in the year when protests were received against the gross overloading of trunks and boys that Heath's poor horse was expected to draw. An over-zealous news photographer had easily persuaded the loading party — the traditional 'twelve strong men of each house' — flushed with end-of-term excitement, to pile the load high, and had then unhitched the lead horse for greater effect. A happier gesture was the invitation to the movie film companies to film the nineteenth-century dress rugger match in 1935, when another master, George Bolton, recalls going into Banbury to see himself appear in three different newsreels!

Everything was done in style and for effect. Just as he delighted in his uniform on field days so he donned surplice and hood on the occasions when he preached in chapel, and in school he always wore cap and gown. His wife Muriel was an excellent hostess and they believed in the importance of entertaining, whether it was well-scrubbed and nervous new boys for afternoon tea, privileged prefects for dinner or more important guests, and of course they always dressed for dinner. The annual dinners of the Friends of Bloxham at the White Lion hotel in

Banbury were full evening dress affairs patronised by Oxfordshire society. The prizegiving was made a great social occasion, held in the inner quadrangle, and Founderstide services were so well attended that the parish church had sometimes to be used.

The idea of the Friends of Bloxham was first canvassed by the headmaster at Founder's Day in 1930, though this is not reported in *The Bloxhamist's* account. Nor is it known whether the suggestion originated with Armitage or Dewey, its highly competent and enthusiastic secretary. It was through the Friends that Dewey advanced his own position in the school as a contender for a senior post with C.N. Lawrence, the second master and Wilberforce housemaster, and the incomparable JK, whom Armitage marked as his own successor should he decide to leave Bloxham. The Friends of Bloxham gave the school just the sort of publicity that Armitage appreciated. It was, of course, the golden period for such societies supporting cultural festivals, national libraries and galleries, cathedrals and other institutions. It was a wonderful success. Formed in March 1931 there were 1,000 members by the summer and 1,200 within the year, headed not merely by the provost, bishop H.K. Southwell, the assistant bishop of Chichester, and the bishop of Oxford, but also by Lord Halifax, the lord chancellor, Viscount Hawarden (O.B.), John Buchan, M.P., the author, the speaker of the house of commons and other parliamentarians, and as many high-ranking officers and local aristocracy as Dewey could obtain. There was no subscription. What was sought was the influential contacts which Bloxham so conspicuously lacked among its own old boys, not least in the increasingly difficult task of finding jobs for school-leavers as the national economy worsened. The headmaster began an informal employment agency in the early 1930s and attributed much of its considerable success to the co-operation of both the Old Bloxhamists and the Friends of Bloxham.

Both Armitage and Dewey were anxious to strengthen the ties binding old boys to the school for the good of its whole community which they firmly believed was wider than just those boys at the school, and also to help the school in its many problems of raising funds, finding employment for school-leavers and attracting new boys; Bloxham had few sons of Old Bloxhamists, only eleven in 1934. They suggested, therefore, that the Old Bloxhamist Society might do better not to meet in London every year, and although this idea was not adopted a dinner was held at Liverpool in 1936 and another of the newly formed Bloxham Society, incorporating both the Friends and the Old Bloxhamists, took place at Brighton in 1938. The Old Bloxhamist Society continued to flourish and expand, holding its first cricket festival at the school in August 1937, when one of the three opponents was the South Oxfordshire Amateurs, and the first O.B. Golfing Society meeting in which Dewey played. For those with a taste for historical precedents this was in fact not strictly the very first cricket festival for there had been similar events in 1898 and 1900. The second was poorly supported and the venture was allowed to drop, but the first in 1898, in which the school was only saved by rain and four club sides were defeated, has a familiar atmosphere —

'...most of them were gathered later that Wednesday evening under the roof of

C. J. Wilson, about 1930.

mine host of the Elephant and Castle, that old and famous inn so well known to all historical students; there they made themselves merry, and jest and song was the order of the night'.

The chief link between school and Society was still Wilson, who continued to welcome all visiting old boys, every one of whom he could remember from their earliest days as new boys when he would put their names in his school lists in his habitual neat handwriting, enjoining them to remember the school motto and leaving them with the injunction, 'Be just'. He spent his time maintaining the registers and records and was to be seen daily in hall and frequently in chapel at early service, reading the lesson at evensong or sitting in the choir stalls where deaf but still in good voice he would obliviously be a bar or so behind everyone else. He had been deaf for years, though occasionally could hear very well indeed, and George Bolton relates with embarassment how he and a colleague watching a cricket match were conversing across Wilson, who was sitting between them. 'If only the old man wasn't between us, we could talk much more conveniently', remarked the other master, whereupon Wilson immediately rose. 'Sit together, then you'll be able to talk more easily'. In 1936, after living for a short time in Strawberry Terrace, he unexpectedly decided to go to live with relatives, leaving Bloxham for the first time after 76 years and 228 terms. In correspondence later in *The Times* Dewey claimed this as a record, a claim which has gone unchallenged. It was Wilson who would repeat tales of the Founder and he, of course, contributed largely to the detailed obituaries of early boys now appearing in *The Bloxhamist.* The magazine always contained much news of Old Bloxhamists, from 1931 including the regular features of 'Letter from Oxford', and 'Letter from Cambridge'. In 1933 it printed the first list of members of the Society which had risen to nearly 500.

Jackson Knight's phenomonal success with the O.T.C. and shooting VIII was not equalled in other activities until Michael Craze arrived in 1930 and took over direction of rugger and athletics. This is not to deny that in the late 1920s there were some good sporting teams, fine individual performances and a steady development of fixtures and interests. In rugger the winter of Armitage's appointment was the first occasion when the lingering influence of soccer could be forgotten as all the XV had played rugger for all their school career. One of the intentions of the change had been achieved with the growth in the number of school matches. During the successful 1928-29 season under D.D. Zvegintzov matches were played against Warwick, Northampton, St Edward's and Rugby, while the headmaster was instrumental in encouraging fixtures with Oxford colleges. The subsequent season, partly under R.W. Dougan who played for Eastern Counties Public Schools and is remembered for his gorilla-like embrace, was even more successful with seven victories in twelve matches, and by 1932-33 the list stretched to eighteen fixtures over the two winter terms, half being against other schools. Three boys played the next year for the Oxfordshire Public Schools' side under the captaincy of D.R. Arkell.

The other winter games became more competitive, the 'team spirit' of the times being provided by house competitions in those sports like athletics and boxing where individual performance is more important than team combination. The Cartwright cup in the mid 1920s was awarded for the cross-country run, relay race and tug-of-war, and the traditional Shrove Tuesday paperchases were still held. Occasionally there were cross-country matches against other schools but athletics remained the most neglected major sport of the year, although standards were slowly and erratically improving. When Roger Raymond broke the school record for the shot with 32 feet 1 inch in 1927 the sports still included such village-fete events as a sack race and potato race; a few years later in 1930 when Dougan added seven inches to the record for putting the 16-pound weight the light-hearted events included races for the Old Bloxhamists (won by D.D. Zvegintzov) and male servants (won by Bo Mallett). The discerning spectators might have taken notice of the under-13 winner of the 100 yards, young E.A.C. Lee.

Interest in fives fluctuated but boxing was actively encouraged by the cult of physical prowess and toughness. House competitions appear to date from 1924 and were reported with much detail, not always flattering, in *The Bloxhamist,* and in 1930, perhaps emboldened by coaching from the former European and British bantamweight champion, Johnnie Brown, the school ventured in its first match, against Warwick, the old rivals at rugger and running — and won. In the same year the first swimming match was arranged; other schools were not prepared to accept the challenge, but the Old Bloxhamists provided a team under D.D. Zvegintzov which narrowly lost. Cricket, of course, remained the main summer game and after the good 1924 season the XI surpassed that record in 1927 by being unbeaten. Again the Old Bloxhamists contributed to the success by providing a professional coach, though the captaincy of wicket-keeper A.H. Mead and the high-scoring opening batsman, S.S. Hordern, were notable among a team of great character also containing E.M. Johnson, the all-rounder, E.A. Snow, the fast bowler, and M. Barnes, one of the best school fielders anyone could remember. Against Banbury, who scored 104, the school openers, Hordern and Johnson, won the match, Hordern going on to make the first century for some years.

When the headmaster, complaining somewhat extravagantly that he had not had a holiday in five years, sought a sabbatical term, the Chapter gave him Lent term 1934. Lesser men might have been content with a walking tour in the Alps — he listed 'walking' as one of his recreations in *Who's Who* — but not Val Armitage. He and "Mu" went on a world cruise, while the school with some foreboding anticipated a series of travel lectures on his return, which was when he brought the new hall bell back as a souvenir. The cruise was a landmark in Armitage's career at Bloxham. Towards the end of the summer term 1933 a new boy, J. Tucker, had contracted a virulent form of *streptococcus haeomyliticus* and died in Banbury hospital; his death was followed by that of a second new boy and others were seriously ill at school and later at home. Armitage was shattered. This was publicity of the worst sort, particularly as only a short time before and at the previous Friends of Bloxham dinner he had been proud of the school's good diet and health and had drawn attention to the increase in numbers and the full complement.

He reacted quickly and wisely. Extra nurses were drafted in to help Sister Stent in throat-swabbing and isolating the boys according to the seriousness of their illness, for this was long before antibiotics were available and epidemics could spread fast and be killers. Term ended early and during the holidays the whole buildings were disinfected and fumigated, redecorated and their furnishings washed, the swimming baths and drains were investigated, the water and milk tested. The origin of the disease was never discovered although other boarding schools were also said to have suffered. The tragedy certainly affected Armitage and it was the need to get away from Bloxham that was the real reason for his sabbatical term. At least one Old Bloxhamist discerned a mellowing change in his attitude afterwards, for previously, although basically a kind man, his bullying manner and outbursts of bad temper together with his linguistic ability and physical appearance had earned him the reputation and nickname of "the Hun". This was confirmed, said both village and school, by the fact that the flower bed in the centre of the headmaster's garden was (and is still) in the shape of a swastika — so designed, they said as the war rumours multiplied, to guide German aeroplanes!

Another effect of the epidemic was to encourage the Committee to embark on a building programme, the like of which the school had not experienced since Egerton finished the headmaster's house half a century earlier. Armitage was one of Bloxham's great 'building headmasters', working on the principle of 'build

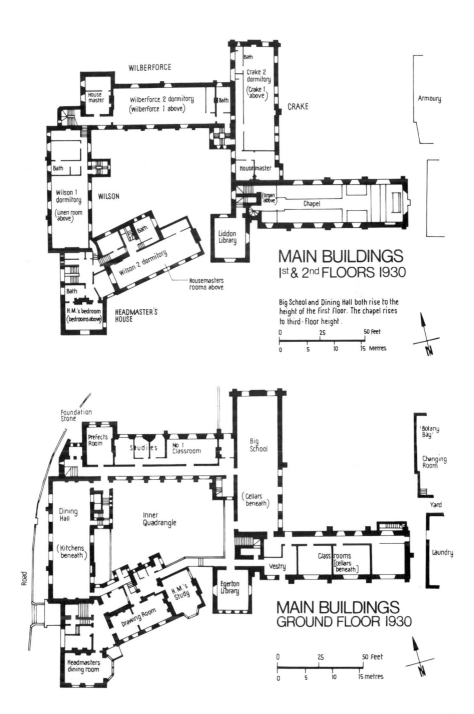

WILBERFORCE

House master

Wilberforce 2 dormitory
(Wilberforce 1 above)

Bath

Bath

Crake 2 dormitory
(Crake 1 above)

CRAKE

Armoury

Bath

Wilson 1 dormitory
(Linen room above)

WILSON

Housemaster

(Organ above)

Chapel

Bath

Wilson 2 dormitory

Housemasters rooms above

Liddon Library

Bath

H.M.'s bedroom
(bedrooms above)

HEADMASTER'S HOUSE

MAIN BUILDINGS
1st & 2nd FLOORS 1930

Big School and Dining Hall both rise to the
height of the first floor. The chapel rises
to third-floor height.

| 0 | 25 | 50 Feet |
| 0 | 5 | 10 | 15 Metres |

N

Foundation Stone

Prefects Room

Studies

No 1 Classroom

Big School

'Botany Bay'

Changing Room

Dining Hall

Inner Quadrangle

(Cellars beneath)

Yard

Road

(Kitchens beneath)

H.M.'s Study

Egerton Library

Vestry

Class rooms
[cellars beneath]

Laundry

Drawing Room

Headmasters dining room

MAIN BUILDINGS
GROUND FLOOR 1930

| 0 | 25 | 50 Feet |
| 0 | 5 | 10 | 15 metres |

N

109

now, pay later'. Although the building debt which he incurred seemed crippling as the national financial crisis dragged on and almost brought about Bloxham's total ruin, it is safe to say that had Armitage not provided the school with its modern facilities in the mid 1930s, there would have been little worth struggling for in 1939-40 when the very existence of the school was in the balance.

Armitage came to a school whose main buildings were at least 50 years old, to which the only significant additions were the gym, swimming bath and science laboratories, all of which were functional rather than beautiful and limited to the minimum essentials. The old buildings were wearing out; the roofs needed extensive repair, the kitchens were appalling, drainage primitive and lighting old-fashioned; the classrooms were antique and as school numbers rose again were also overcrowded. The epidemic drew attention to the risks of overcrowding in the dormitories also.

In Armitage's early years the Committee could do little. The numbers were low, fees were difficult to collect and economy was essential. The regular working overdraft until fees were paid at the beginning of term was £1,000 or more and with the termly profit only £100 or less there was little likelihood of much improvement. For this reason they postponed the installation of the electric lighting plant for over a year in 1925-6, merely discussed modernising the kitchens in 1925 and were grateful for Palmer's generosity in carrying out the work three years later. Of all things this sort of maintenance and modernisation should have come out of the school's own funds, leaving benefactions for new projects, and Palmer, modest though he was, expressed his personal sadness at Founder's Day 1928. 'It has been the dream of my life to add to the beauty of these buildings, but it is the lot of my life to do what is done underground'. At the same time, in 1928-9 the old farmhouse, renamed Wilson in Michaelmas term 1927 when Pym Wilson reached his 80th birthday, was rebuilt from first-floor level and the old studies under the roof replaced by the housemaster's suite of rooms and a new dormitory.

Armitage had more ambitious plans altogether. A Works Committee was formed in 1928 and they invited H.L. North, an architect who had worked for other Woodard schools, to draw up plans for a new block of classrooms, masters' common room and boys' studies on a site between the fives courts and tennis courts. The cost was estimated at £20,000 and faced with this enormous sum and more pressing needs the scheme was inevitably postponed. Instead, money went on maintenance — the dining hall floor laid by the school carpenter, Richard Bartlett (where some time later in 1935 the tables had to be turned from lengthways to east and west to seat the larger school), reroofing the other school buildings, repairing Merton Cottage, putting in new heating, and building a garage in 1929 for the school's Trojan motor car. Subsequently the school was connected to the main electricity in 1933, C.J. Wilson was accommodated in a room in the laundry, closed at last in 1934 when the village laundresses departed from the steaming coppers and yard of drying sheets, and the memorial gateway was built.

This last was the final stage of the 1914-18 war memorial which had taken the form of the processional cross and silver candlesticks suggested by Willimott, the roll of service and photographs compiled by Colonel H.A.R. May, C.B., V.D., new band instruments in 1927, and the chapel memorial designed by L.S. Shuffrey (1865-67), gold medallist of the Institute of British Decorators in 1925. The balance of money collected was originally intended for the O.T.C., but put instead towards the gateway, designed by Thomas Falconer of Amberley, Gloucestershire, and unveiled by Lord Saye and Sele in 1933. Wilson is reputed to have peered up at the inscription, 'The Lord shall preserve thy going out and thy coming in', and with an old man's puckish sense of humour to have muttered, 'And quite right, too, with all this dangerous motor traffic'. Although the gateway was a considerable improvement on the former open approach and iron railings, Falconer's intention to extend the low wall all the way to Palmer house was not carried out, being frustrated partly by a dispute with the village over the width of the Water Lane right of way. The custom of a school bugler sounding Last Post and Lights Out in the main quadrangle, which had apparently started at the beginning of the Great War, was now transferred to the memorial gateway or sometimes the inner quad, a moving and never-missed nightly call echoing from the tall buildings.

Falconer, whose son Peter was at the school, was the Committee's first choice for school architect. As part of the gateway scheme he removed the unsightly fire escape above the main front door and also the porch, as the Friends of Bloxham intended to improve the appearance of the entrance. They never carried out their good intention, so that the school building lost its porch and not until 1977 was the doorway redesigned. He was responsible, too, for the idea of ingeniously inserting the vestry halfway up the chapel steps by building over part of the schoolroom which was truncated for this purpose, and he was engaged to design the proposed classroom block. His unexpected death in 1934 was one reason for delaying that project.

Also, it was a time of much economy. As the country's financial crisis worsened and other public schools were affected, Bloxham actually found its position improving, parents being attracted by fees lower than better known schools. They had been raised in 1927 to £100 and the Committee considered another increase in 1931 to £125, with day boys' fees rising from £30 to £40 and stronger action taken to collect debts. For boys already in the school there was proposed a £10 increase, but even this seemed too much and Palmer gave £1,000 to save existing parents from any increase at all although in 1936 they were actually advertised at £120. These figures may be compared with fees of £175 at Lancing, £185 at Radley and £320 at Eton, very considerable differences when even a £25 increase was deemed large. In addition a sum of £1 a term was charged as an extra towards the building fund, and the entry of day boys was actively sought.

On the other side of the balance sheet various savings were made. The staff were reduced by dismissing one master, retiring the carpenter, Richard Bartlett, and ceasing the engagement of the cricket professional in 1928. The headmaster was instructed to negotiate with the common room for a 5% to 10% reduction in their salaries; instead, they suggested that they should forego their pension premiums, thereby saving £400, which the Committee gladly accepted before reintroducing a revised salary scheme in 1935. The headmaster himself gave up his own salary increment in 1934. At the time the Burnham scale salaries were paid, the headmaster receiving £1,050 rising by £25 annual increments to £1,200 plus £200 expenses. It was not a bad sum, measured against the head gardener's pension of £1 a week, and probably compares favourably with headmasters' salaries today. In 1929 the school bought its own cows to provide cheaper milk — and it was said as a matter of some pride when the school was connected to the mains electrcity that at least it retained its independence and could not be put on 'mains milk'! When the old Arkell fives court collapsed in 1929 it was not repaired and the only way to obtain a pavilion for the second field was for the scouts to build a home-made one in 1934. However, it was all worth it, for the effect of the rise in fees, rise in numbers and savings in expenditure was a much healthier termly balance. From almost no profits in the mid 1920s the school's estimated termly income exceeded expenditure by £2,000 or so a few years later. In 1932, when the masters were asked to accept a salary cut, the audited accounts for the year showed a profit of £736.

The Committee were pleased with the way in which Bloxham was weathering the financial storm in marked contrast, for example, with Ardingly, which was losing money, and Weymouth, which was heading for closure, and they were reassured at the evidence of the numbers in the school. With about 130 boys, all but a handful being boarders, the school was as full as was felt comfortable although in 1935-6 a few more were squeezed in to bring the total up to 146. Accordingly they held a special meeting in March 1936 to consider whether to go ahead with the building programme that they had been contemplating. They also had before them a good report on the school's progress and standards from H.M. inspectors, for 1935 was a year in which one scholarship and two exhibitions were won at Oxford and six out of the fourteen leavers went up either to Oxford or Cambridge. And, too, there was a medical report from the school doctor, Dr Wells, attributing the streptococcal infection at least in part to overcrowding, lack of ventilation and poor heating — a somewhat strange statement since the dangerous 1933 epidemic had occurred at midsummer. They decided to go ahead.

The new classroom block, faced in Hornton stone, was designed in conservative style by Gilbert T. Gardner of Oxford and built by P.R. Alcock of Banbury, whose son was at the school. It was opened on 30 October 1937 by F.B. Palmer. The bare statements conceal a day of rare celebration and varied excitement, brilliantly and precisely organised by Dewey. Palmer's memory was almost as long as Wilson's and he rightly claimed that this was the biggest building development since Egerton's time and indeed the school had not enjoyed a similar festivity since the distant days of the official opening of the schoolroom wing, dining hall and chapel. There were few who could recall those events. Wilson, 90 years old and anticipating his death, had decided unexpectedly not to return to Bloxham after the summer holidays, but Canon

F.S. Boissier was present to assist the new chaplain, J. Sholto Douglas, at the early communion which started the day. Extra carriages were added to the London train, cars filled the quad. From sung eucharist in the packed chapel the procession wound down to the new building. The silver key on its velvet cushion was handed to Palmer, the door opened and the key ceremoniously given to him. The leading guests headed by the bishop of Antigua, G.S. Hand (O.B.), the heads of four Oxford colleges and H.M. solicitor-general passed by the new classrooms, four on each floor, and into the hall.

'Immediately on their appearance in Hall a fanfare of trumpets and loud cheering broke from the gallery, maroons exploded in the garden, the school flag was broken from the masthead, the School and Chapel bells rang wildly and from the glorious steeple of S. Mary's, Bloxham, came a joyous peal'.

Speeches, luncheon in great hall, and more speeches preceded the rugger match against the Old Bloxhamists, an exciting one which the school won 6-3 after being a try down at half-time, and this was followed by a dance in the new hall until midnight.

The building of the great hall and classrooms was only part of a much larger programme. Its completion provided not only light and airy modern classrooms but also a new central heating plant for the whole school and a properly equipped hall and stage for school functions and plays. The first lecture was given there on 14 November by E.F. Hodge, captain of the school, on his £15 five-week European holiday. The first formal function was a dinner for the builders and school domestic staff and that Christmastide the Bicester hunt ball was held there, the hunt later giving the stage pelmet to the school. No longer did the collapsible stage have to be hauled out and fitted to the south end of the schoolroom for plays, the dining hall be cleared for concerts or prizegiving be cramped within the inner quad or gym.

Space was also released in the main buildings for other purposes. The prefects' study in the Wilberforce building was converted into a masters' common room, something which the school lacked although in the early 1920s the Liddon library was also used for this purpose. The school had some doubts as to the wisdom of encouraging masters to congregate and combine. The former no. 1 classroom was subdivided to make new, small studies for prefects and by partitioning part of the schoolroom to make a new vestry in 1937 the old one became no. 9 study for VIth formers. In a further improvement of living conditions the three chapel classrooms were made into house day rooms for the middle school.

Elsewhere in a fever of activity old buildings were replaced by new and every beginning of term was a strange experience. The latrines and laundry were cleared away at the east end of the chapel, carefully preserving the seventeenth-century and Egerton datestones of the laundry and building them into the wall along Water Lane. A new gravelled open quadrangle was created, flanked by chapel and Botany Bay on west and north, and the new classroom and sanitary blocks on south and east.

The row of old stone and thatched cottages and sheds facing the cricket field were swept away. First to go was the tuck shop, originally Egerton's lathe room, and the adjacent sheds. The thatched and stone-flagged tuck shop had been presided over by Bo and Mrs Mallett for years. Chocolates and sweets, potato crisps and ice cream (from the early 1930s), tooth paste and shoe laces, the round blocks of green or white blanco and tins of brasso for cleaning corps kit and uniforms were ranged behind the counter. Bottles of fizzy lemonade — 'a yeller' or 'a pink'un' according to colour, but all tasting the same — were ranked in wooden crates, and here also were sold rugger gear, gym shoes, school or house ties. When Bo Mallett retired in 1934 after 42 years with the school, the Woodard Corporation bursar suggested that the tuck shop be taken over in 1935 by the school outfitters, Messrs Gorringes of London, who would sell school clothes there. The new stone-built tuck shop in traditional Cotswold style was built in 1936 on the site of the sheds between the old tuck shop and the pavilion and under the management of R.S.M. Reg Turner and his wife continued to dispense clothes and comforts for the next thirty years.

The old thatched pavilion, with its whitewashed walls almost entirely covered with the black boards recording the team names for the previous half-century, was rebuilt two years later through the generosity of L.C. Vaughan (O.B.) who had been in the cricket XI himself and was described as 'probably the most useful forward' in the 1887-88 soccer team. His original gift of £1,000 to renovate the pavilion was increased to pay for a completely new and well equipped one, for which the team boards were salvaged for rehanging. Vaughan himself opened the pavilion in 1938 when the XL club visited Bloxham for the first time, bringing a formidably strong side led by Jack Hobbs (Surrey and England) and containing D.J. Knight (Surrey), J.H. Parsons (Warwickshire) and Andy Kempton (Surrey). The school scored 215 for 9 wickets despite the early dismissal of the usually high-scoring opening batsmen, the captain M.F. Parke and S.G. Lester, and although Hobbs mastered all the school bowling the match ended in a draw with the XL club at 159 for 3 wickets at the close.

From the cricket square in 1938, therefore, there was a totally different school skyline from the early 1930s. The untidy and rather ragged collection of old buildings had been replaced by new, clean ones, all faced in the local stone, while the main buildings, gym and armoury had sharp new roofs. Armitage's building ambitions were satisfied, though he was heard wistfully to say that he could give Bloxham the loftiest chapel in the country, even taller than Lancing, if only he might incorporate the ground-floor day rooms into the chapel! The school looked new and go-ahead. Its senior boys were doing well, their successes marked and rewarded by half-holidays and their university activities written in the Oxford Letter, and more briefly, for there were fewer of them there, in the Cambridge Letter in *The Bloxhamist*. The school was widening its horizons, for Armitage was one of those forward-looking headmasters who encouraged individual enterprise and let it be known that Bloxham was a 'school of adventure'. H.D. Eastwood was on an exchange visit in France in 1936, L.A. Bullwinkle in the U.S.A. in 1937 and his brother J.D. Bullwinkle in the U.S.A. in 1939, while in return Bloxham welcomed American and Finnish boys. Eastwood and G. Morgan hitch-hiked to Baghdad in 1937 on a trip well publicised by the headmaster; on their return they appeared on television and could therefore probably claim to be Bloxham's first television personalities. Sporting fixtures were more varied and the school was taking part in competitive public school events at athletics as well as shooting and the corps camps. Armitage himself was serving on the Oxfordshire education committee from 1937.

Much of all this success must be attributed to Armitage and his leadership, ably backed by the men whom he had recruited to his staff. Alone among them from earlier days was C.N. "Lamie" Lawrence, the second master and Wilberforce housemaster upon whom Armitage relied greatly and whose influence on both boys and his younger colleagues was far greater than might be suggested by his quiet and unassuming manner. Despite this it was he whom the younger masters sought out when they wanted a companion for a convivial evening, and after they had taken over the actual coaching of games with conspicuous success, in the background in charge of games and grounds there was always Lawrence, by that time affectionately nick-named "Uncle". Cricket was the charge of Crawshay, who during his Bloxham years played as an all-rounder for Oxfordshire and brought inspiring club fixtures to Bloxham. His own most notable local performance was the occasion when batting for the masters against the school in 1936 he scored 201 runs while the rest of his struggling colleagues mustered 39 between them. He coached some first class school cricketers such as B.C.K. Stark and S.F. Florey, whose 136 not out in 1934 was the first century for seven years. Crawshay claimed that the 1937 team was the best in his time, and it was in that side that P.C. Birse was introduced to the 1st XI as a half-colourman. In the high-scoring summer of 1939 he was the most prolific run-getter that the school had seen for a long time, finishing the season with an aggregate of 576 runs. Jack Hobbs, playing for the second time for the XL club against the school commented that they were 'four wickets better' than their predecessors.

In that match the school opener, A.M. Brassington, was batting in the spirit of the limitless Test matches of the 1930s and took two hours for his 13 runs, 'during which', records *The Bloxhamist,* 'the XL Club made every effort to dislodge him. They stood round him in circles: they tried to make him have a very good lunch: J.B. Hobbs occasionally asked him whether his bat was a good one. All in vain until after lunch the umpire came to the rescue'. The umpire, of course, was Bo Mallett, and he knew his duty when a somewhat high and sharply rising ball hit Brassington on the thigh. Jack Hobb's parting comment to him was, 'You may not be popular here, lad — but they'd love you in Australia'. But the unpredictability of cricket, and especially school cricket, is well reflected in the scores that season, for the side that scored 103 for 1 wicket against Magdalen College School and 144 for 2 wickets against the Revd J. Sholto Douglas's XI, and even 186 for 7 against the XL club, fielding Hobbs, Crawshay and Douglas (who had been a useful bowler for Berkshire), was skittled out for 17 runs against Solihull school. In one way Crawshay's last season in 1938 was of greater significance, for that was the year of the new pavilion and the first matches

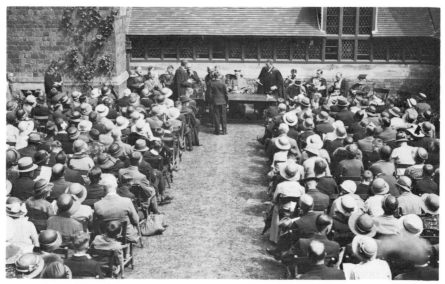

Prizegiving in the inner quadrangle, 1933. Masters facing the camera are (l. to r.)
K. T. Dewey, B. O. Wheel (hidden), Jackson Knight, C. N. Lawrence (standing
by table), Revd C. C. Barclay, M. Craze (partly hidden), V. L. Armitage,
headmaster, 1925-40 (standing), A. T. I. Boggis, C. A. Hodgkinson, F. G. L.
Crawshay, C. J. Wilson. The Provost, the Rt Revd H. K. Southwell, bishop of
Lewes, is seated in the centre and the prize-giver (wearing hat) was Sir George
Arthur, formerly private secretary to Earl Kitchener.

against really strong club sides like the XL club and the South Oxfordshire
Amateurs, who have played both school and Old Bloxhamists regularly ever
since — and indeed the latter sometimes almost appear to have been an Old
Bloxhamist team under other colours.

Crawshay's achievements with the cricketers were matched by Michael Craze's
with the rugger XVs and athletes from 1930. It was he who introduced athletic
'standards' in 1935, so that even the most unathletic might have a reasonable
chance of gaining some house points, and his invitations to Harold Abrahams
and to University athletes for demonstrations gave the sport a new status. The
first school athletics match — against Warwick, as at rugger and boxing — was
won in 1935, while from 1934 the leading athletes competed in the Public
Schools' sports at the White City. B.P. Burbush, holder then of the school mile
record at 4 minutes 46.4 seconds, came fifth in the mile in 1934 and E.A.C. Lee,
who set a school 100-yard record of 10.3 seconds in 1936, was another notable
runner. At the last pre-war meeting Bloxham sent fifteen boys to the White City,
not a bad proportion considering the size of the school, while the school sports,
with the potato and sack races at last weeded out, were spaced out over two days.

It was Craze who was inspired to organise an 1885-style Rugger match to mark

George V's jubilee, an event which Armitage seized upon as a good excuse to invite the national press. The game was a close one, but for once attention was held by the spectators rather than the knickerbockered players, although three film companies recorded the massive set scrums. On the touchlines were F.V.A. Harmer in top hat and frock coat, Hodgkinson in sober grey bowler and coat and Armitage refereeing with a bell in black bowler hat and Norfolk jacket. According to the *Sunday Graphic,* 'one of the masters wore a red beard, top hat and check breeches [Dewey!]. But when the headmaster took off his coat all eyes were immediately fastened upon his braces... They were black braces with chromium-plated tabs, very strong and scholarly.' More seriously, by 1938 when there was a good side with L.A. Bullwinkle and P.C. Birse, the school was fielding four rugger teams and the better players were appearing in county public school sides in the holidays, E.A.C. Lee leading Oxfordshire schools in 1936. Opponents included some Oxford colleges, against whom the school XV could hold its own with credit.

Craze's influence was not limited to the track and games field. He was a scholar (later writing the histories of Felsted and King's School, Worcester) and at Bloxham founded the Egerton Society, a VIth-form literary and cultural society. Two other young newcomers in the 1930s, C.A. Hodgkinson in 1932 and G.M. Bolton, who took over mathematics and the scouts from B.O. Wheel in 1934, are remembered more often in the classroom than outside — Hodgkinson, the refreshing English master who puzzled his forms once by pinning up on the prep board the bald instruction, 'Write a purple passage', and Bolton, one arm on hip, one on his head, pausing in the explanation of theorem or equation. Both men on arrival discovered that their headmaster could be disconcerting. Bolton found he had no headmaster, for Armitage had just taken off on his world cruise, while Hodgkinson had an unnerving welcome for an inexperienced young master straight from Oxford. It was the custom in those days for Armitage (and his two successors) to stand at the foot of the chapel steps to review the school coming out of chapel. Every boy and most of the staff, therefore, regularly passed under the headmaster's eye and the opportunity could be taken for an informal word with prefect or master. On Hodgkinson's first day he duly attended chapel. Coming out, as he reached the foot of the chapel steps, Armitage seemed not to recognise him, afterwards telling him that as an economy he was sacked. Ignoring this abrupt dismissal before he had even started his job, Hodgkinson carried on as if nothing had happened. The matter was never again mentioned!

His own cheerful brand of irreverence is illustrated by the care with which he treasured one of the headmaster's formal notes delivered to him in the common room soon after his arrival and now preserved in the school archives. Armitage wrote,

'I wish it to be quite clearly understood that (except in Masters' rooms) masters are not allowed to smoke or display cigarettes, pipes or cigars, anywhere within the school buildings — Also that the "no hands in trouser pockets" rule applies equally to masters as to boys'.

Armitage liked despatching such notes and enjoyed coining terse phrases and instructions. The long-familiar 'STEADY round the BEND' board was one such, fixed to the outside wall of the school where a lorry had once crashed.

It was a lively common room that worked under Armitage, who became rather more aloof than in his earlier days when JK and Dewey as new young teachers derived so much guidance from his friendship and example. The chaplains of the period contributed much to the spicy and carefree bucolic atmosphere, characterised by the custom of giving Corpus Christi and Ascension days as whole holidays when the school, armed with packed lunches and privileged to visit country pubs provided they bought cider only, could roam and cycle as far as they wished. The Revd R.D. Hudson, who had coached the 1st XV in the late 1920s before his ordination, was chaplain all too briefly in 1931-32 before becoming one of the chaplains of Eton, and he was succeeded by the Revd C.C. Barclay (1932-36) and the Revd J. Sholto Douglas (1937-49). Both were sportsmen, Barclay having played tennis and put the weight for Cambridge, Douglas being a Minor Counties' cricketer, and both brought a wholesome experience of a wider world to the small country boarding school. Barclay had been a priest in Australia for 30 years (and was that the origin of his nickname "Crook", or was it his Chicago-like physique?) while Douglas came of a military family and had been a soldier in the East where, he hinted, he had led a merry and eventful life. He was also a gifted actor both on the stage and in the pulpit, though more accurately it was his custom to preach carefully prepared sermons extempore from the sanctuary steps. His first school production was Galsworthy's *Loyalties* in 1939, after which, year by year, he produced plays for both Bloxham and the Banbury Cross Players. It was the start of a new era in school dramatics, for since the Gilbert and Sullivan performances about 1930 there had been little more than a short-lived revival of house plays and the annual Shrove Tuesday variety show, with home-made sketches by the common room forming popular and slick productions directed by Hodgkinson.

Old boys of the period recall a life of strict discipline under both masters and prefects, whose prestige and powers were enhanced. Armitage had school prefects solemnly initiated in chapel, and once in office they were responsible for much of the daily administration of the school, controlling bounds, keeping order, supervising dormitories, dining hall and chapel, and taking roll call. Two or three times daily, before meals and chapel, the school lined up in the passages for inspection for tidiness, ram-rod straight to the order, 'Get your backs against the wall', and breaches of discipline were swiftly punishable by a beating. School prefects could give up to six strokes with a slipper in the prefects' room, house prefects three strokes. Staff were restricted to imposing extra work or punishment drills, which varied in severity; in the 1930s the school sergeant supervised offenders who had to walk briskly round the track a number of times, but for a dirty uniform after a corps field day JK would order a punishment drill of doubling round the track in full uniform with a rifle held over the head. More serious offences, including lack of effort in the classroom, were dealt with by the housemaster wielding a cane. If a boy dropped his position in class he would be given a report card and for a week his performance in every lesson was assessed by the master. A bad report card with more than three 'VS' or two 'NS' (*vix satis*, 'hardly satisfactory', and *non satis*) earned a housemaster's beating. Armitage himself rarely used the cane unless the offence was exceptional — he did so when boys stole and let off detonators from the railway linesman's shed, and he also clamped down heavily on end-of-term pranks like the occasions when the Crimean War cannon at the gateway was fired or an enraged village was awoken at midnight by the ringing of the church bells.

Daily routine remained little changed for a long time. Early communion at 7.15 and the rising bell at 7.30 were followed by 8 o'clock breakfast and morning chapel. There were four 40-minute periods in the morning divided by a break of about an hour for physical training or runs; on Wednesday and Saturday, which were half-holidays and therefore match days, there was only a short break. In the afternoons were games and two more periods — in the summer term the order was reversed — separated by the short first tea. An evensong service was held at 6.0 followed by second tea, two preparations of an hour and three-quarters and lights out was generally about 9.30. Corps was held on Tuesdays during the fourth period before lunch and on Thursday afternoons when uniform was worn for drill, rifle drill, semaphore signalling and section and platoon exercises in the fields and on Hobb Hill ('the number of times I've assaulted that hill', commented one Old Bloxhamist). Games were compulsory until one reached a very senior position, but with a little ingenuity those who disliked cricket might take up shooting, and if one was not too good at that, then the shooters always needed markers. When the grounds were out of condition there were runs or walks with prefects checking off names at the farthest point which they had reached by bicycle — the four-mile grind round the Highlands and Ells Farm circuit or the six-mile grind extending the route to Broughton and the Wykeham Hill cross-roads were the all too familiar lanes to generations of boys.

By 1938 when the new buildings were complete and academic and sporting successes could be acclaimed, the peak had been passed. The decline was alarmingly rapid. First, the numbers in the school started falling, affected at last by the continued economic crisis of the 1930s and the level of fees which were reduced to £110. From over 140 in 1936 they dropped to about 125 in 1938 and 120 in the summer of 1939 — enough to make all the difference between profit and loss just at the time when every penny was needed to finance the huge building debt of about £14,000, designed to meet the needs of a larger school. Other desirable expansion was postponed, such as the proposed hospital isolation wing and the purchase of Salmon's field east of the school. The Committee was operating on a £4,500 overdraft each holidays and the Woodard Corporation were issuing orders that no school was to seek an overdraft larger than the next term's receipts. For Bloxham, of course, was not alone in its difficulties. Among other public schools Weymouth was forced to close; Rossall and Brighton were only two-thirds full and the latter was heavily in debt; St Bees announced that it would close in 1938 (but in fact survived) and the Imperial Service College was forced in 1942 to amalgamate with Haileybury.

Armitage had reformed and rebuilt Bloxham over twelve years, raised its standards and made it better known. During his headmastership it completed the transition from Egerton's private school for the middle classes to public school, marked symbolically by his appointment to the Headmasters' Conference in 1929. Having achieved so much he now seemed tired of Bloxham, unwilling or unable to cope again with the same sort of crisis that he had overcome with such zest ten years earlier. Even in 1935 he had been privately nominating Jackson Knight as his successor should he leave. After JK departed in 1936 to become lecturer in classics at Exeter university he placed his hopes on Dewey, exhibiting some of his old ruthlessness in obtaining the retirement of C.N. Lawrence as second master in 1938. But that was the year of Munich and Armitage recognised the signs of the coming war.

He was 50 years old but still a reserve officer with military administrative experience and a good linguist, and he cultivated his contacts in the War Office, feeling that his work for Bloxham was over but there would be new opportunities in uniform. The year 1939 passed uneasily. Wilson died on 12 March and his body was brought back to Bloxham for burial in the parish churchyard. The secretary of the Old Bloxhamist Society, E.S. Moore, wrote at the beginning of the summer to enquire whether his school at Felixstowe might in the event of war be accommodated at Bloxham. At the end of term, while some boys were taking higher and school certificate examinations, nineteen others were obtaining air raid precaution certificates. As Britain hastily mobilised for war at the end of August, Armitage received his call-up papers. He left Bloxham without hesitation.

CHAPTER VIII

K. T. DEWEY
1940 — 1952

When Armitage went off to the war towards the end of the summer holidays he left his wife in residence and warned his second master of his departure. There were three weeks before the boys were due back, three weeks in which the nation daily expected massive aerial bombardment. Dewey hastened to Bloxham and set about the enormous task of preparing the school against war, without instruction from either his headmaster or the Corporation and with a host of unanswerable questions facing him. Would the buildings be commandeered by the military, the government or be needed for a school like the Woodard ones on the vulnerable south coast? How many parents would wish to keep their sons at home rather than split their families? Where did one construct air raid shelters for 150 boys and staff? And how on earth could Street's gothic or Gardner's broad modern windows be blacked out and prevented from splintering in bomb blast?

In Dewey Bloxham had the right man at the right time. Imperturbable and a first-rate organiser; shy, without close friends, somewhat lonely and therefore disinclined to delegate, but wholly capable of making his own decisions; a bachelor, deeply loving his work at the school and entirely committed to devoting his whole time and attention to its well-being. With the help of Miss R.A. Garnar, the bursar, and the domestic staff, such masters as he could muster and local friends like the Apps family of White Cottage, he got the school ready for the beginning of term, contriving air raid shelters in the cellars beneath the schoolroom and chapel and completing the black-out for the whole scattered complex of buildings. The school Committee, when it met at the end of September, appointed him as acting headmaster for the term, and it was in this role that he loyally greeted Armitage when he fleetingly visited the school for Armistice Day weekend. The latter had secured a posting as an intelligence officer at army corps headquarters in France where he had organised part of George VI's tour to the British Expeditionary Force. That apparently was his last view of Bloxham, until many years later in 1953 as a visitor. In the intervening period he had served in the Middle East and Italy as officer in charge of military government education offices and after his demobilisation in 1947 spent two years in Germany as chief staff officer to the education advisers of the Control Commission. He formally resigned his position as headmaster in the summer of 1940 and his wife moved out of the headmaster's house. Dewey was confirmed as headmaster.

The problems facing Dewey were tremendous. There were all the "normal" difficulties attendant upon the war. Armitage was the first master to be called up, but he was followed by J.N. Shaw in the summer of 1940 and others later as the armed forces were mobilised and expanded in 1940 and 1941. Teaching had to be rearranged and Sholto Douglas, for instance, found himself brushing-up long-forgotten Latin for the junior forms, and new staff had to be engaged. Some were hardly appointed before being spirited away by the forces, and G.H. Bletchly was one who was at Bloxham for less than a year in 1941. As 25 years previously the headmaster had to rely on various expedients to retain staff, calling on those who had retired, choosing some who lacked the ideal qualifications and experience, and even going to the extraordinary extreme of appointing mistresses. The domestic staff were also hard to recruit and it was, therefore, with a great sense of relief that Dewey reappointed Sister Stent in the hospital and Bo Mallett as hall steward at the outbreak of the war.

Food supplies, their shortage and rationing were one of the immediate problems, but here Miss Garnar proved an adaptable and unshakeable housekeeper, while the school had the advantage of being in the country and therefore able to increase the produce of its own farm and gardens, and a diet committee gave the boys a chance of understanding the restrictions and co-operating in the running of the household. They had to help in other new ways also — in cleaning their own boots and shoes (and woe betide anyone with dirty shoes spotted by the chapel prefect), in working in the gardens or on playing field maintenance, or serving as dining hall orderlies. And as Dewey pointed out to the Committee early in 1940, all these necessary new chores were also economies for the school.

For, in addition to the wartime problems, Dewey was also faced with the inherited crisis of falling numbers and the unwieldy building debt. From 154 boys when the Committee had embarked on its development plan in 1936 — the same size as Hurstpierpoint — the school had dwindled to 111 boys at the beginning of 1940. Furthermore at this critical moment F.B. Palmer said that he could no longer carry on as chairman because of his age and ill health. He was dissuaded from resigning in September 1939, but although his service and love for Bloxham continued he no longer possessed his earlier energy and in 1941 he had to give up. Dewey was alone in the fight for survival.

The nature of that fight is now obscure since most of the participants are dead and the Committee minutes are uninformative. However, the Committee were despondent at the beginning of the war. At that first wartime meeting on 30 September they had no headmaster and a thorough review of the finances was not cheering. They desperately needed more boarders but did not know how to get them, seriously considering resignation from the Headmasters' Conference in order to avoid its restrictions on advertising. They had before them letters from St Felix School, Felixstowe, requesting accommodation if they were evacuated, and it is said that the Committee were also actively contemplating amalgamation with either Ardingly or Hurstpierpoint. Dewey pleaded to be given a chance for one year to pull Bloxham through, and Miss Garnar remembers him coming out of the meeting, fuming. 'They want to close Bloxham! Over my dead body!'[1].

The first priority was to overcome the financial crisis, aggravated in those uncertain days by the local tradesmen demanding prompt payment and by the rising prices. The Corporation bursar, R.C. Freeman, secured better terms for the outstanding £13,100 building debt, thereby reducing the loan charge; Palmer house was let for a year and then in 1941 taken over by the army; the run-down in maintenance coupled with the growth of the school farm was a useful economy; the staff offered voluntary salary cuts, Sister Stent, for example, giving up her first term's payment when she returned in 1939. Most important of all, the number of boys in the school started to rise. From the low point of 111 the numbers crept up — 121 in the summer and 135 at Michaelmas 1940, 157 and 181 a year later — and reached the 200 mark in Michaelmas 1942, being joyously celebrated with *Te Deum* in chapel.

This extraordinarily rapid recovery came about in two ways. Once the early uncertainties of the war at home were over Bloxham possessed the very real advantage of being a boarding school in the country away from military targets. It was specially popular to parents from the blitzed cities of the nearby Midlands and a whole generation of Old Bloxhamists from 1940 to 1950 has this strong Midland connection. Secondly, Dewey deliberately lowered the entrance requirements, both academically and in age. The junior entry was enlarged, the eastern part of the former masters' house becoming a junior house named after Egerton in 1940. Whereas Armitage had wooed the prep schools, Dewey waived common entrance qualifications when he saw fit and in particular increased the proportion of local farmers' sons. This was a return to Egerton's original aims brought about by necessity, but the school benefited in more ways than the purely financial. In any case, as Dewey himself used to say, 'It was not so important who came into his school; it was how he turned them out that really mattered'. These newcomers broadened the outlook of middle-class urban boys at the very time when young men of every background were being thrown together in the armed forces, and they contributed in many ways to the character of a country school, bringing closer links with the neighbourhood and an understanding of its environment. Their less fortunate friends envied their sporting ability, their skill on the school farm and welcomed the arrival of home farm produce to vary the school diet! More boys, more income from fees, was the first need. The restoration of academic standards could follow.

Dewey was successful in his aim. By 1942 the school was asking the army to release Palmer house, needed for extra science laboratories and additional staff. In that year the Committee restored the salary cuts offered by the staff, started repaying the arrears of salaries and considered payment of bonuses, and as the

---

[1] This story has been related by various reliable sources, all of which seem to be derived from Miss Garnar, who as bursar and secretary attended and minuted Committee meetings. She herself was not certain in 1975 when this event took place. It was a meeting at Bloxham and in 1939-41 the Committee rarely met at the school. Their minutes record no such discussion and the only time that they considered an appeal for accommodation from Ardingly was in February 1941 when they met in Oxford. It seems most likely that the occasion of Dewey's vow was this first wartime meeting of 30 September 1939.

The former captain of the school, P.M. Kirk, recalls a similar conversation when he travelled to London with Dewey, who was on his way to a meeting. The latter told him that he intended to take 'a bold line' over a proposal to merge Bloxham with Hurstpierpoint.

K. T. Dewey, headmaster 1940-52.

school went on growing they had the welcome new worry of overcrowding. Every available place for a bed was used, overflowing into Merton Cottage, spilling over to the great hall balcony, while the school could only worship together in chapel by congestion in the pews and placing chairs in the organ loft, probably the most popular seats of all except for the coveted post of organ blower (retained in case of electricity failure) which offered even more opportunity for mischief.

The measure of Dewey's success is marked in the minutes of the school Council (as it was restyled in 1945) when it is recorded that in 1946 the bank loan on the pre-war building programme was finally discharged. It was a landmark as worthy of a *Te Deum* as the 200th boy in 1942, but only a select few knew about it. In the end it had taken only ten years to repay the debt.[2] Dewey has been called 'Bloxham's second Founder', a title he would have disclaimed but one of which he would have been immensely proud. His right to the title rests on the school's successful survival and the fact that this was very largely a personal triumph which has gone down into school legend with some pardonable exaggeration and inaccuracy — it was widely but erroneously believed that he gave up his own salary, for instance. The Council certainly recognised the scale of his achievement, formally recording in their minutes on his retirement 'the

---

[2] By comparison it may be mentioned that a 20-year period for the repayment of capital expenditure was common at that time. In the 1970s capital expenditure by local authorities on state schools, who can offer better security than the private sector, is funded over a 30-year span.

invaluable results of his single-minded devotion to the interests of the School, and the quite remarkable way in which the financial position has been built up by him'. His own determination to keep the school alive and the popular legends of his personal sacrifices to do so won him the loyalty of his staff and boys. At a time when the sense of national unity and purpose was strong, Dewey successfully fostered a similar team spirit in the school and he could always rely on support in showing off Bloxham to its best. His boys remain loyal to his memory and of Bloxham's headmasters only Egerton has commanded comparable regard and affection. He earned their respect not only because of his obvious interest in each one of them but because of his ability on the right rare occasion to acknowledge when he was wrong. S.G. Lester, for example, recalls the episode when as a senior prefect Dewey ordered him to beat any boy who left clothes lying around in the changing room. There were 87, and he did. Loud complaints followed and Dewey prepared to demote Lester, until faced with the resignation of all his prefects pointing out that his own orders had been carried out precisely, and he was wise enough to change his mind.

As a man of solitary disposition Dewey was not given to sharing decisions and had no confidant in the common room except perhaps Sholto Douglas. Certainly the chaplain shared the burden of showing parents over the school as well as the headmaster's hopes and thankfulness as the crises were successively overcome from the early tentative, 'if we play our cards properly we should be 120 next term' to the happy *Te Deum* marking the 200th boy. The school's Anglo-Catholic traditions continued unaltered, for on that neither Dewey nor Douglas was prepared to compromise his principles for the sake of a few more fee-paying parents. Full sung eucharist remained the central service, Sholto Douglas's histrionic sense ensuring that sung eucharists were dramatic and well drilled, compared with which all the other services seemed colourless and lifeless. In 1942 he persuaded both headmaster and the bishop of Oxford to permit the reserved sacrament in chapel, kept in a pyx designed by Dykes Bower and a symbol of Bloxham's adherence to Anglo-Catholic beliefs.

Chapel attendance was still largely compulsory with the whole school going to the short daily evensong or mattins as well as Sunday sung eucharist and full evensong. Saturday evening compline, confession and the daily holy communion were voluntary, the morning 'early' heralded by the ringing of the angelus — the village's rising bell just as the bell rung at the elevation of the host in the sung eucharist was both the village's Sunday dinner bell and the signal for Mrs Douglas to put on the chaplain's breakfast in Ivy Cottage. Neither chaplain nor boys would have considered breaking their fast before communion, such small denials and rules for life being regarded as a form of totally acceptable self-control and self-discipline. Other outward signs of Anglo-Catholic traditions were also observed, such as the use of vestments, making the sign of the cross in chapel and at the short Latin grace for meals, and genuflexion to the reserved sacrament at the altar.

The chaplain was also in effect the director of chapel music, there being no doubt under Sholto Douglas, who was both knowledgeable and strong-willed, that organ and choir were properly subordinate to the service of worship, and the choirs whom he trained were required to lead the congregation or sing anthems without the distraction of a conductor. Once a week there was congregational singing practice, and the emphasis was always on corporate worship with everyone joining in as much as possible. Individuals took little part in services except for school prefects reading the lessons and taking the collection, but the choir was comparatively rarely given the opportunity to display its virtuosity while everyone else sat to listen. This was not because of any decline in choral traditions. The choir joined the public schools' choir festival at Gloucester cathedral for the first time in 1943 and under G.R. Watts as organist the school made three B.B.C. broadcasts in 1945, while Douglas himself composed an All Saints' *Requiem* in 1941 and a *Gloria.*

In ordering services he was assisted like his predecessors by a succession of sacristans and teams of servers, who possessed considerable skill in conducting a well-ordered but unobtrusive ceremonial. The server rang the daily angelus but on other occasions bell-ringing was the duty of an appointed ringer or ringers. The chapel bell in fact was silent for much of the war, first in 1939 so that it could be used for air raid warnings and then in common with other church bells so that it could warn of invasion. The chapel prefect was responsible for drawing up the seating plan, increasingly necessary as numbers grew and the pews filled, allotting each boy his fixed and regular place; only at early service could one sit in any place and even then there were conventions to observe, so that no junior would dare to move back, as it were, above his station, towards the more senior pews at the west end. The chapel prefect could also quickly note absences from gaps in the pews seen from the organ loft, so that chapel attendance acted also as a roll-call, and he would also ensure (if necessary) that silence, reverence and tidiness were observed.

The prefect of hall, who was second in the hierarchy beneath the captain of the school, exercised similar authority over the dining hall, inspecting the line-up before meals and ensuring orderliness in hall. As in chapel, every boy had his fixed place at table, each house having three tables, with one for Egerton house, presided over by a master at lunchtime but by house prefects at other meals. One sat according to seniority, slowly working from the foot of the tables under the windows to flank the master at the head, the junior boys taking it in turn to serve as orderlies for their table. School prefects sat at the high table with the headmaster, chaplain, and Miss Garnar, again in hierarchical order. School prefects in general carried out routine daily administration and discipline, picking games teams and appointing the afternoon's activities in consultation with the master-in-charge, who was in turn in close contact with the groundsman when he was not actually acting as groundsman himself. As the numbers expanded the prefects and senior games players undertook more and more coaching of junior games as well as corps instruction, without which the staff could not have coped.

Some of the more rigid rules of pre-war days were relaxed. Boys not only enjoyed the freedom of the north Oxfordshire countryside on free afternoons but even juniors were allowed to visit the village shops with their housemaster's permission. Wartime clothing shortages led to variations of uniform requirements, already refreshingly few. Armitage had allowed the boys freedom of choice in shirts, ties and pullovers, worn with sports flannels and ginger tweed jackets for daily wear, a licence kept within reasonable bounds by Dewey's own abhorence of slovenliness.

Discipline by school and house prefects remained strict, even fierce, and the stern regime of P.M. Kirk, captain of the school in 1939-40, is still recalled as perhaps the peak of the old style of the prefect system. The smallest misdemeanour might be followed either by immediate summons to the school prefects' study and summary justice or the more formal invitation issued at the end of meals of 'I should like to see the following in my study now...' House prefects' jurisdiction was unchanged and limited mostly to minor offences committed in dormitories, though pyjamas were not much protection against a slipper wielded in the house bathroom. The school prefects, on the other hand, extended their rights partly because the shortage of staff gave them additional responsibilities and partly because Dewey did not curb their privileges as strictly as Armitage. Sometimes they might use the cane or military swagger-stick for punishment, and with the headmaster's permission could inflict a formal prefects' beating in the Liddon library for outstandingly serious offences. The growth of their privileges was partly due also to the quality of staff, for although Dewey managed to increase the size of the common room with that of the school, the ability to maintain discipline was not always among the talents of the teachers obtainable in wartime.

The young masters went off to war, J.N. Shaw, R.A. Cruse, Ivo Payne and "Wisti" Longden in the first couple of years, followed in 1942 after his eleven years at the school by Alan Hodgkinson and G.H. Bletchly. A few Old Bloxhamists helped out either before or after their military service, like P.J.A. Kirk, Richard Martinek and Spencer Lester. For the rest Dewey had to fall back on older men: G.A. Scott, M.B.E., a cultured teacher of three European languages and master of English prose, poetry or conversation, who had memories of Russia in the early days of the Bolshevik revolution; A.G. Brock, M.C., a retired headmaster, one of whose earlier pupils at St John's, Leatherhead, being E.J. Kahn, who had providentially taken up his appointment at Bloxham in 1939; C.T. Apps was another retired headmaster and J.E.K. Esdaile an erudite scholar who was perhaps surprised to find himself in the role of schoolmaster.

They were supplemented by men with teaching experience but lacking formal qualifications. F.V.A. Harmer had spent a few years under Armitage when his unhurried manner earned him the nickname of "Hurricane"; having returned from South America only to be rejected for military service he came to teach geography and took over the athletics coaching. Charles Packwood, dapper and mischievous, taught junior forms, coached boxing with growing success and acted as host and confidant both to informal groups of boys of all ages and to the junior school social club, the Gould Club, formed in 1940 by J.D. Bullwinkle.

Probably the weakest area was science teaching. Dewey introduced biology as a full-time classroom subject in 1940 and still taught chemistry himself, but he was not an outstanding teacher and his headmaster's duties now interfered with his teaching timetable so that a considerable load fell on R. Gillies, who came in 1941. Even more extraordinary to the school than the enlistment of men once retired or those without degrees was the appointment of mistresses, of whom Miss Naish and Mrs Pindar (for biology) were the first to arrive in 1942 and Miss Usher (1942-53) the longest-serving as a teacher of junior mathematics.

Inevitably most of the burden fell on the few experienced men who remained — the headmaster and chaplain, Alan Hodgkinson, housemaster of Wilson, George Bolton, housemaster of Wilberforce, and E.J. "Sam" Kahn, rapidly promoted as first housemaster of Egerton in September 1940 and then moved to Crake the following year when Cruse joined up. It would be impossible to over-emphasise the debt which Bloxham owed to both Bolton and Kahn. The span of their combined full-time service to the school totalled 70 years and indeed remains unfinished since in 1977 both live in the village and Sam Kahn still holds office as librarian in what is somewhat imprecisely classed as a part-time capacity and can also be found doing relief teaching. The very important element of stability and continuity which they provided was rivalled only by Wilson and was variously expressed on Bolton's retirement in 1967, when *The Bloxhamist* reported that he had worked with 94 masters and 18 mistresses, and at the Old Bloxhamists' presentation to Kahn in 1975 when the chairman said that rather than enumerate the many positions that he had held it was easier to list those he had not.

Both men were from Jesus College, Cambridge, Bolton habitually wearing an Oxford B.A. gown so that he could use its sleeve as a reserve blackboard rubber. Respectively housemasters of Wilberforce and Crake and heads of mathematics and classics, Kahn succeeded Bolton as second master, while Bolton as scoutmaster and coach of numerous colts' teams guided the early careers of hundreds of boys who later progressed to Sam Kahn's care in the corps or senior teams. Inevitably, memories of each generation of boys differ, but both men have left lasting impressions of "Flossie" Bolton's darting energy and penetrating voice and Sam Kahn's genial and ceaseless work in study, no 4 classroom used as his office, pavilion or library. Typical perhaps of each was the sight and sound of Bolton, hand on hip, megaphone raised, announcing athletics results, and that of the heavy roller being started up between lessons and lunch, lunch and opening of play, as Kahn drove it out to the cricket square.

Compared with the adventures and disasters that befell some public schools, wartime at Bloxham was uneventful. Dewey quickly assessed the risk from bombs in the first September of the war when after an air raid warning one night the school had taken to the cellars. Observing the upheaval and disturbance he pronounced, 'This is the last time. They are better in bed'. Since the school was not in a danger area for air raids parents did not remove their boys for safety in fear of an aerial holocaust at the outbreak of war. Similarly it was safe from coastal bombardment and the needs of the military, unlike Lancing, evacuated to

Denstone and Ludlow, or Malvern, commandeered twice and forced hastily to move first to Blenheim Palace and then to Harrow with disastrous loss of numbers and destruction of character and tradition. Early in 1941 the threat of invasion put Ardingly under short notice to evacuate and Dewey offered emergency 'floor accommodation for sleeping, say 200 boys for seven days, providing they brought mattresses, and also some help could be given in arranging for them to have meals under cover, providing they brought rations'. The offer sounds a little grudging, but Dewey was jealous for Bloxham's independence and he was not in fact put to the test. The only sacrifices that the school had to make were the temporary loss of Palmer house to the army, the cultivation of gardens, tennis courts and second field, the loan of gym and sports equipment to military units based in the immediate neighbourhood and a disruption of sporting fixtures. At Bloxham the war was invigorating, bringing a remarkable increase in the number of boys and encouraging a closer community spirit.

There was, of course, difficulty, discomfort and sadness. Once again the pages of *The Bloxhamist* were devoted to the exploits of old boys on active service and obituaries of those 52 killed in action, so clearly remembered as recent prefects, colour-men and schoolboys. As in the Great War 25 years before, the Old Bloxhamist Society decided to give up all formal meetings so that it was *The Bloxhamist,* strongly encouraged by Dewey, that tried to keep the old boys in touch with each other and with the school by giving more space to their news. Restrictions on the use of paper limited its issue to once a year throughout the war and post-war period, but the layout introduced by Harmer in 1936 gave more words to the page and featured its first pictorial cover, an attractive drawing of the memorial gateway by F.R.H. Darke (O.B.). In other respects the magazine deteriorated, its style and contents becoming scrappy and of necessity strictly limited to school news, though in 1944 both the *Oxford Mail* and *Banbury Guardian* held it in high esteem for its news content. Literary composition found an outlet instead through 'The Fortnightly', a broadsheet started in 1940 by Hodgkinson and published less frequently than its title would suggest by display in the Egerton library, and 'Still Waters', a title chosen by its originators about 1950 to signify depth rather than stagnation.

Although it was rare for the school to take to the cellar air raid shelters, a regular fire-watchers' patrol was maintained by the common room and senior boys. The black-out was checked and a watch kept for aircraft and air raid warnings, and the duty rather enjoyed as a break from routine and an opportunity to catch up with marking and reading. Hodgkinson instituted a firewatchers' log book in the summer term of 1941, which after two nights of formal entries was transformed by Sam Kahn into an entertaining outlet for common room wit recording an uneventful night spent partly in reading Cicero and taking down the cricket nets before 'Owing to an unfortunate misunderstanding the firewatchers both retired to bed but any unforeseen incidents would have been noticed as the senior firewatcher suffered from insomnia'. A not untypical night was 19 June.

[In C.A. Hodgkinson's hand].'Preliminary note. Let me remind the junior watcher of last night that the Masters' Common Room has been kindly let to the A.R.P. authorities as a headquarters, and that his comments are rather impertinent.

[In J.R. Moore's hand]. After joining my senior partner, we toured the buildings on a blackout patrol, during which we had a look at the swimming bath where we met Mr Payne. After a short chat, he departed to bed. We returned to "G.H.Q." after a while and about 0100 hrs Mr Hodgkinson went to his room to boil some water. Just as he returned Mr Kahn joined us for a cup of tea, & we devoured the excellent sandwiches. At about 0220 hrs, the Common Room lights suddenly gave out, & have left us "surrounded by a sea of darkness". P.S. Gloom has descended upon me! Mr H. is correcting my Latin Prose!!! [Continued by C.A.H.]. (Exit 3.15)

Gloom unjustified. Early record should have included the throwing of several pails of water on the newly-laid bit of turf by the Sanblock. Recommend this practice to subsequent watchers, if turf is to grow at all.

Climbed Chapel steps at 2.45 to see ghost of former matron. Not at home.
Continued correcting Latin Proses by the light of Seventeen Candles.
Aerial activity absolutely all anglican.
Lights restored at 3.30.

4.0. Last round completed. The glowworm shows the matin to be near, and 'gins to pale his ineffectual fire. Northern sky filled with dawn light. 4.1. bulb passed out. 4.5. Drank glass of port to the success of the General Inspection.

4.15. I have just dipped my pen in my glass of port by mistake. I trust I shan't pick up the red-ink-bottle to drink out of.

4.30. semi-daylight. Bed.

C.A. Hodgkinson'

A rare example of Dewey's personality is revealed in the entry for Monday June 2.

'Patrol began with silagers to supper. One of them (the one with a ?dog) left us a pint of beer which we shared (equally) after the midnight patrol.

The larger member of the patrol ascended the big ladder in Central Quadrangle: grand view from top.

Patrol drove H. Doran to bed with a drawing pin, and chased cat out of Poofery [the headmaster's drawing room].

List of School scholarships, Diocesan Magazine, Saki, Old Bloxhamists' addresses, Hugh Walpole's obituary notice and the Universities Mission to Central Africa made the night all too short: the tea and good sandwiches were attractive.

Quiet night except for Whitsun Monday road traffic.

Smaller member retired at 2.35 a.m. fresh as a daisy, and very hearty: (*larger member still rosy and cheerful*) No sirens, no fires, good night. (L.M. retired 4.35 a.m.)

K.T.D.
L.D.W.'

In the very first hot summer of the war in 1940 Dewey contacted as many farmers as possible to offer schoolboy labour at harvest, and in subsequent years masters ran an agricultural camp in the summer holidays to help the local farmers, the first being organised in 1941 by Hodgkinson and E.F. Hodge. The accounts kept by George Bolton for the 1943 fortnight's camp have survived, revealing that 28 boys joined the camp for a week each and that a formidable total of 1,379 hours were worked, almost entirely for eleven farmers, though some jobs were done for the school, chiefly when the weather was bad. With wages of 9d. to 10d. an hour, half of which went for board and keep, most boys earned about £1 for the week's work — a quite considerable sum for pocket money in those days. A somewhat similar rate of 1s. a day was paid for those boys who helped stoke the school boilers, while the school contributed to its self-sufficiency by expanding the school farm.

There were many other small ways in which the school community helped the war effort. Scouts collected waste paper and the whole school contributed to the various savings campaigns, like Warship Week, Wings for Victory and Salute the Soldier. The corps band not only led the village Armistice Day parades according to custom but took part in wartime fund-raising activities elsewhere in north Oxfordshire. The O.T.C. itself was disarmed at the outbreak of the war, such was the shortage of weapons, being left only with a miserable collection of obsolete and replica rifles, while in deference to changing times its title became the Junior Training Corps and slowly battle dress replaced the old uniforms. At first the corps had joined with the village Local Defence Volunteers and after the L.D.V. was restyled the Home Guard, the school formed a Home Guard detachment, these primitive responses to the alarms and fears of blitz and invasion being an important ingredient of the nation's morale and belligerence. Although boys in the J.T.C. did not automatically obtain a commission on joining the armed forces the experience was valuable, and the corps enjoyed the additional variety of training available from the wider selection of courses and special demonstrations arranged by army units stationed nearby. In 1941, for instance, boys cycled to Tadmarton to see British and American tanks and the artillery troop at Palmer house and in the nissen huts opposite wheeled out its guns and wireless equipment for inspection on the field. Overhead the newly invented Gloster jet aircraft made strange sounds on test flights from Barford aerodrome.

On VE Day 1945 the corps band led the victory parade through the village and the school started to prepare for the return of peace. Masters started to trickle back from the armed services — J.N. Shaw for a short spell as housemaster of Wilson before his death, Wisti Longden, limping and with hand damaged by war wounds as housemaster of Egerton, G.H. Bletchly as Wilson housemaster, and for shorter periods Hodgkinson and Lee, the former captain of the school and athlete who had spent four frustrating years in prisoner-of-war camp. After a term of laborious levelling, raking and stone-picking the second field was resown for rugger pitches, while Dewey, with the pre-war building debt extinguished, made plans to continue the interrupted development programme as a war memorial — the new hospital envisaged by Armitage, new changing rooms and

131

armoury and (that old ambition) a better school entrance.

But Bloxham recovered from wartime conditions as sluggishly as the nation. Building restrictions, food and clothes rationing persisted for years with diminishing intensity and once again the lack of reserves and endowments proved a handicap. When Mr. A. Heath retired from farming and offered Hillside Farm, above Merton, to the school in 1947 it was a purchase that could not be missed although the Council had no clear idea how to use the site. A new hospital was a priority since Palmer house was used for masters and laboratories, and the rooms in the headmaster's house were unsuitable for wards and could not be used for this purpose indefinitely. The Council, however, debated for some time whether they should convert the headmaster's house properly or build at Hillside. In the end the building licence from the Ministry was so delayed that Dewey never saw a new hospital and instead Hillside farmhouse was converted as a married master's house. Even more disappointing for the long-term development of the school was the failure in 1950-51 to defeat the local district council's plan to build houses on the field flanking the east side of the main cricket field. This was the obvious expansion area for the school, who had unsuccessfully negotiated for it before the war. The School Council took their case to a public inquiry but in post-war Britain with urgent housing needs and a socialist government the appeal went against the school, which thus found itself effectively blocked from expansion on all sides. With hindsight one wonders why the Council did not negotiate to exchange this site for the second field, which was near existing council houses and more convenient to the village, but farther away from the school buildings.

Years of minimum maintenance on those buildings had now to be made up, although the school was exceptionally fortunate in having carried out so much new work and alterations immediately before the war. Once again the kitchens needed modernisation but a greater anxiety were the signs of outward slippage at the east end of the chapel. Mr (later Sir) Frederick Snow, father of two boys at the school, examined the weakness and in 1949 Booths of Banbury carried out the remedial works of adding buttresses at the east end, one of which unavoidably obscured Egerton's foundation stone, replaced by a replica built into the buttress. To prevent the lateral walls spreading, tie rods were inserted and as part of the scheme the ceiling of the sanctuary was painted white to give better light. In 1951 the dining hall and day rooms were refurbished but other building work was held back while Dewey hoarded reserves to develop the Merton-Hillside site as soon as plans and a licence were approved. At the same time he launched an appeal for a new chapel organ as a memorial to the Old Bloxhamists killed in the war and in memory of F.B. Palmer whom the headmaster with good reason named as the school's greatest benefactor since Reginald Egerton.

The reserves did slowly mount up even after the purchase of Hillside for £3,900 and the transfer of £500 to the tuck shop after Miss Garnar took over direct control from Gorringes in 1951, so that in the financial year 1950-51 the Council transferred some £5,500 to reserves before the Corporation asked them to keep a good balance in the bank to aid other schools in the Southern division. There was a steady increase in fees; in 1944 they stood at £120 a year, rising to £150 in 1947 and £195 in 1952. The increases not only paid off the debts and prepared for a future building programme but also enabled the Council to be more generous to their staff. Not until the summer of 1944 did they repay Sister Stent her term's salary which she had volunteered in the financial crisis of 1939-40, while Dewey's salary remained unaltered from the time of his appointment as acting headmaster in 1939 until 1948 The headmaster and divisional bursar then reviewed all the common room salaries and improved them to about 13% higher than standard Burnham scales.

By then the composition of the common room was altering as men released from the forces completed their degree and training courses. The wartime masters left or retired and in their place were welcomed a galaxy of new men between 1946 and 1949 — E.P. Gibbs, D.E. Hood and H.C.M. Large; C. Armour, L.A.B. Beecher and D.R.G. Gwynne-Jones; J.M. Edwards, D.J. Skipwith and J.F.G. Sootheran; and in 1949 also, to replace Sholto Douglas, the Revd C.G. How. It seemed a massive changeover of staff not entirely acceptable to the school, for the new and younger men expected sharp discipline and a keen attitude to work. In fact the change came later to Bloxham than to larger public schools who attracted the men released first from the forces, and visiting teams to Radley or St Edward's learnt of unpleasant reforms which they were not yet experiencing. Once again Bloxham was suffering the handicap of being a minor public school. Its wartime advantages of security and empty places were past. Now it was the large and more famous schools which, having returned to their old buildings or freed from the dangers of warfare, were building up their numbers and competing for parents' interest at the expense of the smaller and weaker ones. Bloxham no longer benefited from Armitage's flair for publicity and compared with pre-war days was weaker academically.

Dewey himself was increasingly suffering from ill health, becoming greatly over-weight and afflicted by gout. His loyalty and determination had saved the school in 1939-40, but neither he nor his Council were thrusting enough in post-war conditions. They were, of course, difficult times of shortages and socialism. Not since the late Victorian age had there been such a huge advance in state interest in education, following the Fleming Report and R.A. Butler's Education Act 1944. One of the Fleming Report's recommendations had been the award of state bursaries for appropriate pupils from local education authority schools to public schools, and in anticipation of being required to accept boys under such a scheme Dewey persuaded the Council to fix an all-inclusive fee in place of the many extras which amounted to about 10% of the total fees. In fact, enquiry of the Oxfordshire county council received the reply that it was unlikely that any places would be sought. The Fleming proposals generally were rejected because the local authorities had no wish to see their best pupils creamed off to subsidise independent schools outside the state sector and their control. The Council's planning defeat over Salmon's field was perhaps unavoidable, and the need to maintain income, and therefore numbers, was paramount. Nevertheless, the school was too small and too young: Egerton junior house should have been scrapped even before the end of the war and a stronger effort made to raise both entrance and leaving qualifications. The Council was certainly not exempt from blame, for although they are largely chosen on the recommendation of the headmaster of the day, the wartime and post-war members were increasingly content to let Dewey run the school in his own way, and they accepted uncritically his generalised reports of unspecified good progress.

Dewey was perhaps almost too exclusively devoted to Bloxham without looking far beyond the school's own small community or narrow interests, but in one respect he did forge new links. Despite occasional public disclaimers from headmasters, Bloxham had always felt isolated from the Woodard Corporation because of its first allegiance to Egerton rather than Woodard and its distance from the three other schools of the Southern division, all within a few miles of each other in Sussex. In 1948 the newly formed Southern Division conference was invited to Bloxham and the full Corporation came the following year. Dewey's genial hospitality and customary meticulous planning showed Bloxham at its best, and common room and prefects entertained the visitors at lunch, tea, and sherry with calm self-assurance. In the following year the first rugger match against Hurstpierpoint was held, the only other school in the division to play the game.

He also started to try to improve academic standards, so important for the good reputation of the school to attract parents. There was, of course, still an intake of boys from preparatory schools though proportionally fewer than before the war. The Liddon interviews were introduced in 1940 when each boy's progress was formally reviewed by headmaster and housemasters, and Dewey reported record-breaking school certificate results, but without reminding his hearers that the larger size of the school demanded new records. In fact, the results were not too good. In one of the better pre-war years in 1938 three higher and twelve school certificates were obtained from a school of 125 boys; in 1941 with a school of 180 five higher and thirty school certificates were won, but in 1944 with 230 boys there were only six higher and twenty eight school certificates. The results fluctuated wildly but 1950, the last year before the school certificate was replaced by the more flexible General Certificate of Education system, was average with ten higher and twenty school certificates. The slight improvement in higher certificate results reflected a rather stronger VIth form of between 40 and 50, still less than a quarter of the senior school. Compared with the high-water mark of the mid 1930s when a third of the school leavers went up to the universities, with about twenty in residence at Oxford and Cambridge, the post-war record was weak. With a senior school half as large again only half a dozen usually headed for the universities each year and though *The Bloxhamist* records are incomplete it would seem that less than a dozen were in residence together at the same time. It was, therefore, overdue for the Council to be told in 1951 that 'a sterner policy of failing the less promising in Common Entrance Examination has been embarked upon'. Dewey, however, retired before the effects of this policy were discernible, although it was gratifying for him to be able to name a

Unbeaten rugby XV, 1947, under L. J. Anderson (captain), with E. J. Kahn (on left) and E. A. C. Lee (right) as coaches.

dozen boys with places at Oxford and Cambridge in his last year.

If academic standards suffered from the low qualifications for entrance there was every excuse in the need to increase numbers from the 1939 low base and to maintain the size of the school in the highly competitive early post-war years. Probably at no other period in its history did Bloxham come so near to being a 'county school' in the sense that Egerton had envisaged, closely identifiable with its neighbouring countryside and providing an education in the Anglo-Catholic principles of the Church of England for boys proceeding straight into business rather than the universities. After the long depression agriculture was prospering, the more substantial farmers were attracted by a public school education for their sons and a significant proportion of the boys were sons of farmers in Oxfordshire and the surrounding counties. In the late 1940s and 1950s the most flourishing school society was the Young Farmers' Club, annually winning Oxfordshire public-speaking and stock-judging contests. Membership of the club was much wider than those from farming homes and in other ways also the presence of young farmers broadened the experience of the other boys — heated support for the fox-hunting petition against abolitionists in 1948, knowledgeable tips for point-to-points in the Easter holidays and a certain dare-devil attitude to activities acceptable at home but against school rules, whether they be scrumping expeditions or clandestine smoking. They also contributed largely to the vigour of the school and its ability to compete at sport on reasonably level terms with schools two or three times its size, though parents' habit of taking their boys away at the age of fifteen or sixteen when they became useful on the farm meant that the school did not get the full benefit of their ability.

The first major sporting triumph after the war was the unbeaten 1947 rugger

XV, the first unbeaten XV ever and a well deserved reward for Sam Kahn's careful coaching. It was a surprisingly young team to do so well under L.J. Anderson's captaincy from the front-row, the vital linking half-backs, P.C. Jones and J. Godfrey being newly promoted colts who had the advantage of having played together in younger teams and the Wilberforce house sides. A third XV was also unbeaten in their four matches in which they amassed the extraordinary total of 145 points against 5, and since the second XV also had a good season the school ended the year with sixteen senior matches won, two drawn and only two lost. The colts had an unbeaten season in 1941 and matured to make a good first XV under A.S. Lees in 1943, but did not enjoy a comparable one until 1952, a disastrous year for the senior teams, best forgotten. By that time Bloxham sides were increasingly handicapped by the small size of the school and the heavy drain of early school leavers compared with their bigger and older opponents, and at rugger Bloxham scrums were consistently lighter and younger than those they faced.

Not surprisingly, therefore, the school tended to do better in minority sports where the odds were less uneven or where the skills of the individual counted for more than teamwork. In athletics school matches were revived in 1947 and as a sprinter Peter Maisey won three junior events at the Woodard schools' meeting in 1949 and two years later equalled E.A.C. Lee's sixteen-year old 100-yard record. New shooting records were won in 1947 by J. Turner, who won the Bisley XX Club competition and was chosen for the national team of 40 cadets out of the 31,000 eligible, while the school VIII came fourth in the *Country Life* competition. A few years later in 1951 J. Young obtained the highest individual score in the Ashburton shield competition at Bisley, for the second time that a Bloxhamist had done so, P.G. Hunt coming first in 1929. As a contrast in shooting standards generally, in 1929 the Bloxham VIII had been sixth with scores of 454 and 94 for the cadet pair; in 1951 the scores of 482 and 113 were unremarkable, and over 500 was needed to be among the top dozen schools.

The boxing squad did remarkably well for several successive years. Since the 1930s it was customary for almost all boys to box, though no doubt some were pressed unwillingly to take part in what always remained nominally a voluntary sport. In 1945 210 boys took up boxing out of the 233 in the school and half boxed in house competitions. These, of course, were fought out keenly if sometimes unscientifically, and to improve the sport generally 'standards' were introduced as in athletics. Charles Packwood became master in charge of boxing in 1944 and steadily transformed a rather rugged form of combat into a well trained and well disciplined sport which continued to attract such large numbers of boys that Bloxham could compete on equal terms with much larger but less enthusiastic schools. The first matches after the war were in 1948 against Malvern and Cheltenham and in 1951 the school challenged Eton for the first time. Each year the standard improved until in 1952 under the captaincy of G.B.H. Wightman there was an unbeaten season against Eton, Radley and Malvern, a success repeated the next year under M.J.B. Cort when the same three schools and Pangbourne were defeated.

The other voluntary games of fives and tennis did not command the same interest in the early post-war years and the loss of the tennis courts for great hall and vegetable gardens was not made good. On the other hand the return of peace restored the cricket fixture list and in place of Royal Air Force and regimental teams — including once in 1941 the unlikely sight of the Gordon Highlanders, who were skittled out for 33 runs by J.H. Whiting and P.J. Florey — there came the clubs once more. The XL club had continued to bring teams whenever possible and in 1946 returned for a regular annual fixture, as also did the South Oxfordshire Amateurs. A more significant landmark was the first match against the M.C.C. the following year and the rejoicing when the school XI under J.W. Butler beat them in 1948. That was one of the most successful cricket seasons for years for the XL club were also beaten and strong sides from the South Oxfordshire Amateurs and J.H. Whiting's XI held to draws.

In other ways the return from wartime conditions was expressed in a wider range of social activities, though the school remained monastically isolated. In place of the rare permission to walk into Banbury to see a wartime film the senior school societies like the Saye and Sele, current affairs and scientific societies went on expeditions and outings, while in the middle school the Gould club flourished under Packwood's relaxed and benevolent care. Visits to concerts in Banbury and the theatre at Stratford were again possible and as the world opened to a generation brought up amid wartime restrictions Brock took a select party of VIth formers to Paris in 1949, and individual boys set out on the sort of adventures which Armitage had encouraged and publicised so well before the war; in the April 1950 *Bloxhamist* were recorded the selection of Roger Denney as schoolboy trainee by the Ski Club of Great Britain, M.T. Howkins obtaining his pilot's licence while still a house prefect, and D. Bayly-Jones being the first Bloxhamist to row in an Oxford University trial eight.

Dewey was wholly a Bloxham man and one of his main objects as soon as the war ended was the revival of the Old Bloxhamist Society. He had done his best to preserve its links during the war, allowing old boys' news to fill one-third of *The Bloxhamist,* maintaining sports fixtures and always warmly greeting visitors and correspondents. He encouraged and prodded to such effect that Richard Martinek (later Kern-Martin) organised the first post-war gathering at the Dorchester Hotel, London, in January 1947, when about 120 Old Bloxhamists attended. Spencer Lester was elected secretary and the other elections included those of Wisti Longden as resident secretary and Roger Raymond as chairman. In one capacity or another those three served the school for the next thirty years and by 1951 they had obtained 600 members for the Society, which was holding meetings not only in London and at Bloxham but at Birmingham, Bournemouth, Leamington, Liverpool and Oxford. Much of their inspiration came from Dewey personally, for he was firmly convinced that the Bloxham community embraced those who had left as well as those who were currently and briefly at the school. Dewey furthermore instilled into the post-war Society a sense of responsibility to assist and support the school and to preserve its fundamental traditions. No doubt in the late 1940s he was privately already looking forward to the time when

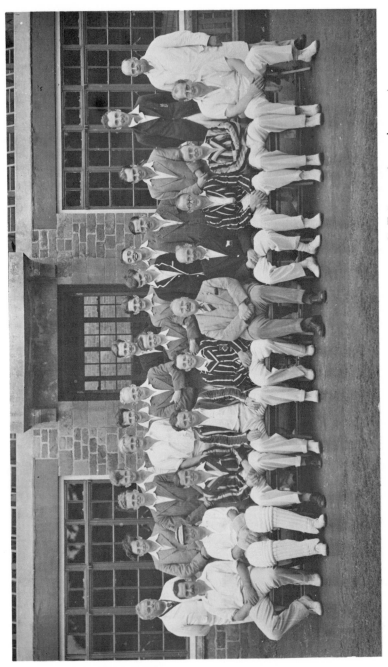

Old Bloxhamists v. South Oxfordshire Amateurs, 1947. In the group are K. T. Dewey (seated, centre) with (on his left) F. G. L. Crawshay and R. M. Raymond; Bo Mallett (standing on extreme left of picture) and S. G. Lester (standing immediately behind Dewey).

he would no longer be perpetuating and defending those traditions himself, but it was a role destined to lead to misunderstanding and controversy in later decades when the pace of innovation alarmed the conservatively minded Society.

It was certainly an unexpected shock to most when Dewey announced his retirement in 1952. Although he had been at Bloxham for 27 years and its headmaster for twelve he was still only 50 years old and was so closely identified with and devoted to Bloxham that it was inconceivable that he should retire at such a young age. What he did not reveal except to his few closest friends, among whom were Val Armitage and Sholto Douglas, was his worsening health. To the gout that had afflicted him from an early age was added cancer and a sense of exhaustion from the struggle of the war years, and his concern for Bloxham was such that he would not carry on as a sick man. As early as 1950 he had shared his intention with Armitage. Two years later he told Bloxham and left at the end of the summer term. He died in Devon in 1961, jubilant to have defeated his affliction with the words, 'Well, it hasn't robbed me of the Centenary year', when he attended every commemorative event.

CHAPTER IX

R. S. THOMPSON
1952-1965

Bloxham looked forward to the arrival of Dewey's successor with some foreboding. The school had been led for longer than almost anyone could remember by a "Bloxham" man familiar with its ways. Among the masters only George Bolton could recall clearly the pre-war days under another headmaster, although of course the memories of Bo Mallett and Arthur Neal, the head gardener, went back much farther. A newcomer would change things, and although it was widely recognised that the time for change was due there was an understandable apprehension of the future. Common room gossip and contact by the newly acquired long-range corps wireless set with Sherborne, where Stanley Thompson was a housemaster, indicated that the new headmaster might be a formidable character. He was also married. The school accepted that a few junior masters might be married and live in the village with their families and had made allowance for the apparent eccentricity of senior men like Sholto Douglas and George Bolton, but it remained essentially a bachelor community which distrusted the distractions of family life as had Beetle in *Stalky & Co.*

Stanley Thompson had been educated at Lancing, where he had been captain of the school, and as his career progressed his main ambition was to become a headmaster, preferably of a Woodard school. He had read history at Oriel College, Oxford, teaching since 1922 at Sherborne, where he had been a housemaster for the previous seventeen years, in which time he had played cricket and hockey for Dorset. He had been disappointed at not being chosen as headmaster of either Ardingly or Worksop, but the Woodard chapter had noted his interest and when Bloxham became vacant his persistence was rewarded.

Like Armitage in 1925, six years after the first World War, Thompson's first days brought him to the conclusion that the school was still living under a wartime siege mentality, illustrated vividly when he looked out of his study windows on to flower beds planted with carrots and beetroot. In the quadrangle stood a vast and unsightly heap of boiler fuel, for the coke had been delivered in bulk to overcome wartime supply difficulties, such prudence actually being justified in the bitter winter of 1947 when even that supply gave out before more could be delivered through snow-blocked roads; in 1952 it was unnecessary. He was horrified to discover the lack of anti-tetanus protection for the boys, although the north Oxfordshire soil was reputedly a source of infection. The low academic standards were as clear to see as the coke pile, but Thompson had not anticipated that they would cause Bloxham to be struck off the Headmasters' Conference. The headmaster, not the school, is elected to the H.M.C., and once elected he remains a member. However, before a new headmaster is elected his school has to satisfy certain conditions, among which are the levels of examination work and the size of the VIth form. It was on these conditions that Bloxham failed in 1952. The unexpected rebuff was a severe blow to the school's pride, and therefore to Thompson's, who although he was unfamiliar with the workings of the H.M.C. had been looking forward to meeting old friends and new colleagues. Nor had he expected to find his Council so ill-informed about the state of the school, some not even being familiar with the layout of the buildings, with their obvious deficiencies like the lack of living quarters for married staff and the appalling laboratories. The weakness of the science side, the lack of art and music facilities in which Thompson was especially interested, and the early school-leaving age all contributed to the poor academic record, but beneath the surface he discovered a further contrast with Sherborne, the extent of prefects' privileges and a carefree sense of discipline.

This last was the more unexpected because both on his previous knowledge of Bloxham and on his arrival he was aware of the well deserved reputation of the boys for their behaviour and courtesy. Bad manners and slovenly dress were among the few things which angered Dewey. Thompson himself had experienced Dewey's discreet and well organised hospitality on his first visit to the school when, driving into the quadrangle, he had sought directions from a couple of boys who happened to be there. By the time that he had walked to the gate leading to the headmaster's house, Dewey was strolling across the lawn to give his customary beaming greeting. It was a good introduction to Bloxham, a characteristic that impressed him, and one that he was determined to maintain. Dewey had also built up a powerful community spirit in the school as a whole and Thompson inherited an intensely loyal common room, of whom he has written:

'I don't know when it started, but I suspect in Dewey's time, that the common room became a byword for devotion to their job; nothing too much trouble; courtesy and hospitality to strangers and visitors. They were perpetually on the job, yet buoyant withal and wonderfully good company. I have never seen anything quite like it in any other school I have visited. The Chapel, the masters and the boys between them created an atmosphere which could be felt and which was often noticed by visitors, especially prospective parents. It was something I was terrified might be lost through my fault.'

That was a very real danger. Reform was overdue. In the uncertain and hostile post-war world of the welfare state Bloxham was poorly equipped to compete either with the larger and more prestigious independent schools or those expanding and newly built by the local authorities. This was perhaps more evident to an outsider than to Bloxhamists, who withdrawn in isolation had not fully appreciated the realities of post-war education. Thompson himself, knowledgeable in the ways of a larger public school, took some time to adjust to the close-knit community of a small one. His previous experience of old boys' societies did not prepare him for the type of association that Dewey had cultivated with the Old Bloxhamist Society, which he later described 'must be unique in public school history'. He failed to take them into his confidence as they had been accustomed, which led to misunderstanding, for instance, over his policy to raise the school-leaving age, widely misconstrued as designed to exclude farmers' sons, or the decision near the end of his time for voluntary chapel.

Once again, though, the school was fortunate in being given the right headmaster at the right time. Stanley Thompson was a firm disciplinarian with long experience of schoolmastering, a staunch churchman and a family man possessing a wide range of friends, contacts and outside interests. From these the school began quickly to benefit and equally soon learnt that there were advantages in having a married headmaster. He could talk to parents as a parent himself and Barbara Thompson had an important influence as the school emerged from bachelor seclusion. He was also sensitive to the isolation with which a headmaster is necessarily surrounded. One of his first acts was to move out of Dewey's study because of its dark and forbidding approach. He wanted to be as easily accessible as possible, his study welcoming and cheerful. To this end he announced shortly after his arrival that, with the exception of the sacrosanct daily quarter of an hour when he listened to his favourite B.B.C. radio programme, "The Archers", any boy could come to him in complete confidence at any time. Previously, school prefects had enjoyed ready access to the headmaster but others rarely, and many boys took advantage of the offer, his own interest in them as individuals being also witnessed in the careful briefing he gave new boys on their arrival and his invariable custom of greeting every boy's birthday whether in term or holiday. Similarly, teaching colleagues were invited to his 'beer and baccy' evenings to talk over educational problems and school affairs and in return he enjoyed their hospitality in the common room or fives court, where he was still a useful player and coach. Like Dewey he was to be seen constantly on the boundary or touchlines of games fields, daily at Bloxham and at home or away matches, his presence the more essential as he was the first headmaster in modern time not to live within the confines of the main school buildings.[1]

Although the new headmaster could diagnose the school's weaknesses and within a fortnight of his arrival gave the school Council a typically detailed and blunt exposition of them, like both Ward and Armitage he sought the objective view of expert consultants to confirm and support his own diagnosis. Accordingly a formal inspection by H. M. inspectors was invited and took place in the autumn of 1953. It was the first inspection for eighteen years and their four-day visit was both sympathetic and thorough. It was also one of the most significant events in the recent history of the school, for its post-war development was based on the inspectors' report.

Not that Thompson had been idle for his first twelve months before the inspection. Nothing and no one escaped his scrutiny. The Council were bombarded with reports, budgets, suggestions and recommendations, and discovered that they were expected to work harder for their school lunch! Thompson was not afraid to take his own decisions, and indeed more than once forestalled his Council, but he wanted the Council to be well informed and fully concerned with the administration of the school. Similarly he shared his ideas

[1] Boissier had lived in the masters' house (Egerton house) when the Founder as warden lived in the new headmaster's house, 1886-90.

and objectives with the parents, distributing a termly newsletter containing a mixture of past news and future intentions but also, as he stood firm against the spreading habits of an increasingly permissive society, rarely omitting an outspoken reproof about leave requests, boys' behaviour, pocket money, provision of tuck, or dress and appearance, as in 1955:

'Last term I noticed a few variations from the official pattern [of blue suits], which makes me think that some parents do not realise that there is one. It is most undesirable for there to be any deviation. Once this starts, we shall have liberties of great variety being taken, which will be disastrous. . .

Closely akin to the types and patterns of clothes is a matter of hair styles. At the beginning of each of the last two terms a few boys have come back with their hair very different in appearance from the normal. From the little conversation that I have had with parents so far, I formed the impression that they were as displeased about this particular piece of individualism as I was. Lest boys should try to play off parents against me and vice-versa, I want to make it clear that I dislike it and will not countenance it here. What boys do in this matter in the holidays is not my business, but what they do here is. I have told the School that any boy who returns here in future with a hair style different from the normal will go home until such time as it is normal.

One final point, but an important one. The Tuck situation has got out of hand and needs tidying up. Several parents have remarked to me directly or by implication that they are surprised at the freedom allowed in the matter of Tuck. . . I think it ought to be restricted in both kind and in amount. I therefore propose to ban all tinned foods except jam and to ban from the mid-day meal all accessories to what is provided by the School. . .'

Repeatedly he wrote about the school-leaving age, for Bloxham suffered in many ways from its small size and the small proportion of boys in the senior range. He returned to this subject again and again. He warned the Council in 1953 that of the 229 boys only 79 were over sixteen; 40 were under fourteen. As a practical step he converted Egerton to a senior house with Kahn as its first housemaster in 1956. To parents he pointed out that there was little advantage in paying fees to a public school if you removed a boy just when the public school education was becoming superior to that provided by the state, and particularly to those parents who were farmers he drew the analogy of gathering the harvest on a fixed date regardless of whether it had ripened.

Within the school he backed his own judgement and overturned every activity, beginning with classroom work. The boys returned in the autumn of 1952 to find that the work timetable had been completely and ingeniously reorganised by Kahn, dividing the school into A and B streams throughout and allowing no one to avoid a distasteful subject before reaching the upper school. Some staffing changes were made immediately to strengthen science teaching and to reduce both the size of classes and the work-load on the common room. Other changes followed as some of the wartime members of the common room left — R. Gillies (science and organist) since 1941, Miss Usher (mathematics), the last surviving full-time mistress of the war period since 1942, and Charles Packwood (English

Park Close, about 1959. Oriel Cottage is in the top left hand corner partly masked by trees and to its right the tall large house is Stone Hill House.

and junior teaching) since 1943. It is a reflection of the extent of their teaching activities as well as staffing deficiencies that they had to be replaced not on a one-for-one basis, but by a team of younger but experienced men — B. B. Kemp, who was actually appointed by Dewey at Thompson's request to succeed him in teaching chemistry, T. A. Grocock (science), J. V. Fiori (mathematics and science), J. M. Lerrigo (French and German), J. E. Gardiner (organist), E. J. Summers (English and art) and I. A. Watson (junior teaching). The newcomers greatly strengthened the miserably defective science side and were able to start serious work in art and music for which, wrote Thompson in his first report to the Council, the only provision made was the advertisement in the *Public Schools' Year Book* that such facilities existed.

Without suitable buildings little could be achieved, and while financial crisis and wartime building restrictions persisted there could be little hope of erecting new laboratories to develop science teaching. D. E. Hood, Gillies and Dewey himself, together with their classes, had had to make do with what they could, and though Thompson was impatient to press ahead with building plans, first the Council had to be won over by the evidence and recommendations of H. M. inspectors. The Council had only recently cleared the debt from the 1930s development and though reserves were growing they had been raided already to buy Hillside where the new hospital was planned. There were other immediate building needs: a new organ and enlarged organ loft as the F. B. Palmer and war memorial, changing room improvements and the creation above them in Botany Bay of an art room, and, more urgently, somewhere for the head-master to live. Originally the Council had thought of converting Hillside, which had the merit of convenience, as had Bennetts which was a possible alternative. However, by coincidence Hill Cottage in Workhouse Lane was for sale and bought as a temporary residence; it could obviously not serve for long if only because its rooms were too low for the tall headmaster to stand upright comfortably. He renamed it Oriel Cottage. At about that time J.F.G. Sootheran was seeking somewhere for a new hockey pitch and, enquiring whether the paddock at Park Close might be available, Thompson discovered by chance that the owner was thinking of selling the house. It was one of the few in the village suitable for a headmaster's residence and its adjoining paddock would be a useful asset. Additionally it was a pleasant thought that Hubert Egerton's old home might again be connected with the school. On Thompson's urgent call, the Council wasted no time. After viewing it with the provost the chairman called a special meeting and Park Close was bought early in 1953.

The boys, especially the seniors, also felt the impact of the new headmaster's reforms. He radically curtailed prefects' privileges and tightened up on their right of beating. Dewey had allowed his prefects wide freedom to punish and rarely intervened personally. From the start Thompson sought to make his own standards clear to everyone and warned that he intended to deal firmly with cases of breaking school regulations. Most public schools were suffering a rash of such behaviour, with the attendant bad publicity, and Thompson was striking at escapades which an earlier generation of senior boys had come to condone. Similar control was enforced over the middle school where dayroom boys had been in the habit of terrorising juniors, particularly the weaker and more vulnerable ones, and 'to be had in the day room' became no longer a form of unchecked bullying.

In other ways also he challenged existing customs and, where he found them wanting, changed them. The school list, the 'Blue Book', had only been published annually since 1941 and therefore rapidly became out-of-date. Henceforth it came out termly, reverting to the 'Grey Book' colour of its early years from 1926. *The Bloxhamist* likewise was published two or three times a year from 1953 instead of annually (another wartime necessity) and was changed in style and format. In his first year he ordered the wearing of formal blue suits on Sundays and special occasions and the sartorial freedom in the choice of ties and pullovers was stopped.[2] Even such minor customs as the seating of the high table, with the headmaster flanked by the school prefects in order of rank, were altered, much to the consternation of the traditionalists.

Many of these changes and reforms could be justified by the urgent need to restore the school to the Headmasters' Conference and meet the deficiencies

---

[2]Many of the clothing changes were introduced gradually as clothes wore out. The ginger sports jackets, introduced by Armitage, were not phased out until 1966, a few being handed down in families as prestige symbols for a further ten years.

exposed by the inspectors' report. Those who disliked them had few grounds for opposition. It was more important to make a new start and rebuild the school's morale and standards than defend old customs, and parents and prospective parents had to be reassured. One Old Bloxhamist recalls that it was only the sound pleading of the headmaster and a governor which reassured him sufficiently to keep his son's name down for the school — a decision and act of faith which he did not regret. Thompson's intentions were clearly signalled to the independent schools when he turned down weak applicants from preparatory schools, who had hitherto considered it easy to get places. It was this sort of determination and promise for the future rather than any marked improvement in the school's own academic performance which earned Thompson his election to the Headmasters' Conference in 1954.

His policy of raising entrance standards by insisting on a good pass mark in the common entrance examination as well as trying to eliminate those likely to leave early had an adverse effect on school numbers. From 243 boys when he took over, the school shrank in a year to 229, at a time when costs were rising over 10% a year and there was a growing and worrying amount of fees not paid promptly. The Council debated the alternatives of lowering their new entrance standards to fill the school or raising the fees. By 1956 these had risen to £261, which still allowed a profit of only 3%, and were dangerously close to those charged by larger and academically more successful public schools; Lancing's fees, for instance, were £285 that year. However, the year 1953 was probably the lowest point. The old ways of the school had been shaken up — Council, common room, parents and boys. Now the reconstruction could really start and the Council, with a business-like approach, due in part to the presence of one of its new members, Roger Raymond (O.B.), embarked on ambitious plans for development. The cautious policy of saving and minimal spending to be free of debts was abandoned for one of capital expenditure funded by loans and mortgages. The needs were too urgent to wait for appeal funds to accumulate.

An appeal had in fact already started. In his first report to the Council shortly after his arrival in September 1952 the headmaster had catalogued a list of eleven building deficiencies. Some were relatively minor and soon being met: additional seating in chapel, improved changing room and art room in Botany Bay, a music room in the Park Close stables built by Gilbert Clifton of Bloxham, hockey pitches (1957) and tennis courts (1958) at Park Close largely the gift of the Old Bloxhamist Society, extra dormitory and masters' accommodation there, better dining hall facilities so that the whole school could again feed together at the same time, conversion to oil-fired central heating, and a new carpentry shop (1954). This is an impressive list of minor works, largely covered by mortgaging Park Close and paid off in only six years, and mainly carried out by the school itself; J. V. Fiori, with his experience from the Royal Engineers, designed many of the alterations and Ted Source and the maintenance team carried them out. The chief exception was the chapel alteration where the delicate structural problem of extending the organ loft was designed by the school architect, F. R. Jelley, in consultation with Frederick Snow & Partners, and carried out by

Booths of Banbury, who also put in extra choir stalls. The organ itself was rebuilt and installed by Percy Daniel (O.B.) of Clevedon, being formally dedicated at a crowded service on 30 September 1954 when a recital was given by Sir William McKie, M.V.O., Master of the Choristers, organist of Westminster Abbey and by virtue of that office Director of Music for the Queen's coronation the year before.

By the time of his first Founderstide (introduced by another innovation, the versified prologue read by the captain of the school) Thompson's catalogue of new building needs had been further amplified and refined — a larger masters' common room, more laboratories, more classrooms, more playing fields, the modernisation of Egerton house and, to relieve over-crowding, a fourth senior house. Appreciating the size of his shopping list, the target of the approaching centenary and the unique opportunity offered by his first Founder's Day speech, he threw out the challenge:

'1960 is the centenary year of the foundation of this school — seven years from now. People launch appeals for £18,000 or £20,000 and get it, but that is not enough for us. What we want is £70,000 — or £10,000 a year for the next seven years. From this moment forward anyone can stop me at any time of the day or night and make their contribution. . . My wife and I will be pleased to start off the fund, here and now, with £100.'

One cannot relate in detail the progress of what the *Banbury Guardian* called 'perhaps the biggest local appeal ever to be launched', or the course of the building programme, but the main landmarks must be sketched in. The first appeal ran effectively from 1953 to 1960 when it reached over £30,000, a sum far short of Thompson's hopes but up to the Council's estimate of £20,000 from the appeal, topped by £50,000 from a loan fund. The chief contributions came from the parents' committee led by H. J. Badger and J. Thewlis, Old Bloxhamists, £10,000 from the Dulverton Trust and £8,900 from the Industrial Fund for the Advancement of Science in Schools, both obtained through the intervention of a new Council member, Lieutenant General Sir John Evetts, the industrialist, from school fetes run by masters and boys, while few visitors could avoid the cheerful salesmanship of centenary pencils by George Bolton. Free professional advice was immeasurably valuable. It was on J. V. Fiori's report on the first proposals for the laboratories that Roger Raymond endorsed the choice of S. T. Walker of Birmingham (the parent of one of Thompson's Sherborne boys), as architect for the laboratories in 1957 and then of the new house two years later. And while the rest of the Council viewed with growing dismay the widening gap between their budget and the builders' estimates for the new house, Raymond appraised the bills of quantity and made the whole project feasible.

The new laboratories adjoining Egerton House in Water Lane were opened by Sir John Evetts on 24 January 1959. They contained physics, chemistry and biology laboratories, the latter largely the gift of Dr. T. H. Sanderson-Wells (O.B.), an expert on soil fertility. The new house for Wilberforce was handed over at Christmas 1961 for occupation the following term. Together they were the first major additions to the school since 1936 and regrettably on the grounds

Science building (1959), with Wilberforce House (1961) on right and gym (1902) and squash courts (1974) on left, 1975.

of cost Hornton stone could not be used even as a facing material. Both buildings are therefore brick-built and plain — the Council had demanded that they should be 'spartan although of good appearance' and *The Bloxhamist* records them as 'strictly functional . . . but little individuality', while the authoritative Sir Niklaus Pevsner's *Buildings of England* volume on Oxfordshire comments tersely 'simple and utilitarian'. On aesthetic grounds, that is the best that can be said for them, with some being offended by the pale pink shade of the brick chosen, and it is ironic that one of the arbiters of architectural taste and defender of Victorian enthusiasm for embellishment, Sir John Betjeman, should have been a member of the Council which approved the design.

The inhabitants of the new house were entirely approving. Wilberforce under Wisti Longden revelled in their new surroundings and spacious well-lit house rooms, rapidly discovering a new unity in the isolation of their separate building. Others, chiefly those left in the old school, regretted the division of the school community. Much of the character and close-knit spirit and pride in Bloxham derived from the fact that the school had always lived, dined and worshipped together. Bloxhamists firmly believed that the fragmented house system of larger and more famous public schools was much inferior to their own school family unity. The new Wilberforce House was the first important step into a new way of life.

The removal of Wilberforce from the old school allowed a whole series of desirable improvements to the 100-year old main buildings. Greater privacy and more living space were expected in the 1950s, and by ingenious subdivision of the old dormitories and schoolroom, together with many other moves and changes, each house obtained three day rooms (henceforth known as house-rooms) for all its boys, and the outlying Wilson and Crake dormitories in Merton and Park Close were brought into the school. More studies were contrived in the former Wilberforce junior dormitory, replacing the study passage which in turn became a Wilson senior house-room and enlarged masters' common room. In 1962 the purchase of the former Co-op hall in Workhouse Lane provided a meeting place for societies and clubs as well as the history department. For the necessary guidance of Old Bloxhamists, bewildered by the new geography, *The Bloxhamist* wisely summarised the changes in its June 1962 issue.

In describing the new Wilberforce house the editor of *The Bloxhamist* commented 'that it is not the building, but its inhabitants who make a house what it is', a view echoed by an American exchange student in 1961 who was appalled by his first sight of a disorderly and ugly conglomeration of buildings until set at ease by friendly and well-mannered hosts. To him the two were an unlikely combination. Somewhat similarly Thompson had also remarked when launching the appeal fund in 1953 that 'fine buildings do not make fine scholars'. The new studies and house-rooms encouraged the better attitude to work that Thompson was seeking, as well as providing greater comfort and privacy for the growing collection of possessions, tape recorders, record players and typewriters that boys brought back to school. The task of rebuilding the school's academic record, though, was even harder than constructing new living and teaching space, and both were incomplete on Thompson's retirement in 1965.

Not until 1957 did the headmaster detect much improvement in work standards when entrants for the common entrance examination were also of a higher calibre, but there were diverse factors hindering a more rapid recovery. One, beyond the school's control, was the threat of large-scale ironstone mining in the immediate neighbourhood in 1960-61. Another was the size of the school, which was always too small. In order to enlarge the numbers first to 260, when Wilberforce house was opened, and then to 270 in 1963 there had to be some lowering of entry qualifications; it was the same problem that had faced Dewey twenty years earlier. Moreover all public schools were suffering from rapidly rising fees, especially those without endowments like Bloxham. In 1962 the fees were £495 a year, an increase of 350% since 1939. Schools in a similar position, like Dover College and Brecon, also experienced massive increases of about 300%; by contrast the increase at Eton, well-endowed and therefore partly protected against inflation, was little more than 100% over the same period. There was also increasing competition from the slowly rising standards in state education as the teacher training colleges turned out more and better trained teachers and the local education authorities embarked on large-scale building programmes with government assistance. Understandably from their point of view Oxfordshire county council turned down a renewed offer in 1954 to take selected boys from county primary schools, but the underlying reason for the rebuff seems to have been little appreciated at Bloxham even when repeated in general terms by the Labour minister of education in reply to a House of

Commons debate in 1961 — the ministry had no interest in a partnership between the state education system and the independent boarding schools which though it might benefit a small minority of individual children could only weaken the state schools to the advantage of the independent ones.

Examination results, therefore, remained depressingly poor with no more university awards than ten years previously despite all the schemes to improve them — competitive stars and prizes in 1953, an extra week on the summer term in 1958, the appointment of house tutors to discuss with boys the fortnightly assessments of their work as well as leisure and moral matters, the discouragement of frivolous spare-time activities, a reorganisation of upper school studies and a revival of VIth-form privileges in 1961, together with first discussions with neighbouring schools for linked VIth-form studies in 1963. Then in 1964 *The Observer* published a table of the 'best buy' in education compiled by the Advisory Centre for Education and based on the GCE A-level examination results of 70 public schools in 1961-2. Bloxham was placed at the bottom of this list with a mere 8.1 passes per 100 boys.

The publicity was singularly ill-timed in putting off parents just as the prospects were brightening. The Bloxham results that year had been no worse than in previous years, and within months of its publication the school could prove the table to be wholly misleading. By 1964, and using the same scale, the A-level pass rate had risen to 27.7 passes per 100 boys and the measure of Thompson's hard fought achievement is seen in the statistics given in *The Bloxhamist* in 1965. On his arrival in 1952 there were 24 boys over seventeen, 12 Old Bloxhamists at the universities, 18 VIth formers and 7 A-level candidates. The comparable figures when he left were 49 over seventeen, 20 at the universities, 46 VIth formers and 52 A-level candidates. It was still far below the target he had set himself, for in 1965 only about 6% of the school-leavers were entered for the universities compared with over 50% from Rugby and Winchester. Nevertheless it was a very notable improvement which promised well for the future.

It proved as difficult to attract good staff as good boys, and for many of the same reasons, so that as the common room grew in size there was a bewildering succession of faces among the junior masters, which must have had some effect on teaching results. From his own difficulties in finding a suitable house Thompson was acutely aware of the inadequate living quarters within the school now that the days of unmarried masters living in bachelors' rooms were past, and of the shortage of property in the village as it became increasingly attractive to Banbury commuters and retired people. A core of the older, experienced men gave continuity and stability among the many changes — George Bolton as second master and Wilberforce housemaster; the ubiquitous Sam Kahn, moving from Crake to become first senior housemaster of Egerton in 1956 as years earlier in 1940 he had been the first housemaster of Egerton as a junior house; Philip Gibbs who took over the corps and 1st XV from Kahn and then succeeded him at Egerton in 1961 to become Bloxham's first married housemaster.[3]

---

[3]George Bolton, housemaster of Wilberforce (1938-48) married after becoming housemaster.

The continuity provided by these men became increasingly valuable as other long-serving staff left. In 1955 Miss R. A. Garnar left, the soft spoken and imperturbable bursar who had kept the school fed, heated and looked after through all the trials of wartime and post-war rationing and restrictions and in addition had with Dewey wiped out the pre-war building debts. Not only had she coped with these formidable housekeeping problems but she had necessarily been school hostess and chief wardrobe mistress for school plays, duties taken on by Barbara Thompson and the growing number of other masters' wives. As bursar she was succeeded by Commander C. A. Jenkins, O.B.E., formerly of Wycliffe College, near Stroud, whose unobtrusive but far-sighted business-like skill Thompson found invaluable as the school embarked on its first building expansion for 20 years.

In the same year J. M. Edwards (1948-55) was replaced by another cricketing geographer, H. Ll. Pullinger. Other masters who left included in 1956, D. J. Skipwith, the ever cheerful Wilberforce housemaster and boxing coach; in 1957 the Revd. C. G. How, one of the school's great chaplains, 'ever ready to seethe with righteous indignation at the iniquities of a master, prefect or other petty tyrant', accompanied everywhere, on the rugger touchline, at base camp in Welsh mountains, even on one mistaken occasion at the altar, by his diminutive black poodle Pēpē; in 1958, E. J. F. Roughley (1950-58), mountaineer and English master, and in 1959, J. F. G. Sootheran (1948-59), cricket and hockey coach; and on the grounds of ill-health in 1965, G. H. Bletchly, who had first come to Bloxham before his war service and had been the kindly and dependable Wilson housemaster from 1947 to 1963. He was an inveterate note-taker, reducing everything to order neatly on paper and in his mind. Dewey had soon seized on his organising skill to run the wartime Dig for Victory campaign, which the school had rapidly and happily turned into its own slogan of 'Bombs for Bismark'. The nickname came from his history teaching, and he was a historian both in the sense of teaching the subject and being anonymously the author of the pictorial history *All Saints' School, Bloxham: brief history of the school and its progress*, published to mark the centenary in 1960. If only his many notebooks had survived they would have been a rich source for this history. Less laudably, such was his passion for recording events, his is the handwriting which defaces many of the old photographs and school archives.

Among the newcomers appointed in 1953 were J. V. Fiori, who succeeded Kahn as master in charge of the playing fields in 1957; B. B. Kemp, Crake housemaster from 1956 to 1978 and the longest serving housemaster the school has ever had; J. M. Lerrigo, modern languages master, and T. A. Grocock (died 1961), who taught the boys physics and demonstrated to everyone the ease with which *The Times* crossword could be finished before the end of morning break. To these may be added I. A. Watson (1953-60), who was ordained in the parish church shortly before he left; E. J. Summers (1953-61), teacher of English and art, and temperamental producer of a seven-year run of Shakespearian plays; who, when Gibbs and Roughley led parties to battle with the wind and rain of Welsh mountains, headed south with Geoffrey How and groups of boys for the

*'Bo' Mallett beneath the portrait of the
Founder in the dining hall, about 1955.*

warmth and art treasuers of Spain and Italy; J. E. Gardiner (1953-62), organist and director of music, who was responsible for the revival of music to such effect that by the time of his leaving there were not one but two school orchestras; A.D. Pickering (1959-67), Oxford boxing blue who also played cricket and rugger for university and county, who took over direction of games and became Wilson housemaster in 1963; R. C. Theobald (O.B.) (1962-67) who has the distinction of introducing a new most attractive and informative style for *The Bloxhamist* in 1964.

In the same period Bo Mallett retired, successfully at the third attempt in 1955, and he died three years later. His brother Jack died in 1964, having been groundsman in the 1930s, and with their passing the school lost two of its regular cricket spectators from the Water Lane wall, as well as two of the few who could remember Reginald Egerton himself. Bo Mallett and his wife had run the old thatched tuck shop for years in the 1920s and 1930s, overlooking the cricket square where he umpired countless school matches, an upright, stocky figure in his white coat, deftly tucking a bowler's sweater under the stump of his arm. His unhesitatingly sharp 'Not out' to the most intimidating appeals from club cricketers was unequivocal. Most of his working life was spent in the dining hall, where as a young waiter he had lost his arm, and it was there, setting out the high table, controlling the queues or organising the orderlies that most will remember him. There he was partnered by Mrs Emery and Miss Ida Heath who left in 1963 after twelve years' supervision together of the dining hall. Mrs Emery had served the school since 1940 — and for once the word 'served' is indeed correct — running the hall from the empty days of 1940 to the double sittings of the 1960s. It should be a sobering thought for many schoolmasters that the cheerful comradeship and reliability of a countrywoman like Mrs Emery or the gruff discipline of a man like Bo Mallett is often more effective and longer recalled than all the careful classroom expositions and chapel sermons!

In the 1950s dining arrangements were complicated by the necessity of having two sessions for every meal because the hall was not big enough for the larger school, while Thompson's emphasis on more and better work had led to other timetable changes. The day still began with a daily early communion service at 7.15 followed by two breakfasts for seniors and juniors at 8.00 and 8.20. Five periods were squeezed into the morning, except on Mondays when one was still given up for the corps, compared with the four periods of Dewey's time. After the double lunch sittings there were two more periods and games, as in previous years with the order varying according to the season of the year. Evensong was followed by the two suppers at 7.00 and 7.25 and first and second preps of one hour and 35 minutes respectively. Junior dormitories' 'lights out' was at 9.15, senior at 10.00. On the half holidays of Wednesdays and Saturdays, again as in the past, there was morning chapel and four periods, an afternoon free from lessons, but prep as usual. School matches were normally restricted to half holidays, and Thursday afternoons were devoted to corps, scouting and similar activities.

This pattern was changed by 1965. Meals were pushed forward about quarter of an hour and supper by half an hour, partly in response to the difficulty of obtaining domestic help in the evening, made possible by the use first of a classroom and then the former big schoolroom as a dining hall annexe. There were still two preps on a 'normal' day, but now no prep at all on Saturday. Wednesday afternoons were occupied by corps training, and Tuesdays and Thursdays became half holidays of a sort, with six periods and morning chapel, allowing school matches to be played on those afternoons as well as on Saturdays.

The sporting fixture list was becoming increasingly diverse with boys showing more interest in individual competitiveness and minor sports in addition to the traditional team games. Of these the milder winter weather of the 1950s and 1960s, together with the completion of the new pitches at Park Close, encouraged a revival of hockey, which Thompson himself had played for about fifteen years for Dorset. Rugger, on the other hand, went through a bad time for match successes, despite some inspiring coaching from Northampton club players. Eventually in the successful season of 1961 the match against Hurstpierpoint was won, and in the same year a new "needle" fixture was arranged against Allhallows, usually a weaker side and played at Richmond as the last match of the season; in 1965 the school entered the Oxfordshire seven-a-side competition for the first time and despite inexperience survived to the semi-final. The woeful record of well played matches but poor results makes for depressing reading in *The Bloxhamist*. Some of the blame could be attributed to the unequal size of school opponents, who were commonly larger schools with an older school-leaving age, and the long term effect of repeated defeats on morale generally.

To some extent this was equally true of cricket, where strong club sides were still challenged, the XL club under Andy Kempton, the South Oxfordshire Amateurs and the M.C.C. There were some good seasons — R. E. Towner's team of 1955 was one — but it is striking that even outstanding individual players tended to lack support. One thinks, for example, of D.N. Adey and C.C.W. Rodgers who scored 420 and 282 runs respectively in 1957 in a season in which only one match was won. Their partnership of 287 against the XL club in which Adey scored 183 and Rogers 101, both not out, and the school declared at 297 for 1 wicket ranks with the score of 289 for 1 against Magdalen College School in 1901 when Tordiffe scored 181 not out. The centenary year produced another good side under T. R. Hand, who was also a high-scoring batsman, but the outstanding cricketer of the 1960s was A. T. Tame. He was rapidly promoted from the colts team in 1962, when he also played for the England Schools under-16 XI. In the successful 1964 season, when the side defeated all the other schools played and lost only to three clubs, Tame's personal tally was 56 wickets and 367 runs, and he had already taken over 100 wickets for the 1st XI. The school anticipated new records in his final summer term, but although as captain he could not beat his previous scores among his 42 wickets were those of D. L. Murray, the West Indian test cricketer, and he finished his school career with a total of 1,137 runs and 165 wickets, a most exceptional 'double'. He also played for Southern Schools and the Northamptonshire 2nd XI before the close of the 1965 season.

The cult of the team game, at which many boys do not excel, was slowly giving way to the encouragement of individual effort and enterprise. In games, a revival of gymnastics owed much to R. C. Stancill, and there were more matches in tennis, fives, swimming, and the first school matches in sailing in 1962, fencing and judo clubs in 1963 and golf in 1965. Boxing continued successfully with unbeaten seasons in 1954, 1956 (when an 'A' team lost), 1961, 1964 and 1965, matches in the intervening years generally being in Bloxham's favour; much of the credit was due to the keenness of the boys, the prestige which the long run of successes gave the sport, and the coaching of Skipwith, Pickering and Sergeant-Major Adams. A more serious interest was taken in athletics, junior records falling more easily than senior, though Soulsbury established a new pole-vault record of 9 feet 8 inches in 1956 and D. R. Mence was the best all-round athlete that the school had seen in action since before the war. He ran the mile in 4.43 minutes in 1959 and in centenary year also broke both the quarter and half-mile records and equalled E.A.C. Lee's 1936 record in the 100 yards. At the White City inter-schools' meeting that Easter he came third in the half-mile, the first time that a Bloxhamist had broken the two-minute barrier for the race. He, however, was already being chased by a junior sprinter, N. T. Prakash, who at last reduced Lee's 100-yard record to 10.2 seconds in 1962.

The other team and individual sport of shooting had for ten years been Kemp's particular speciality, obtaining sixth place in the 1955 *Country Life* competition, when there was a new school record of 485 at Bisley. That record lasted only five years before being broken in the centenary year by a high score of 500, some consolation for missing the royal visit at school. Even that score only put the VIII 49th out of 103 schools, but in another four years Bloxham was 19th with a new record-breaking score of 507 in the Ashburton shield.

Shooting was technically still governed by regulations about the size of the corps, which having become the Combined Cadet Force in 1948 was changing in character to meet post-war conditions, the phasing-out of conscripted National Service at the end of the 1950s and the new emphasis on initiative training. The massive public schools' camps with their competitions, large-scale exercises, spit-and-polish and comradely rivalry gave way to leadership courses and venture camps, and the new style attracted both staff and boys. From 1953 Gibbs, Roughley and Pym Hall led small groups of boys on expeditions, camping, climbing and trekking in Welsh and Lakeland mountains. The enjoyment of these adventures decided Gibbs to abandon the traditional public schools' camps in 1958 and carry out with military assistance his own training schemes in Wales, becoming one of the pioneers of the so-called 'Greenfields' camps, for which he was promoted Lieutenant-Colonel above the proper complement of the relatively small Bloxham corps. After that the corps varied the larger military-run camps with its own and Fiori continued the practice after he took over in 1961. He had already in 1956 formed an engineers' section in the corps, replacing the signals section, and under his guidance bridges tended to appear miraculously quickly over Welsh mountain streams and at general inspections. As commanding officer he was faced with post-conscription changes imposed by the War Office, restricting the age limits and length of service of cadets, so that the 'Forty' was reorganised and civil defence, Duke of Edinburgh awards and public works introduced. The cuts reduced the corps contingent from eight officers and 272 cadets to 6 officers and 170 cadets. No one much cared for the change at the time, and it is interesting to note in passing that although imminently faced with the interruption of their lives by conscription, senior boys not merely accepted but approved of National Service. Twice, in 1947 and 1953, the current affairs society had debated the subject, and voted overwhelmingly in favour.

While striving to improve academic standards, Thompson also set out with customary vigour to widen cultural pursuits in what he rightly termed on his arrival as a philistine school. Indeed, his enthusiasm for music tended to attract too much time and too many resources, and for a few years there was some imbalance, for instance, between the number and value of musical and open scholarships. One of his first staffing requests in 1953 was for a director of music and the conversion of the Park Close music school in 1956 was the most important minor building project following that appointment. For nine years John Gardiner was an energetic director, enjoying the whole-hearted support of his headmaster. In his first year the long-established music society, which was for

Chapel with choir under J. E. Gardiner, director of music, 1957.

appreciation rather than performance, was joined by a choral society, a madrigal society, and the tentative beginnings of a school orchestra formed by a small group of performers decidedly short both of instruments and somewhere undisturbing to play them. By July 1954 the choral society had joined forces with Tudor Hall, the neighbouring girls' public school at Wykeham Park, and at Christmas 1955 they sang choruses from Handel's *Messiah* in Banbury church, the first breach of the monastic separatism of both schools. In the following year a house singing competition was begun, in 1957 and 1958 the school again broadcast chapel services, and in 1956 Gardiner produced *Trial by Jury,* the first Gilbert and Sullivan opera since 1931 — when Longden had played the title part of the Mikado.

The programme was extended in subsequent years. *Patience, Mikado* and *Iolanthe* followed the short *Trial by Jury;* in the winter of 1959-60 Bloxham and Tudor Hall sang the whole of *Messiah* in Banbury, and on 6 February 1960 the house singing competition included instrumentalists and the first public performance by the school orchestra. By 1962, when he left, Gardiner had achieved a musical reputation which the school had not enjoyed before, except possibly under Dr. Hain in the early years of the century. He had, moreover, composed minor works of his own, including a setting in 1958 for George Bolton's school hymn, *Lux splendens*[4]; there is, however, no record that Bolton claimed the prize of five shillings offered for a school song in 1935!

There was a parallel resurgence of dramatic and artistic activity under Summers. Like Gardiner, he started from scratch. The repertory company type of plays produced by Sholto Douglas had been replaced by the entertaining but frivolous musical operas written originally for the Gould Club by Charles Packwood, owing something to the then immensely popular American musicals, *Oklahoma* and *Annie Get Your Gun* and something to Gilbert and Sullivan. There was no existing tradition of serious acting in the school. Nevertheless, after only half a term's rehearsal he produced *Twelfth Night* in Michaelmas term 1953, the first full-length Shakespearian play to be performed since F. H. George's series ended in 1924. *The Tempest* and *Merchant of Venice* came next, followed annually by others including, most ambitiously, *King Lear* in 1959. By the time the cycle had been completed in 1964 — when I. G. McV. Crichton's portrayal of Sir Andrew Aguecheek was praised as warmly as Bill Smith's eleven years before — Jeffrey Summers had left, and the producers were the chaplain, the Revd A. J. Gardiner, and R. C. Theobald, who himself had played in Summers's earlier productions. Long before then, the critics had been commenting not only on the acting ability of the cast, but on the clear diction and expression of the actors

---

[4]Bloxham has never adopted its own school song with much enthusiasm. In Egerton's period the Winchester *Dulce domum* was always regarded as the school song and sung at the summer end-of-term concerts, in recognition of the debt and inspiration that Egerton had for his old school. Likewise, the Bloxham school prayer follows the pattern of the Winchester collect of thanksgiving. In 1893 J. H. T. Goodwin had written a song 'All Saints for ever' which W. E. Thomas set to music. It was first sung, with *Dulce domum*, at the midsummer concert that year. Both seem to have fallen out of use when the Egerton kind of concerts and prize-givings were given up by Ward. There was apparently no response to the appeal for a school song in 1935 or in 1953.

which was derived partly from these school productions and partly from the widening experience of the house play competition begun in 1956 and the elocution competition which Thompson had started soon after his arrival.

The kaleidescopic range and variety of other school societies and activities illustrates the ephemeral interests of groups of boys or a solitary master. A new senior and exclusive society, the Literati, replaced the Saye and Sele society of the 1940s and 1950s, and most continuity is seen in the existence of the Young Farmers' Club. Its pre-eminence slowly waned, having reached a peak with a four-year run of success in winning the Oxfordshire Y.F.C. county quiz from 1953 to 1957 and coming away from the Oxfordshire Show in 1955 with a pedigree Jersey calf won in the open cattle-judging contest. The growing affluence of teenagers generally benefited the village shops at the expense of the tuck shop, still presided over by Reg Turner after his wife's death in 1955, and permitted more ambitious excursions by both the school clubs and by holiday parties — trips to factories and coalmines, castles and borstals; travels to France, Italy, Spain, mountaineering in Switzerland and skiing in Norway and Austria. Horizons were widening in other directions as Bloxham welcomed students from the U.S.A., Sweden and — even more novel — from Tudor Hall girls' school, with whom first was arranged a termly dance, then the choral societies' performances and Scottish dancing.

All this was in harmony with Thompson's own outside interests. Dewey spent even his holidays 'sitting on the nest', as he termed it, and reputedly his only reading was Bradshaw's railway timetable and *The Times,* and the latter primarily for news of Old Bloxhamists. Stanley Thompson, on the other hand, took every opportunity to make Bloxham better known. It was through his friends, for instance, that the choir came to sing on several occasions at Gloucester cathedral and that the B.B.C. again broadcast school services, the first occasion in 1958 being well remembered because the technicians failed to put the school on the air at the beginning of the broadcast. He agreed to the school being televised with Harrow, Winchester and Mill Hill in 1961, and he courted the preparatory schools by inviting their headmasters to Bloxham and in return visiting them to preach or give away prizes. As a lay reader he took services in many places and served on the Oxford diocesan board of education, acting as their representative on the Oxfordshire county council's education committee. Locally he was chairman of the Bloxham parish council during the battle against the proposed north Oxfordshire ironstone quarrying and both Stanley and Barbara Thompson involved themselves in village life, making the school do so also. On occasions the school worshipped in the parish church and the choir started the practice of singing in neighbouring churches.

For a headmaster of generally conservative outlook it seems at first extraordinary that he should have been responsible for introducing far-reaching, even revolutionary, changes in the traditional life of the school chapel, of which the only fixed features seemed to be the discreet care lavished upon it by Mrs Bolton and Mrs 'Chapel' Mawle. Although chaplains and organists effected the alterations, the initiative and support came from the headmaster, whose churchmanship was both active and unchallengeable, ever ready to seek new ways of presenting the eternal truths. The long daily chapel services had been shortened in 1899 and reduced to one short service a day from the late 1920s, a custom that had continued unaltered until in 1955 house prayers were started on Monday evenings. In the same year Anglican chants were introduced to vary the use of plainsong, which had been sung, though apparently not on all occasions, from at least Crake's arrival in 1865. The Sunday 'early' and sung eucharist were combined into a single service at 8.20. More prominence was again given to major festivals like ascensiontide, rogationtide and special occasions, but the greatest innovation was the introduction of voluntary chapel services in 1963.

It was, of course, a controversial and daring decision in a school like Bloxham. Thompson had thought long and hard about it, having been concerned for some time at changing attitudes towards the chapel services arising from the outlook of society in general. The chaplain, the Revd. A. J. Gardiner, who had come come from Ardingly in 1957, agreed in principle but left in 1963 before he could put the new scheme properly into effect. The provost had also given his approval, but the Council were largely taken by surprise, for although the headmaster had warned them that radical alterations in chapel worship at public schools were under wide discussion he had assured them that Bloxham's arrangements were satisfactory. Only shortly before the provost had pointed out that 'if any scheme for increased numbers were to be considered, enlargement of the Chapel would have to be a vital part'. They at least, therefore, were still thinking only of the traditional public and Woodard school practice of compulsory chapel, even if it was the practical difficulty of accommodating the whole school in the chapel which reinforced Thompson's case. For some years the school had been able to worship together only by the undignified expedient of having a phalanx of juniors standing by with chairs to march into the aisle after the chaplain had processed to the altar. Certainly the matter of compulsory chapel-going was a subject for debate in the public schools. A large proportion of parents were not regular churchgoers, and their sons were hostile to the notion of compulsory attendance in termtime, and at some schools there was open dissent. Bloxham required all boys coming to the school to be practising members of the Church of England, or willing to become such, and compulsory chapel had been accepted, perhaps sometimes grudgingly, whatever the custom was at home, but in the 1950s the underlying discontent was growing. And although Thompson imposed discipline in other matters, he was not prepared to do so in chapel affairs: Christian belief and worship was a matter of personal self-discipline.

He had already noted with disappointment the poor attendance at the voluntary Lenten addresses in 1960, 'The number of boys who availed themselves of the chance of being absent was to my mind quite staggering, when one considers that this is essentially a Church School and its members are composed presumably of Church people.' The result of making chapel attendance voluntary was similar, the headmaster writing to parents in his newsletter:

'The voluntary principle should not present any difficulty, for it should be perfectly natural for all boys to go to Chapel fairly regularly as a matter of course. In actual fact they don't. Why they don't is speculative. It may be because of the novelty of the situation, or because their personal organisation is bad, as it sometimes is in other aspects of life, or because they do not go to church at home and so don't see why they should go at school. A few go pretty regularly and a few never go at all except when there is the occasional compulsory or part-compulsory service.'

The Old Bloxhamist Society, more conservative than the headmaster, was horrified, firmly believing that the discipline of youth leads to the habits of adult life, although observation of the empty pews of a parish church on Sundays, not notably filled with middle-aged public school men, would lead to a different conclusion.

Attention was directed on the chapel and the aims and beliefs of the Founder during the celebrations in 1960 to mark the centenary of Egerton's school. The headmaster, with the precedent of Sherborne's quatercentenary in 1950, had been looking forward to the occasion since his appointment. The first event of the centenary year was actually the Old Bloxhamists' dinner-dance at the Trocadero Restaurant in London on 16 January, followed later by celebratory dinners at Leamington and Oxford. At Bloxham the year opened on 31 January, the exact anniversary of the arrival of William Pearce a hundred years earlier, with a commemorative sermon by the Founder's great-nephew, the Revd P.V.M. Allen (O.B.) This same blend of enjoyment and thanksgiving, which had characterised Egerton's own life, formed the basis of the summer celebrations. A fete for the village children and a 22-over cricket match against the village, won by one run, was a sort of prologue to the main events, suitably heralded by a dramatic thunder storm early on the morning of Thursday 23 June. All Friday was filled from the 7.20 'early' to the centenary ball in Banbury for 500 guests including some boys and their Tudor Hall partners. Throughout the day were exhibitions and displays, sporting matches against the Old Bloxhamists, prizegiving and the first of several performances of Jeffrey Summers's *The Masque of the Reluctant New Boy*.

On the next morning the thanksgiving service was held in the parish church, with even that large building overflowing from its congregation of 750 people and the service relayed to 100 more in the school chapel. Bloxham had not witnessed anything like it since the jubilee or even Egerton's own well staged foundation ceremonies. Three bishops, Exeter (president of the Woodard Corporation), Chichester (the Visitor) and Oxford went in procession the length of the village street with the school and staff, fellows of the Corporation and representatives of the other Woodard schools. The customary skill of school sacristans, on this occasion A. J. Franks, T. R. Hand and P. C. Butler, in unobtrusively and with dignity directing ceremonial services was superlative in dealing with so many clergy in strange surroundings, and to the favourite hymns of 'Hail thee, festival day' and 'For all the saints' was added George Bolton's *'Lux splendens'*. A small but pleasant detail was the gift of half the collection, which appropriately came to £100, to the new church of All Saints, Dar-es-Salaam in the diocese of Zanzibar, with which Bloxham had anciently been linked by W. M.

H.M. Queen Elizabeth the Queen Mother during her visit to the school in 1960, with R. S. Thompson, headmaster 1952-65.

Richardson, master from 1876 to 1879 and second bishop of the diocese. Later in the morning the bishop of Exeter blessed the new house, then no more than a vacant site and concrete platform, and after the celebration lunch at which Sir William Hayter, warden of New College, Oxford (Egerton's college) was guest-speaker, one of the strongest Old Bloxhamist cricket sides had the satisfaction of beating the school XI. Fireworks and *Te Deum* on the second field brought the memorable weekend to its finish.

This was not, however, the end of the celebrations. A month later (and fittingly close to the old Founder's Day of Egerton's birthday) H. M. Queen Elizabeth the Queen Mother paid a formal visit to the school on 20 July. Drizzle turned to sunshine as the red royal helicopter landed by the cricket square, and in one crowded hour Bloxham's first royal visitor inspected a guard of honour, viewed chapel and Liddon library, called on Sister Skillington and took tea with headmaster, his wife and school prefects, visited the site of the new Wilberforce house on her way to the laboratories, and planted a maple tree, *acer goldsworth purple* between chapel and classroom block under the critical eye of the head gardener, Arthur Neal, commenting as she sprinkled on the obligatory spadeful of soil, 'I will put three shovelsful on just for luck'.

The centenary marked the climax of Thompson's original appeal. The Council now took stock, and looking ahead further Sir John Evetts summed up the priorities in a paper in which he prepared the Council and school for the Second Development Plan, launched publicly in 1962. His original four 'Priorities at Bloxham' were for quality of boys not quantity, a new classroom block, new playing fields and more domestic quarters. These proposals were to be translated into doubling the laboratories by building on a classroom wing, levelling the land above the second field, building on accommodation for a married housemaster of Wilberforce and a new sick bay for up to fourteen cases, and providing a larger library. Expenditure of £60,000 to £70,000, even up to £100,000 was envisaged, of which the first priority of the classrooms designed by S. T. Walker would take about half.

Since the first appeal had only just closed with a total of £30,000, a sum of this magnitude seemed impossible, and the Council decided to employ a professional fund-raising company to organise the appeal with a target of £40,000. It was not a success. Administrative costs swallowed up the income, and after a year and a half only £15,000 had been raised. By reverting to more traditional methods and personal contacts chiefly through the housemasters, Old Bloxhamist Society and Sam Kahn the fund rose more rapidly to £30,000. In Thompson's last term a carnival fete opened by one of the reigning popular disc-jockeys, Pete Murray, raised nearly £1,000 in one day, a day which included a cricket match against the strongest XI of famous players ever seen on the square. Everton Weekes, then at his peak as a West Indies test cricketer, brought a side containing three test and seven county players, who scored a modest 219 for 6 wickets in reply to the school's 215 all out, a surprisingly large score engineered by the gift of 150 extras. Stanley Thompson was umpiring for the last time, the grass was growing on the newly levelled third playing field and, as he moved out of Park Close to his Worcestershire retirement home, Brackley Builders Ltd started work on the laboratory classrooms. In the thirteen years of his headmastership he had laid the new foundations for his successor to build upon.

CHAPTER X

D. R. G. SEYMOUR
From 1965

Derek Seymour had little desire to become a headmaster. He had been a junior housemaster at Leatherhead from 1939 to 1944 and a housemaster of two different houses at Marlborough from 1944, and above all things in schoolmastering he enjoyed boys and running a house. But the world of public schools is small and the contacts many, through the Headmasters' Conference, corps camps (where Bloxham had first impressed itself on Thompson), academic courses and sporting fixtures, and the links forged by the Woodard Corporation are, of course, especially extensive. It was unlikely, therefore, that the abilities of a successful housemaster would be undetected and in Seymour's case his headmaster at Marlborough, J. C. Dancy, had formerly been headmaster of Lancing. Marlborough under Dancy was noted in the 1960s for new attitudes to boarding school education and Seymour, who had taught chemistry as head of science, had led the way with his own house. The experience of two years' teaching at a leading Australian public school had further fashioned his ideas about boarding school education with its isolation and restrictions on the freedom of teenage boys who were maturing at an earlier age. Accordingly he had been one of the first to convert his house's accommodation to study-bedrooms and to seek out-of-school interests and activities for his boys, both features which he was to translate on a larger scale to Bloxham. When it was suggested to him that a small school, with its friendly family spirit preserved by Thompson, was really very similar to a house in a large public school, he put it to the test. After visiting the school and staying with the Thompsons in the spring of 1965 he saw that this was indeed true.

On the other hand, the extent of Thompson's achievements was not so immediately apparent to him. His first impressions were summed up in almost the same words as those of his predecessor. Compared with Marlborough, Bloxham seemed old-fashioned, introspective and academically backward. This last impression had been confirmed by the Advisory Centre of Education report which had been published early in 1964 before Seymour had heard about the Bloxham post and strangely enough it had not registered with him. Reading it again in a new light was as unwelcome a greeting for the new headmaster as unkind a farewell for Thompson. In fact, the better results were just coming through as a measure of Thompson's success in raising academic standards and to prove the report wrong. By 1968 the number at the universities had grown to 48, compared with 20 in Thompson's last year, but those 48 were boys selected by Thompson. Unfortunately the damage was done, both to the morale of the school and confidence of parents just at the period when the flow of entrants from the steep post-war increase in the birth-rate was dwindling.

Seymour's vision of a full education embraced excellence in balanced academic work (including the sciences where as a scientist himself he judged the deficiencies to be greatest), excellence at games, and also excellence in all those cultural interests, religious teaching and practice and social responsibilities which together created his concept of the 'whole man' — or what in the older language of the school prayer made 'profitable members of the Church and Commonwealth'. Additionally he aimed at a completely new standard of living conditions throughout the whole school, comparable more with those of modern university halls of residence than traditional boarding schools.

He set out to achieve these aims in a series of five-year plans, their length determined by the period for which plans can in practice be forecast and put into effect as well as the usual span of each generation of boys passing through the school. In each case he did not move to the next series of targets before completing the current ones, although sometimes, of course, there were changing priorities. The progress of each stage is charted in *The Bloxhamist,* but there are difficulties in reviewing chronologically such recent events which necessarily are ingredients of a continuing strategy. Bearing in mind Seymour's long-term objectives, the broad themes of his five-year plans were, first, further to improve academic standards; second, to overcome boarding school isolationism; third, to fulfil the education of the 'whole man'. This is a gross over-simplification of thirteen years' uncompleted headmastership and there was, of course, much overlap and interaction between the main objectives and others less important; throughout, there was a continuing programme of building development, throughout there was an advance in academic results, throughout a growth of social and cultural contacts and influences outside the school.

These plans could not have been carried out effectively without the vigorous support of the school Council. Since 1960 it had been under the chairmanship of Dr George Parkes of Keble College, Oxford, a well-known don and estates administrator for the university, and on his retirement in 1967 he was succeeded by J. B. Schuster, D.L., T.D., of Nether Worton as acting chairman. It was rapidly evident that Schuster and Seymour made an outstanding team, both in their vision of education and in the determination to attain it. The full significance of the Council's policies in the 1970s will not be seen in perspective for some time and unfortunately by then it may not be so clearly remembered, nor will the formal minutes adequately record, that it was Schuster's personal leadership and inspiration which prompted so many of the bold decisions and developments. Both in their proposal and execution he had the shrewd support of Roger Raymond (O.B.), a long-serving member of the Council, and of J.A.H. Wolff, C.M.G., the bursar from 1964 to 1977. As the headmaster has said, 'One sometimes would not have gone on if the enthusiasm of Schuster and Raymond had not carried one over the rough spots'.

The latter deserves recognition with Egerton and Palmer as one of Bloxham's most generous benefactors, with a special inclination towards helping those who help themselves and for making his gifts when all other means have failed. Of the many examples that could be quoted, two typify this generosity. He had viewed critically the frugal plans for a junior common room in 1969 and, calling for the creation of something entirely new, increased his own gift to £3,400 to make it possible to start without delay. Similarly in 1975, when eleven acres of Ridgeway field west of Brickle Lane were sold at auction, the school could only afford to buy about eight acres for playing field extensions and then dropped out of the bidding. The remainder was knocked down to another bidder. The successful purchaser then came up to say that he had been acting on Raymond's instructions, and gave the land to the school.

Bursar and headmaster necessarily work as close partners and Wolff had a more important role than any of his predecessors because he supervised every detail of the largest building programme since Egerton's time and during the worst inflationary period of the century. His colleagues valued him for both his organisational qualities and wicket-keeping ability, being a Cambridge University cricketer and hockey blue, and the importance of his post was also enhanced by the adoption of contemporary business methods in administration. Seymour made use of management groups of senior masters, delegated much of his authority and actively sought good publicity through the press, the nomination of Philip Howard (1966-71) as the school's first press officer being a novelty among public schools. The second master's post became a full-time administrative one, giving Kahn (1966-76) a range of responsibilites which Bolton, who had seen Seymour over his first two years, never enjoyed under Dewey and Thompson. In 1970 Seymour created the post of director of studies, a major innovation among public schools, appointing the head of mathematics, B.A. Clough. These two, together with the bursar and chaplain, formed the new management team who directed policy within the school, the secretarial staff being increased correspondingly in response to the growing complexity of the administration. Similarly the housemasters met together regularly, while the heads of teaching departments administered their affairs with greater freedom and were closely involved in the selection of new colleagues. By 1976 that teaching staff had grown to 34, partly in order to sustain more levels of VIth-form work, but only four in 1977 had not been selected by Seymour, although two-thirds had been at the school five years or more. The great majority were young, which has varied implications — in the provision of living accommodation for young married families or single men who make Bloxham their home, in the comradeship and outlook of the common room (which even of this size could produce a rugger XV capable of beating the school team and Old Bloxhamists), and in the reduction of the so-called generation-gap between teachers and VIth formers.

Among those who left or retired in Seymour's early years were some who had contributed much to the revival of the school. There were the Pullingers (1955-66), teaching geography and art; George Bolton (1934-67), second master for 25 years who had written for *The Bloxhamist* so many appreciative and choicely worded farewell tributes to his colleagues; A.D. Pickering (1959-67), a man of many parts, but remembered by most as a lively history teacher, games master and Wilson housemaster; D.G. Wisti Longden (O.B.)(1938-67), whose 'Out, out, damn, spot' — with that punctuation as he cancelled fractions on the blackboard — sticks in the memory longer than the fractions. Bolton wrote in *The Bloxhamist* of Longden's weakness for gadgets, citing the Heath Robinson arrangement of hooks, string, pulleys and mousetrap by which his alarm clock would switch on the bedroom light and kettle. No less ingenious was the 'Thank you' sign which dropped across the rear window of his car as he overtook a slower vehicle.

In replacing them and in enlarging the common room, Seymour's first priority was to strengthen the science side. He had made it a condition of his appointment that Thompson's proposals for the new laboratories should be speedily carried out and that the school should continue to be firmly committed to teaching the courses for the GCE O-level and A-level syllabus, since an early analysis of classroom work had suggested to him that there were boys better fitted for CSE (Certificate of Secondary Education) courses. Warning the Council that he intended to raise the entrance qualifications further and that this would reduce the numbers for a short time, and thereby put pressure on the school's financial stability, the headmaster shared his hopes and plans with the preparatory schools. He believed that, shown the evidence, they, like the school Council, would support him and provide a genuine cross-section of their leavers to produce in about three years a greatly improved VIth form; in about five years the school would be in that sound academic position which alone could enable it to withstand future competition.

This, broadly, was the main feature of the first five-year plan. It took time to work through the school generations, but it succeeded. Although at first no entrants justified the award of scholarships, compared with nearly 20 in 1977, boys in the late 1960s had the great advantage that the common room had been strengthened in preparation for the standards being aimed at. In 1970 P.A.G. Morrison, A.T. Porter and W.R. Swinbank won the first Oxford and Cambridge scholarships since B. S.Smith in 1951. Seymour also put forward a new target that all boys should obtain at least six GCE O-level and two A-level passes before leaving, a target largely fulfilled by 1977 as a statistical average and often exceeded by individuals.

In his first year Seymour had organised the school along the traditional academic lines of the better public schools, allowing the more able boys who were expected to reach university to take their O-levels in two years before proceeding straight to a three-year A-level and university entrance course; others took the more usual three years to O-level followed by two years A-level work. By about 1975 half the school was in the VIth form and were comfortably above the national average of pass rates at both A-level and university grades, giving Seymour the opportunity for a second and major educational reform to eliminate the two remaining points with which he was dissatisfied. First, the two-year course to O-level led to early specialisation by the more scholarly boys — one of the weaknesses of the GCE system compared with the broader requirements of the old school certificate — and they entered the VIth form at too immature an age. Second, the whole school only had a choice up to O-level of courses in physics with chemistry or biology with chemistry and no boy could do all three sciences. By changing from the two-three year organisation of 1966 to two-one-two year courses for the scholarly, both problems were removed. All boys take the three science subjects over three years while the more able, having taken their arts subjects and mathematics in two years, have a further year to enlarge their experience and education with a broader range of subjects before specialising for A-level work. A by-product has been greater flexibility in middle-school setting; every subject is individually setted and forms exist in name only, so that a boy can work at different subjects at his own pace and ability. The whole reorganisation reflected the improved confidence in the academic strength of the school.

Many factors contributed towards achieving this first priority of the original five-year plan. The higher entrance standards and the enlargement of the common room were two. The curriculum development and extension of VIth-form teaching through the North Oxfordshire Scheme also contributed. This last educational experiment had been tentatively discussed in Thompson's time in 1963 and developed from day conferences, becoming fully operational three years later when, largely at the initiative of Seymour and H. Judge of Banbury School, the five schools of Bloxham, Banbury, North Oxfordshire Technical College, Sibford and Tudor Hall joined to share resources for VIth-form studies and conferences, especially in teaching minority subjects on one afternoon a week. Together the schools could attract speakers and generate discussions which none could have done alone and the Scheme had the added attraction of bringing together students of differing outlook and social background. Unfortunately, the political campaigns in education and the reorganisation of the Oxfordshire local authority schools hampered even such a modest attempt at integration between state and independent schools, and it was left to Bloxham and Tudor Hall alone to continue the principle with VIth-form 'minority time options' teaching.

Banbury School had also participated in starting the Nuffield science course in the new Bloxham laboratories in 1965 and in addition to some VIth-form teaching Tudor Hall girls and other schools have joined in some of the academic conferences, field courses and projects reported in almost every issue of *The Bloxhamist;* the magazine, however, omits mention of the reading parties attended by one or two prospective university scholars annually at Villiers Park, Middleton Stoney, the first being P. Morrison in 1970.

Among the conferences were those of the Industrial Society, the first of which was held in 1968 following an earlier experimental one at Marlborough. It was then a novel idea for industrialists and trade unionists to explain to schools the problems and challenges of industry but the early conferences were so successful that they have been repeated at intervals since. Likewise visiting lecturers and careers officers have supplemented the advice on careers from the school's own staff, who under D. E. Hood have widened the guidance available, making use of sophisticated aptitude tests and involving parents in the choice of VIth-form studies.

E. J. 'Sam' Kahn, 1939-76.

Hood himself retired from teaching in 1976 after 30 years as head of biology from the days when science teaching was concealed in distant and antiquated laboratories in and near Palmer house. Other members of staff who had been responsible for the academic improvement had also left by then. They included the Egerton housemaster, D.G. Guard (1961-74) and the first housemaster of Raymond, Frank Willy (1967-74), J.M. Lerrigo, (1953-76), modern languages teacher, house tutor and choirman, and Brian Clough (1966-77) head of mathematics and first director of studies. Finally, Sam Kahn (1939-76), second master, also retired, having over the years been housemaster of three houses, in charge of classics, rugger, cricket, the playing fields and the corps, and generally tackled single-handed with infinite patience, good humour and efficiency the number of tasks that fully occupies four of five lesser men. Both the chairman of the Old Bloxhamist Society in making a presentation and a contributor to *The Bloxhamist* gave up trying to enumerate the posts that he had held, the latter writing, 'It might be easier to state that to the best of our knowledge he has NOT been responsible for the Science Department or School Hockey, but all other available posts including that of Acting Headmaster, Sam has filled with distinction at one time or another'.

The parting speeches to M.J. Folliott (1963-74), history master, first head of the new politics and economics department and Wilson housemaster from 1969, were premature, since a year later he was back to succeed Kahn as second master. There are others still teaching at the school who have advanced Seymour's aims, among whom, not mentioned in another context, must be included the head of science from 1967, R.A.H. Hillman. When Seymour was first appointed he had to make the time to teach chemistry at VIth-form level himself. After he obtained Hillman as his own replacement there was established a science team who have in recent years published half a dozen books between them and become so well known by 1974 that Bloxham became only the second school in the country to act as hosts for a residential science project week for VIth formers, financed by Villiers Park. Their names and those of their colleagues are listed in *The Bloxhamist* and Woodard Corporation *Kalendar* and in due course of time *The Bloxhamist* pays tribute to their achievements when they leave. In a small school there are necessarily relatively few opportunities of internal promotion, but the academic quality of the common room is indicated by the fact that in the last decade Bloxham masters have taken eleven senior posts in major schools or other fields of education.

Neither *The Bloxhamist* nor the *Kalendar,* fully conveys the character, skill and spirit of the common room as a whole, and such lists omit others essential to the well-being of a boarding school, like the doctors, hospital sisters and matrons. Here also, one cannot include them all. Sister Stent's energetic reign of eighteen years (1932-38, 1939-51) was rivalled by that of Sister Skillington (1953-72), an equally competent disciplinarian and organiser in times of crisis. It was the ever-resourceful "Skilly" who, when Spanish kitchen staff with no English arrived in the early 1970s, bought Mrs May Smith a dictionary; characteristically, Mrs Smith replied that it was quicker to use sign language. With 35 years' experience as matron and dining hall supervisor she could remember the pre-war days when at 6*d.* an hour she had to brush the boys' dark suits for Sundays, but that recollection of a bygone era is surpassed by the image of 14-year old Arthur Neal starting work as boot boy under William Payne in 1923. He graduated to the gardens and did not retire as head gardener until 1974, by which time their heyday as pre-war pleasure grounds and wartime vegetable plots had long passed, and new buildings invaded all but the headmaster's lawns and the swastika bed. His counterpart was groundsman Don Green (1946-66), while the administration of the school owed much to the long experience of Mary Pritchard, headmaster's secretary (1960-73) and Nell Eagles (1954-76) in the bursar's office.

From the very beginning of the school masters had also habitually coached games and some had been notably good sportsmen; there had also been periods when professional coaches had been employed, mostly only for cricket. The growing size of the senior school and the academic demands on the teaching staff made it increasingly difficult to rely entirely on such part-time direction of games. The generally low morale of school teams, despite some fine individual performances, led Seymour to create the new post of head of a physical education department in 1967, a post held first by I. Moffatt, an English Rugby trials cap, and since 1970 by M.J. Tideswell, who played cricket for Hertfordshire and hockey for an England under-23 side, winning his 100th hockey cap for Hertfordshire in 1975. Both were also responsible for the growing acreage of playing fields and the complex coordination of the multiplicity of games, school, house and individual, available to all boys in the 1970s. There is a recognised interaction between high academic standards and good sporting results and, although some public schools have sometimes had the reputation of pursuing excellence at one to the detriment of the other, it is more common for success to breed the confidence and morale to obtain good results in both. Certainly in Bloxham's history the two previous outstanding periods for academic success under Egerton between 1865 and 1875 and under Armitage were also the times when games were played well. Tideswell, therefore, has made a great contribution to Bloxham's standards in the 1970s by his leadership of the considerable sporting talent in the common room and by his own coaching, not least by choosing himself to concentrate on the younger players rather than the first teams. In this he has been aided by his colleagues, Folliott, Clough (also secretary of the South Oxfordshire Amateurs), N.C.W. Furley (Oxfordshire rugby and cricket player) for rugby, cricket and hockey, and P. Howard (a double Blue) and C.D. Stewart for tennis and fives.

The one sport at which the school had been consistently successful since the end of the war had ended twenty years later in 1967 when boxing was dropped after Pickering left. For some years there had been growing difficulty in obtaining fixtures as other schools gave up in response to medical criticism of the sport and Bloxham was one of the last public schools to keep it alive. In 1964 there had been doubt whether the Eton match would continue because of the opposition of a new head there and Bloxham had to seek opponents far afield — Lancing, Tonbridge and Ratcliffe were new matches in 1962, Haileybury in 1966, and in Pickering's last year of 1967 the only fixtures that could be arranged were the long-established one against Nautical College, Pangbourne, and the two new ones of Haileybury and Downside. So ended a great sporting record for such a small school, with 23 out of 27 matches won between 1961 and 1967, mostly against much larger schools. A prime source of sporting pride in the school was lost and for a time was not replaced by comparable success elsewhere.

Rugger seasons remained depressingly poor until a victory over Hurstpierpoint in 1971 heralded the good 1972 season when the six school teams won 33 and drew eight of their 55 matches. The first XV coached by Folliott beat both Hurstpierpoint and St Bartholomew's, Newbury, at that time the highest scoring school side in the country. They lost only two matches, one being the excitingly narrow 19-20 defeat by the last kick of the last match against King's School, Parramatta, Sydney, one of Australia's great rugger-playing public schools. Reputedly they only go on tour when their habitually good sides are exceptionally strong and the school was lucky to have the chance to meet them because Ian Humphreys (master, 1956-60) was their manager. It had been 25 years since the school's undefeated season of 1947 and at last that record was again within reach; by a happy coincidence T. Civil played in the 1947 team and his son Neil in 1972. Four boys played for the Oxfordshire under-19 team and J. Bulow was reserve for the South of England trial, while the captain, Bruce Thomson, had the high individual score of 126 points to his credit. In 1974 there were again four Bloxhamists playing for Oxfordshire and G. Phipps played for South of England schools.

Better results were also gained at cricket. The 1967 and 1968 seasons were perhaps better than the 1969 one under N. F. Defty, when an unbeaten record was preserved only by some desperately fought draws, but of 1970 there could be no such qualification. Defty, who had played for a Public Schools Colts XI in 1967, again captained an unbeaten side. This time there were only five drawn matches, including a score of 246 for 6 wickets against the M.C.C. when Defty and N.H. Gotch had an opening partnership of 210 runs. Defty himself scored

Record opening partnership of 210 runs v. M.C.C. by N. F. Defty (109) and N. H. Gotch (104).

569 runs that year and Gotch 516 in 1971; Simon Smith came within two runs of the 500 mark in 1975 and six runs over it in 1976 when he also played for the Worcestershire C.C. 2nd XI.

There was a foreseeable revival of interest in Tideswell's own game of hockey and the division contained 140 boys in 1972; the 1975 season was particularly successful with only eight defeats in 28 school matches and eight boys playing for the county. The popularity of hockey was also helped by the milder winters of the 1970s and by transferring athletics to the summer term from 1971. This decision had further repercussions, putting the 543-yard track round the cricket field out of use. When made in 1885 it had been one of the first school cinder tracks in the country, but with the introduction of metric distances and changing views on the merits of grass over cinder tracks a new 300-metre athletics track was marked out on the dead-level second field — that climb up the hill to the final sprint on the cinder track was not just physical exhaustion! In addition to giving the athletes a more pleasant part of the year for their training the reform also inaugurated a new era of metric records, which should give the mathematicians some entertainment in comparing old and new times and distances. The minority sports allowed ever-widening variety for most tastes — badminton, basketball, cross-country running, fives, golf, gymnastics, life-saving, pentathlon, sailing, softball, squash, swimming, tennis and volleyball. Even so, the demand for the more popular ones was greater than the facilities: at first, one-third of the school wanted to play squash and the courts were over-booked for coaching until demand settled down and the village courts were hired, while in tennis until the proposed new all-weather hockey pitch and tennis courts are ready only about 30 of the 80 applicants can be accepted.

The 1969 shooting VIII under the leadership of M.J.S. Edwards produced a new Bloxham record at Bisley, coming fifth in the Ashburton with a score of 509, the previous best being in Jackson Knight's time just 40 years earlier when D.C.B. Harvey's VIII had been sixth with 454. The 1974 VIII was tenth and in the interval R. Towse won the Spencer Mellish cup for the best individual shot in 1971. K.A. Spring coached the shooters for many years, assisted by R.Q.M.S.I. Bill Adams, formerly of the Worcestershire regiment. The latter's patience with small boys struggling with the wayward behaviour of heavy .303 rifles was legendary, and his work with the corps since 1950 was rewarded by a commission in 1969. He had replaced an equally legendary instructor, Reg Turner, ex-Royal Marines R.S.M. who had arrived as school sergeant and tuck shop manager in 1936 and died in 1974, having instilled into many recruits something of his own smart and upright bearing with the injunction, 'Heads up! You won't find no sixpences lying about in the quad!' Successive Ministry of Defence orders, issued at the speed of drill commands in 1967 and 1968, reduced the size and altered the character of the corps. It became affiliated to the Royal Green Jackets, losing its distinctive brass cap badge of the school arms and the black and white shoulder flashes, though the former has been restored in 1977. Defence spending economies further weakened cadet corps in general, but the school contingent continued to flourish, inspired by its Greenfields camps and training visits to military units overseas in Norway and Germany and ever more complicated field days and general inspections under Lt. Col. K.A. Spring. Ambitious but typical was the 1972 NEWD (a phrase coined by Fiori for Night Exercise Without Darkness) assault of Broughton Castle by canoeists, skin divers, paratroopers dropping by aerial ropeway and engineers borne by rafts. On his retirement as commanding officer Spring was awarded the O.B.E. and replaced for the first time by a master appointed primarily for his military experience, Major S. McCloghry, M.B.E.

When, soon after coming to Bloxham, Seymour had told the Council that his first priority was to raise academic standards, he had pointed out that the school was too small to justify and afford the full range of facilities and staff necessary for VIth-form teaching, especially on the science side. At this point it is interesting to look back to the letter from F.S. Boissier to the Founder early in 1893 when he said exactly the same things — that with a small staff the school could not aim at university, army and navy entrance, that for educational purposes there should be 300 to 500 boys, with better science and library facilities and an investment in new buildings. Boissier had recognised in those days that for domestic and religious reasons Bloxham had to remain a single household which limited its size to 150 to 170, and Egerton from the outset had aimed at 150 boys to make a profit; Dewey in the 1940s had needed 240 and had still, just, retained the single household for most purposes. Thompson had removed the traditional constraints on further growth by using a dining hall annexe and by giving up compulsory attendance at chapel — among others a good practical reason for doing so. In the late 1960s further growth was essential and Seymour forecast that when the expected better examination results came through it would lead to an increased demand for places. This in turn led to the unavoidable conclusion that a further building programme would have to be undertaken. There was a pause while the Council hesitated, waiting to see whether the forecast was accurate. In the meantime they made some important improvements, necessary whatever decision was eventually reached about the size of the school.

First they fulfilled their promise to Seymour on his appointment by doubling the science building in 1966, adding six classrooms with workshop, library and other subsidiary rooms, designed like the first part by S. T. Walker according to the brief prepared by Fiori. At its formal opening by Sir Peter Runge the diverse displays of maps and geology, livestock in the biology room and physics equipment and experiments were ample evidence of the already growing strength of science in the school, further emphasised by a second major science exhibition in 1972. On the arts side the former tuck shop was converted into a working library in 1968. Two other developments in the old main building were of great long-term significance. In 1966, largely by inserting an extra floor in the lofty schoolroom and other internal works, Crake and Wilson houses were given studies and extra day rooms for about half their boys, similar to Wilberforce and Egerton and bringing the whole school up to the prevailing public school living standards, while the cramped senior common room was considerably enlarged and improved. Then in 1967 the arts and technical activities centre was contrived in the cellars beneath the chapel and schoolroom, which will be remembered by older generations as the gloomy holes for boots, tuckboxes, air raid shelters or maintenance workshops. Their previous purposes were revealed by the archaeological discoveries during the alterations of a 25-year old 2s. 6d. postal order and an antique packet of hidden cigarettes! ATAC (a typically weird acronym of the period) owed much to the generosity of two parents, F. Defty and J. R. Greenhaulgh, and from its highly equipped workshops are poured pottery, sculpture, models, woodwork, radio and electronic equipment, far exceeding the early hopes and imagination of Egerton when he fitted out the original lathe shop a century before. Under A. J. Griffin's guidance several sophisticated if deceptively simple devices have been made — three being the electronic school clock and bell system invented by R. Youngson in 1973-4, the Bloxham Electronic Random Number Indicator Equipment (BERNIE for short) and the electronic cricket scoreboard. BERNIE was commissioned and paid for by the Old Bloxhamist Society to draw the monthly lottery of their 200 Club. Though then not fully developed, the scoreboard, also paid for by the Society, was first used in the 1976 cricket match between the school and the Old Bloxhamists; its final completion and installation took place during the summer of 1978.

By 1969 the headmaster was becoming restive, urging the Council that the signs were favourable and asking them to take the vital decision to build an additional house. It was the most important decision in the recent history of the school made at a time of much change and uncertainty both in state education, affecting the schools in the North Oxfordshire Scheme, and within the Woodard Corporation, but Bloxham decided for itself the style of its future development. It was a decision which will deserve the careful examination of a future historian seeing the events in long-term perspective. Schuster, then acting as chairman of the Council, summarised the story:

'We had long known that for educational and financial reasons we must ultimately increase the size of the school from 250 to 320 boys, and that this would mean building a new House. In October 1969 the Headmaster told the School Council that the time for this had now come, since the annual demand for places had reached a level which, if satisfied, would make a new House by September 1971 an absolute necessity. Unless the Council could guarantee him a new House by September 1971 he would have severely to reduce the intake in September 1970 and, since a low intake takes five years to work its way through the school, this would mean goodbye to further thoughts of expansion for that long period'.

The chairman continued this speech at the opening of the house by explaining how quickly the Council reacted, making a prompt decision to accept Seymour's argument.

'Consultations with our architect produced the answer that the whole project, including a Housemaster's house and one or two consequential items, would cost around £120,000 and that the contract would need to be signed at the very latest by June 1st, 1970, if the House was to be ready on time. So it was we had eight months to find the money and then but fourteen months to build the House'.

It was an impossibly inadequate time. Schuster first had to convince the Woodard Corporation to win their approval and support, and then had to raise the money. Within three short months he had achieved the impossible. Three large anonymous benefactions and a loan from the Corporation were assurance that the building could go ahead, the Council naming it Raymond house in gratitude to Roger Raymond for all his many gifts to the school.

There remained the choice of style for the building. Seymour had a firm belief that in the 1960s mature and intelligent young men required privacy and comfort, and that parents were right to expect such conditions in return for high fees. Some of the earliest modern study-bedrooms to be built in a public school, similar to those in the halls of residence at colleges and universities in Britain and overseas, had been in his house at Marlborough. Therefore, when the Council were considering proposals for Raymond house he put it to them that to build a Wilberforce-style house would be out-of-date within ten years. The dilemma was obvious. If the new house were built with study-bedrooms an expensive conversion of all the other houses and the original school buildings would have to follow. The Council chose to look forward and Raymond house was built in 1971

Mrs Margaret Thatcher, M.P., at opening of Raymond House, 1971, with D. R. G. Seymour, headmaster from 1965, and F. J. Willy, housemaster.

with study-bedrooms for about two-thirds of its 60 boys.

Externally it was designed in the same functional style and pale russet brick as S. T. Walker's other new buildings for the school, thrusting its angular south front above the pitched roofs of the stone village houses falling away to the valley beneath. Inside, its plan was revolutionary. Small house-rooms and dormitories were retained for the junior boys to establish their sense of community, but all 40 seniors were given study-bedrooms, with common room and house library. Matron's and house tutor's quarters were included in the main building and the housemaster's residence linked to it by his study. Like Egerton house a few years earlier, the first housemaster, F. J. Willy, drew boys from other houses ready for the formal opening on 29 October 1971 by the secretary of state for education and science, Mrs Margaret Thatcher, M.P. The other houses were converted on the same principles, Wilberforce in a very similar manner in 1974, Egerton enlarged and faced in Hornton stone in 1977, leaving the more complex architectural problems of altering the old building for Crake and Wilson.

The plans for that final and most difficult stage in converting the whole school on the principle of study-bedroom accommodation were announced at Founderstide 1978, remarkably rapid progress since the decision to build Raymond house only eight years earlier and during a period of excessively high

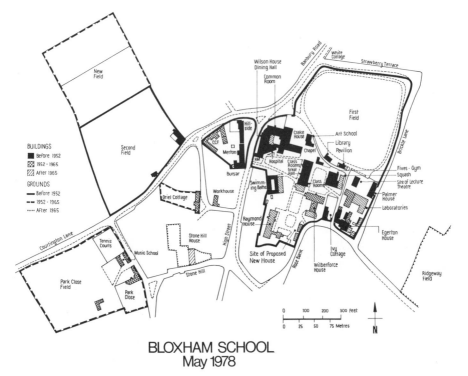

BUILDINGS
- ■ Before 1952
- ▨ 1952 - 1965
- ▧ After 1965

GROUNDS
- —— Before 1952
- – – 1952 - 1965
- ···· After 1965

New Field

Second Field

Oriel Cottage

Courtington Lane

Tennis Courts

Music School

Park Close Field

Park Close

Stone Hill House

Stone Hill

High Street

Workhouse

Swimming Baths

Bursar

Merton

CCF

Hillside

Wilson House Dining Hall

Common Room

Banbury Road

White Cottage

Strawberry Terrace

First Field

Crake House

Hospital

Chapel

Class Rooms Great Hall

Class Rooms

Raymond House

Site of Proposed New House

Rye Bank

Wilberforce House

Ivy Cottage

Art School

Library Pavilion

Fives - Gym Squash

Site of Lecture Theatre

Palmer House

Laboratories

Egerton House

Brickle Lane

Ridgeway Field

0   100   200   300 Feet
0   25   50   75 Metres

N

BLOXHAM SCHOOL
May 1978

inflation. At the time of going to press strenuous efforts to begin the first stage of these plans were being made and it is anticipated that building will start again in the quite near future. In the meantime the demand for places had brought the size of the school to about 350, making it necessary to introduce cafeteria arrangements in the dining hall in 1970, extend the hall into the inner quadrangle in 1977 and open Stone Hill house under N.W.C. Furley in 1976 as a waiting house to take up to twenty new boys who later moved on to their senior houses. It thus became the latest, and by far the most comfortable, of the various overflow annexes which had been dotted about the school buildings since Dewey had started to build up the numbers in the 1940s.

By concentrating on enlarging and improving the living quarters in the 1970s, on which £420,000 was spent, some other desirable building projects were held back. For these a further appeal was launched in 1978, to which £62,000 had been contributed by Founder's Day. The most important, starting that autumn, was the replacement of the 1923 laboratory, later used as games equipment and machinery store, by a lecture theatre with demonstration room and audio-visual aids, science library and chaplain's room. At Park Close the music school is to be extended and on the second field an all-weather pitch for hockey, to be used also for tennis, will be laid.

Seymour's forecast in 1969 had proved correct. The pressure for places had

176

Raymond House in 1978.

strengthened due to the academic successes, impressive living conditions and broad educational aims and facilities of the school. Much of the headmaster's second five-year plan, while continuing with his academic aims and the building programme, was concerned therefore with introducing ideas further to break down isolation from the local community and to bring school and home in closer partnership. To some extent these trends were happening anyway and were evident in all boarding schools, and Seymour based his policy on Marlborough's lead in this country and his experience in Australia, where one-third of the school that he had taught at had been day-boarders. This relationship was easier to foster with many of the staff being family men themselves living in the neighbourhood with wives involved in various aspects of school and local life. This applied particularly to housemasters' wives and to Betty Seymour. Her hospitality and entertainment of visitors and senior boys, especially prefects and the Literati Society, is renowned, but her unobtrusive influence on senior boys, friendship to colleagues and their families and support of the headmaster has, like that of her predecessor, Barbara Thompson, been of greater significance than this *History* has suggested, and is perhaps best expressed by the headmaster when referring to his post as a dual appointment.

Parents were offered more opportunities of visiting and taking part in school activities and it was hoped and intended that parents of day boys, whose entry

Study-bedroom.

was no longer discouraged, would take a lead, as indeed they did. The day-boarders became an important minority, with B. Thomson being the first day boy prefect in 1971 and C. Whitley captain of the school in 1978. As parents became generally more frequently and closely involved in school life so the distance between home and boarding school became an increasingly important consideration in the choice of a school. In 1950 most parents had usually been seen only at half-term leave and the major events of All Saints, the school play and Founderstide, though some visited for both school and house matches. Twenty-five years later there were some fifteen events a term — house dances, leaves, matches, plays and concerts — to bring not only boys and parents together, but sisters and friends as well. This sort of relationship, made possible by the extension of private motoring compared with 1950 when many boys still travelled between home and school by train, is only feasible when the travelling distances are not too great. There was, therefore, a steady contraction in the school's 'catchment area', with an increasing proportion of parents living within 50 miles of Bloxham. This was a return to the situation in Dewey's headmastership (though for different reasons) in contrast to Thompson's when a large number had come from the Home Counties and London area.

Egerton House, enlarged 1977, with Ivy Cottage. Compare with P. 40.

Distance of new boys' homes	*1965*	*1967*	*1969*	*1971*	*1972*	*1977*
Under 50 miles	21	21	42	47	50	59
50-150 miles	35	20	19	22	24	9
Over 150 miles	1	5	1	0	0	0
Overseas	6	6	13	19	14	18
Total	63	52	75	88	88	86

Distance of all boys' homes	*1969*	*1970*	*1972*	*1977*
Under 50 miles	83	106	146	204
50-150 miles	104	93	129	54
Over 150 miles	11	3	3	5
Overseas	41	44	40	71
Total	239	246	318	334

Apart from the growth in the number of those living relatively near Bloxham the tables also reveal an increase in overseas entrants, about half of whom come from British families living abroad. Although in the early days of the school

Egerton had a few African and Burmese boys, until about twenty years ago it was rare for Bloxham to have boys of nationalities other than British. The American and African boys of the earlier part of the last decade have been largely replaced by those from Asia. One feature not revealed in the tables is the importance that all boarding schools place upon providing an education for those who will benefit specially for family reasons, including those whose parents have died, are separated or have a frequently changing home because of business, service or personal reasons. These benefits are only obtained, of course, if there is only a small minority in these circumstances, and in recent years Bloxham has aimed at not more than 20% including the British expatriate families.

Another feature of the broader entry to the school was a small but persistent demand for a post-O-level entry; in 1973 M. McBride was the first senior entrant to become captain of the school and in 1978, Jonathan Bridgwater, another senior entrant, was the first Old Bloxhamist's son to become captain. This demand to some extent prepared the way for the more radical innovation of girls in the VIth form. Other boys' public schools had already experimented successfully, notably Marlborough at the end of Seymour's time there, and it was part of his long-term strategy to broaden Bloxham's education in a similar fashion. By the time that Bloxham accepted its own first VIth-form girls in the school in 1973, the school had long been accustomed to feminine company. With encouragement from successive headmistresses of Tudor Hall, the girls' public school only two miles distant, the two schools combined VIth-form work and met frequently on social occasions, started in Thompson's time, such as concerts, choral society evenings and dances. The formal links between the schools were strengthened when Seymour was elected a governor of Tudor Hall in 1966 and the Revd L.F.P. Gunner appointed its chaplain in 1970. The North Oxfordshire Scheme and other working conferences brought together VIth formers from other schools, both boys and girls; the two daughters of the Wilberforce housemaster, Elizabeth Fiori (1965-68) and Jane Fiori (1968-69) were accepted in the VIth form as an exceptional case, and Georgina Haselden was similarly accepted for a one-year A-level course in 1972-3. It was the satisfactory result of these experiences, social and academic, which led Seymour formally to announce that Bloxham would take day girls into the VIth form from September 1973. The names of the first two, Jane Stansbury and Teresa Wormington, deserve to be recorded as much as Egerton's first boys. They were attached to Raymond house but given their own modernised quarters in Merton, where eventually there will be about a dozen; Clough acted as their housemaster until 1977 when Mrs C. Hall, teaching mathematics, became Bloxham's first senior house-mistress. Being such a small minority even in the VIth form and therefore chosen with care, they have been rapidly absorbed into the life of the school, their regular daily presence leading Bloxham and Tudor Hall together to open membership of VIth-form societies to each other and jointly encourage brothers and sisters. Even the Old Bloxhamist Society survived the shock and opened its membership to Old Girls in 1974.

It is only from the 1970s that an analysis of the occupations of parents has survived and, although a century is too great a span to distinguish trends, it is of some interest to compare the 1975 figures with those given by Egerton in 1870, to judge how far Bloxham still meets the Founder's intention of providing a Church of England 'middle-class' education. Only ten years after he had opened the school Egerton found that he was attracting the sons of parents who were of a higher social standing than the tradesmen and farmers that he was aiming for, with about half the parents being professional people and half businessmen and farmers. The proportion of the old-established vocations of the church and law has dropped, as has that of the farmers. In the 1970s the majority of parents are in business and managerial positions or belong to the new professions unknown or almost unknown in Victorian times.

Occupations of parents

	1870	%	%	1975
Clergy	21	13	2	6
Lawyers	10	6	1	3
Doctors, dentists	7	4	6	19
Services	4	2.5	6	18
Business and trade	42	26	40	123
Farmers	50	30.5	9	30
Professions (accountants, architects, banking, engineers, surveyors, veterinary, etc.)	30	18	20	61
Teachers, lecturers	0	0	2	6
Widows, etc	0	0	6	18
Unclassified	0	0	8	24
	164	100	100	308

The demand for additional places occurred despite the improvement of educational standards by the state and, nearer at hand, the opening of a county comprehensive school, Warriners (named after an old-established village yeoman family), at the corner of the Bloxham Grove road in 1971. Fear of state intervention under Gladstone's Liberal governments in the affairs of private church schools had been expressed by Reginald Egerton, and in post-war Britain the educational freedom of the independent schools was a theme which recurred constantly in formal speeches on the opening of new buildings or at Founderstide. Following the Newsom report of 1965 to examine ways of integrating the public schools into the national education system Seymour had endorsed the view of the Headmasters' Conference that government policy would allow some cooperation, saying in 1968,

'At no time had the climate of opinion among all headmasters of public schools been more favourable to change, because we honestly believe that we have something of vital importance to contribute to the nation's education. For over forty years now the Headmasters' Conference had repeatedly declared their willingness to open doors to boys who cannot afford the fees. It would be a sadness to them if the Newsom Report died through lack of finance as did the Fleming Report'.

Finance was not available, nor the political will. Even most Conservative local authorities, who might have been expected to be sympathetic to the idea of cooperation, preferred to invest in their own schools rather than spend money on giving a small minority of their pupils the opportunity of a public school education. In fact the sustained attacks by Labour governments on the principle of selection in education, combined with the financial constraints on putting such a policy fully into practice, have probably benefited the public schools, although in considering the history of one small public school it is perhaps as well to keep their contribution to national education in perspective. All the Woodard schools together had about 6,200 pupils aged over eleven in 1977. Even the relatively small Oxfordshire local education authority was then responsible for 47,516 secondary school pupils.

The destruction of the grammar schools in favour of comprehensive schools alienated many parents at a time when improved living standards enlarged the number of those who could afford fee-paying education. Some were offended by the sheer size of the comprehensive schools, others disappointed at their inability to build up strong VIth forms; Warriners, being new, was especially unfortunate in having to defer the creation of its VIth form for financial reasons in 1976. With hopes for cooperation between state and independent education unfulfilled, although Bloxham and Warriners combined for some minority subjects, and with public opinion coming to accept the philosophy of non-selective education and to question the role of the school, rather than parents, in setting moral and religious standards, Seymour delivered a series of thought-provoking Founderstide addresses in the 1970s. He warned of the threats to the independent schools from government policy — in 1974 and 1975 the threat to freedom for parents 'to educate their children as they wish; to spend their money as they wish; to have their child brought up in a school where religion is of real importance; freedom for efficient schools to operate outside of the maintained system' — and in 1976 and 1977 he exposed the basic difference between the government policy that selection in education is harmful 'and the independent school system, based on a belief that selection *is vitally essential*'. He further emphasised his belief that education is more than academic learning and 'that "development of character", and of "the whole man", and "retention of moral standards" are not just empty platitudes'.

The demand for places proved that parents agreed with these beliefs despite the rise of fees in the inflationary years of the 1970s. Compared with fees of £861 at Radley and St Edwards in 1973 those at Bloxham were £780, before leaping that year to £870. By 1975 they had risen to £1,230 and in 1978 were £1,935. The fees for day-boarders had increased proportionally. The first day girls' fees were £510 a year in 1973, but by 1977 the cost had become £1,137 and the VIth-form intake of both boys and girls was affected despite generous scholarships such as those given for girls by a member of the Council, Laurence Robson. In Boissier's letter of 1893 already quoted he had made the plea that there was every justification for Bloxham to raise its fees and aim at a higher grade of education. It was perhaps unfortunate that Egerton and his trustees clung to the original aims of the school at a time when the pattern of middle-class education was changing, and it was not until the 1970s that Boissier's remarkable vision was fully realised — both for the size of the school, its upgraded standards and the recognition that parents are prepared to pay for quality. This embraced that 'thirty per cent' of education upon which, with work and games going well, a constant demand for places and a building programme rolling forward, Seymour next wanted to concentrate, perhaps the least tangible and most difficult target that he set out to achieve in his third five-year plan.

In an unsettling period of religious change Thompson had preserved intact the fundamental and focal importance of the chapel in Bloxham's life and had established a high quality of interest and performance in music, art and drama. Continuing that policy, a notable musical landmark was the first Bloxham Festival by Brian Judge (1966-73), spread over a winter weekend in 1970 with performances, instrumental and choral, at Tudor Hall, Bloxham parish church, the school chapel and great hall, repeated twice more before Judge left and described in one of the Banbury newspapers as 'the artistic highlights of the year'. At his last festival the programme included the *Dream of Gerontius* in Banbury church, a children's concert in the great hall and an organ recital in the chapel. By that time virtually the whole school participated in some musical activity and by 1974 his successor Martin Roberts had revived the house singing competition to include every boy. Over a quarter of the school performed in the autumn concert of 1976, and by forming a joint Bloxham and Tudor Hall choir in 1974 to replace the trebles lost through earlier maturity, Roberts greatly restored singing in chapel. At one level the joint Bloxham and Tudor Hall choral society continued its ambitious programme of Verdi, Elgar and Mozart and the choir featured on Radio Oxford and sang at five cathedrals in the midlands and south of England, while at another there flourished a succession of house dances and wierdly named pop-groups. The school could talk of its great musical tradition — and in retirement Stanley Thompson could be satisfied that it was a tradition which he had created, and he might well be proud that his Concert Club, had grown to a membership of 250 season ticket-holders by 1978.

In drama the Shakespearian cycle of Thompson's headmastership under R.C. Theobald's able direction was replaced by modern playwrights with plays chosen for their social message as well as dramatic entertainment. Theobald cast Tudor Hall girls for the first time in 1966, and in response to repeated requests by the local newspaper critics to give public performances the school did so in 1968 with P. R. Mayes's production of *An Inspector Calls*. One of the lead parts was taken by Patrick Ryecart, who in 1977 received what can only be described as rave notices in *The Observer* for his West End performance in Shaw's *Candida*. The top stars with whom he was playing were full of praise for his early training at Bloxham and throughout the 1970s Brian Joplin's series of productions earned

Great hall (1937) with examination tables set out and during rehearsal for school play under B. M. Joplin, 1978.

excellent reviews in the press and were reckoned to be at least equal to those of public schools with a much larger choice of cast. The quality of school plays was supported by the talents of the common room and other staff and helpers as producers, stage directors, designers and wardrobe mistresses, on almost continual call as the house plays came in 1976 to be performed at intervals throughout the year in preference to a single night's marathon of one-act plays, and a junior school play, reminiscent of the Gould Club in the 1940s, was produced from 1975. The historian again looks back, this time to the 1930s, to find a parallel for the common room Christmas revues. *The Bloxhamist* concluded its report on the 1976 one, 'The Bloxham revue is a bit more than a good laugh; it also serves as an outward expression of the good relationship that exists between boys and masters, and this it has expressed better than ever before'.

This relationship had always been fostered through school clubs and societies, which numbered 35 by 1976 and required a directory to guide the newcomer. They have become too diverse to catalogue here, the purely recreational (such as the Motor Club or Rough Shooting Club) mixed with the academic (like the Modern Language or Science Societies) and cultural (like the B.S. Film Appreciation Society). The most prestigious was the Literati, started by

Thompson after the demise of the similar Saye and Sele Society, while another long if erratically successful tradition was maintained by the Debating Society, with one or two notable speakers like M. Johnson in 1969.

Almost every day of the term had its special event and a perusal of the terms' calendars brings the conclusion that there is no such thing as a typical week to serve as an example. The pattern of the daily timetable becomes equally complex with variations on the normal theme of a daily early communion, five morning periods, two afternoon periods and games, a two-hour prep, and half holidays on Wednesdays and Saturdays. On Mondays there was a short morning chapel service, no evening chapel but house prayers later in the evening; on Wednesdays there was evening communion. Thursday afternoons were allotted to corps and its related activities, and Friday mornings to minority time options. Academic, VIth-form and choral societies met in prep time and on Saturdays, when there was no prep, the evening was given over to drama, films, school and house plays. Other societies met on Wednesday afternoons and Sunday afternoons and evenings; on Sundays also the Concert Club met and minority sports were played in the morning after chapel.

In the daily social life of the school two special schemes of Seymour's devising early in his headmastership were, however, particularly important. First was the opening of the ATAC workshops in 1967, intended primarily to extend the theoretical science of the classrooms into the applied practice of everyday life, while at the same time linking arts and sciences outside school work. By chance the workshops proved to be something of a new social centre partly filling the place of the old tuck shop. But the headmaster was seeking something more positive than this: his ideas for a junior common room, which had been turned down at Marlborough, were translated into reality at Bloxham in 1970, largely through the practical support of Roger Raymond. S.G. Lester had suggested the site and at Founderstide that year the Raymond Society opened its doors in the Vaughan pavilion to its first members, to boys over seventeen and, at their suggestion, to masters. The lower part of the pavilion, which was enlarged at the same time for more changing rooms and games storage space, was made into a reading room and lounge, with an office for the Old Bloxhamist Society. The historically minded may care to turn up the first issue of *The Bloxhamist* kept in that office to discover that a reading room in the pavilion was first suggested in April 1875 and that H. E. Platt, the editor, pleaded for such an office in 1876! Upstairs, the open balcony was enclosed to make a large club room with licensed bar as an informal meeting place, unique among public schools, for a youthful staff and adult senior boys. 'For me', commented Seymour, 'the Junior Common Room is no luxury but a vital part of this new educational concept'.

Young people of the 1960s and 1970s possessed a strong social conscience. Both the headmaster, who was local chairman of Voluntary Service Overseas for some years, and successive chaplains awakened that conscience. In 1966 the Revd D. C. Dowie started exchange visits with Northorpe Hall, a home for deprived and delinquent boys near Mirfield, Yorkshire, and initiated a 'social services group'. By chance this coincided with reforms both of the cadet corps and the scouting movement (the latter eliminating those troops like Bloxham's which operated for only part of the year), thus releasing the necessary pool of labour for community work in and about the village. In 1971 Dowie's successor, the Revd Laurence Gunner, began a pilot scheme for service to the local community in Milcombe. Energetic fund-raising paid for a minibus and a variety of equipment and tools, with which in the first full term of operation the community service volunteers paid 400 visits to 45 clients in eight neighbouring north Oxfordshire villages. Within three years there were 60 clients and a second 'bus was bought to transport the increasing number of boys taking part in community service, not only as an alternative to organised games but in addition to them.

It is perhaps surprising that no chaplain before Dowie had organised this sort of enterprise as part of the Christian mission of the school, and this emphasises the old isolation of the school from the local community. Dowie was a 'progressive' priest, who acknowledged that 'he favoured a radical approach to the teaching of Christianity' at a time when the whole Church of England was in a turmoil of overturning long established attitudes and forms of service, and his enthusiasm for every kind of liturgical and ecclesiastical innovation probably compounded his difficulties. He had come to the school in 1964 immediately after voluntary chapel had been introduced when the understandable first reaction of many boys was to avoid attendance as far as possible. He made changes of his own — a westward facing altar and congregational participation in ordering the traditional sung eucharist, itself replaced by the experimental Anglican 'Series 2' form of service in 1968, the evening eucharist, rogationtide and advent carol services, and evening weekday talks replacing the familiar if repetitive evensong. Traditionalists regretted that plainsong was rarely sung; older generations of Bloxhamists would have had no need to journey to Downside, as did the Clerici Laici group in 1976, 'in order to hear plainsong sung in the traditional manner'. He wrote a service book for Bloxham in 1964 — the first since Crake's a century earlier — and masters preached. The fashion was for ecumenicalism. To Bloxham was invited a far wider variety of preachers and speakers of differing faiths and beliefs while on two Sundays in February 1966 the school began worshipping with the congregations of the village parish and methodist churches.

His most important and long-lasting achievement was the first Conference on Public School Religion of 1967 when 120 headmasters and chaplains gathered at Bloxham primarily to discuss the issues behind chapel attendance, voluntary or compulsory. The conference gave birth in 1969 to a Committee for Research into Religious Education in Boarding Schools, financed by the Dulverton trust and with which the school has remained closely associated ever since. It became known as the Bloxham Project for short, with Seymour as its vice-chairman, and a subsequent conference was held at Bloxham in 1972 to discuss the first research report of the two directors, subsequently published as the book, *Images of Life*. Both the research and the conference disclosed a rather sad, perhaps alarming, picture of no more than a general token observance of Sunday religion throughout boarding schools and the Headmasters' Conference then decided to finance research for a further five years. This concluded with a third three-day conference at Bloxham in 1977 with the theme 'Towards a New Vision', when one of the distinguished visitors to address the 183 chaplains, heads and other staff was Stuart Blanch, archbishop of York. At its close they asked the Bloxham Project to continue its work for three years more.

The Bloxham Project had the effect of making the school widely known by name and as a host, and as a direct result Seymour served on both the Durham Commission and the Carlisle Commission, reporting on religion in education, and on the Farmington Trust on Religious Education working on day school religion. Bloxham itself, however, had so moulded its own long tradition of Catholic teaching to avoid the situation that was causing such anxiety to other heads and chaplains. Much was due to the Revd Laurence Gunner, who succeeded Dowie in 1969. Many of the latter's unsettling innovations have become accepted — about half the common room continued to deliver chapel sermons or talks, of which J. M. Lerrigo's were published in 1971 as *Love is never wasted,* and the following year the altar was moved forward to permit either eastward or westward facing celebration, while Gunner has also continued to vary the diet of daily services and preachers. The upper school are expected to attend the weekly talk from the visiting speaker but the other three weekday services are voluntary. One of the three Sunday services must be attended, and with Anglo-Catholic doctrines still the basis of the school's worship (if much changed since Egerton's day) the main service on Sunday is still the eucharist. On one occasion in 1976 it was replaced by mattins, when *The Bloxhamist,* commenting that this restless generation was always seeking variety, welcomed the change.

Change alone is not enough to attract or hold the restless. In place of the communal discipline which former chaplains had obtained with success Gunner sought a deeper voluntary involvement. He encouraged boys to take a greater part in chapel services, even to the extent of conducting some weekday ones; he formed the school church council (on the pattern of a parochial church council), and led it and the servers to a wider ministry in the school community; he introduced a stewardship scheme, which also had the effect of increasing chapel collections; and by the Lent appeals for special causes — the 1978 one raising £1000 — he gave the school a greater sense of responsibility to the community in general. Although therefore the chapel is perhaps not such a singular focal point of the school as in the past it still exerts a greater influence than in most other public schools. This is especially apparent in those years when the calendar permits Bloxham to celebrate Easter with a unique and memorable programme of Holy Week services, concerts and plays. The chaplains continue to be appointed by the provost, not the headmaster, and although other masters are no longer chosen primarily as active members of the Anglican faith they are still required to accept engagement with 'knowledge of the object of the Founder and of the Governing Body that all pupils who may come to the School shall be taught, together with sound grammar and learning, the fear and honour of

Liddon chapel (1968).

Almighty God according to the doctrines of the Catholic Faith as they are set forth in the Book of Common Prayer of the Church of England'.

The Old Bloxhamist Society had witnessed some of these early changes with unease. The religious teaching of the school had a profound and life-long effect on boys who remained the most loyal to the school. Chaplain after chaplain had instilled the belief that the chapel was the centre of the school and that while others might change or lower their Christian or moral standards there was no reason for Bloxhamists to do likewise. Members of the Society were aware from their own experience that much of the strong sense of unity in the smaller school of earlier generations was derived from the teaching of the chaplains. Their chapel was familiar to all, whether packed for sung eucharist or containing only a handful of boys at 7.30 in the morning. They had already looked askance at the principle of voluntary chapel and their anxieties crystalised over the proposal for the Liddon chapel in 1967. Four years earlier the provost, the bishop of Lewes, had obtained the Council's approval for a crypt chapel and the following year Miss Beith of Chichester gave £1,000 for the purpose in memory of Canon Julian Bickersteth, formerly vice-provost. The intention was to provide a place of worship of an intimate character suitable for some weekday services, for private prayer, informal meetings and to house the reserved sacrament. It was designed to combat and overcome the signs of apathy and resistance to 'public school religion' with its dangers of a shallow reliance on formal services, evident at Bloxham though in a less extreme form than at some public schools. After some thought of placing the chapel beneath Crake junior dormitory the Council decided that by moving the new working library to the former tuck shop the Liddon library could be used.

The headmaster, knowing that the scheme had been approved in principle before his arrival, was startled at the vehemence of the Old Bloxhamists' reaction, as was the provost. Like Thompson, who had suggested the idea, both were sensitive to changing attitudes in the school, but the Old Bloxhamists were strongly opposed to a proposal which diverted attention from Egerton's 'crowning building of all', and the more so because it also changed the Liddon library, the memorial to Egerton himself. For many the nostalgia generated by that small and overcrowded library which had served the school so well and so long, was summed up in Roger Ostime's sonnet twenty years earlier.

'Tranquility is here. The very chairs
Seem not inanimate, but life at rest. . .
As if they too could sense the hushing stares
Of myriad eyes, that, searching for a guest
Who would reflect their own quiescent mood
Have lighted on us . . . and are satisfied.
The chairs and I, albeit profane and rude,
Catch their approval with a happy pride.
We hope that we shall never give offence
To all those records of the wit of man,
Lest in our aspect their creators sense
Irreverence toward them. 'Tis not our plan;
We feel the honour of their tolerant eye
And give them humble thanks . . . . the chairs and I'.

The eloquence and sincerity of the headmaster and the provost's concession that the reserved sacrament should remain in the chapel did much to mollify the Old Bloxhamist Society, and the Liddon chapel was dedicated by the provost at All Saints 1968, an attractive modern room planned by Dowie, with a central altar, simple furnishings and a sense of lightness and welcome. It came to be used extensively in the way that had been intended and has undoubtedly been an important factor in determining the personal commitment of boys to the Christian life of the school.

It was singularly unfortunate for the new headmaster that so soon after his arrival he should have been embroiled in a controversy, not of his own making, with the Old Bloxhamist Society. Newcomers from other and larger public schools have been surprised, and pleased, at the intense and active interest of the Society. Thompson, handicapped by his experiences elsewhere of old boys' societies of an entirely different type, succeeding a headmaster who had inspired the Society with his own love for Bloxham, and obliged by the school's condition to introduce many changes and reforms, perhaps never entirely overcame those initial disadvantages. The controversy over the Liddon chapel had the benefit of bringing the new headmaster and the Society to a much closer understanding, shown in the events of the last ten years.

This has largely been due to the constant and unflagging support of Spencer Lester and his wife Peggy, the former innocently snared in the year that he taught at the school in 1944, when Dewey asked if he would just bring up-to-date a few of the Old Bloxhamist address cards neglected since Wilson's death. The Society was then being revived after its hibernation during the war and in 1947 Lester officially became its secretary, building up the membership to 1,400 by 1961 when he succeeded Raymond as chairman. He has held that position ever since, with one short break, firmly announcing his intention to resign in 1978. Throughout this period the Society's activities have expanded with its membership — the August cricket festival restored in 1950, provincial dinners in 1953, informal monthly London gatherings since 1959, the masonic lodge in 1960 (having been proposed without success in 1912 and 1930-32), rugger (1962), hockey (1960), golf (1963) and shooting (1952) matches in addition to more contests with the school. In the 1970s school and Society have drawn closer together, beginning perhaps with the annual dinner being held at Bloxham in preference to London in 1968. Admittedly there has been some decline in the character of the dinner if one looks back over earlier menus, for in 1895 and 1897, when the Society was being formed, it was an eleven or nine-course meal, with up to four speeches, four songs (three sung by Egerton) and a musical sketch. In contrast the 1974 dinner was a pallid affair of only six courses followed by two speeches. The Victorians had both more stomach and stamina than the present generation!

In the 1960s much of the Society's energies and resources was spent in supporting the school's development appeals. With the school Council raising its building funds by different methods the Society in the 1970s had the opportunity of pursuing its own interests more directly, especially after its income was greatly increased by J. P. Barwell's formation of the 200 Club lottery in 1970. That was the year in which Arthur Disney began his tree-planting scheme for the school grounds, with 158 new trees planted by early 1978, and also the same year that one of Spen Lester's main ambitions was realised with the provision of the Old Bloxhamist Society office in the pavilion. For the first time the Society now had a permanent home in the school and a place to keep their own files and the older school archives. From cupboards and drawers scattered about the buildings appeared long-forgotten treasures — old score books, Wilson's neat lists of addresses, Egerton's letters, accounts and registers, Boissier's massive log book, a formidable heap of photographs mostly without captions, even a khaki armband of the 1940 Bloxham Local Defence Volunteers. This untidy and unsorted accumulation of historic records was the source of another of Lester's ambitions, the publication of a new history of the school, which will stand as a fitting tribute to his unending service to the school.

The ties between the Society and the school have been immeasurably strengthened by the fact that both Lester and his assistant and successor as secretary, David Boss, live within a few miles of Bloxham, frequently present at all hours of day or night, in common room, headmaster's study, on the touchline or in the 'Elephant' bar, and always ready to discuss the school and its welfare. Together they have raised the membership to about 1,700 in 1978, the enormous work-load being shared by a resident secretary in the common room. For 25 post-war years this was Wisti Longden, followed by J. M. Lerrigo and in 1977 by

S. McLoghry. Dewey taught Lester to see the Society as the guardian of Bloxham's traditions, and in this he has followed the example of Dewey, Palmer, and Wilson in the manner that goes back to Egerton himself. When the Founder spoke to the young Society in 1898, having just given his school to the Woodard Corporation and received the illuminated address of appreciation from his own old boys, he left them with this advice:

'Here let me express my earnest hope that coming generations of Bloxhamists will keep up their connection with the past, by taking part in these Old Bloxhamist gatherings, and keeping up the traditions of the past as *one* School, whether under the old or new regime'.

Egerton had vividly expressed his own fundamental aims for the school in one of his letters to Keble College, written almost exactly one hundred years ago on 18 March 1879.

'I myself should like to leave as large a freedom as possible to the Governing Body — *provided that that Governing Body were staunch & thorough Churchmen.* Even if they thought it for the interests of the Church to alter the *grade* of the school — to make it for a higher class – at higher terms – I should feel not the slightest uneasiness at leaving such a matter wholly to their judgement.

My only wish is to do something, *for the Church* — this is *all* I want to secure — & that I don't want to leave to the judgement of *the State'*.

Throughout a century of vast changes in the history of the nation, in social conditions and in methods of education, Bloxham has remained unswervingly true to its Founder's ideals of independence and Christian teaching. With the powerful preservation of these traditions, with the shining light of the unique strength of the Bloxham community, with the stimulant of academic excellence and delight in buildings renewed, the school can be proud of its past and confident of the future.

Aerial view looking west. From right to left are Egerton's original buildings, classrooms and great hall, Wilberforce and Raymond houses, and science laboratories. In the background, the second field, Park Close and Stone Hill.

APPENDIX

HEADMASTERS

Revd J. W. Hewett	1853-57
Revd P. R. Egerton	1860
Revd F. S. Boissier	1886
Revd G. H. Ward	1899
Revd A. R. M. Grier	1915
Revd F. H. George	1919
V. L. Armitage	1925
K. T. Dewey	1940
R. S. Thompson	1952
D. R. G. Seymour	1965

SECOND MASTERS

Revd A. D. Crake	1865
W. W. Bird	1868
Revd A. D. Crake	1872
Revd W. M. Richardson	1876
Revd A. L. C. Heigham	1879
Revd G. F. Garwood	1881
Revd A. L. C. Heigham	1883
Revd F. S. Boissier	1885
Revd W. A. Marshall	1886
Revd R. A. Ransom	1889
C. N. Lawrence	1925
K. T. Dewey	1938
C. A. Hodgkinson	1940
G. M. Bolton	1942
E. J. Kahn	1966
M. J. Folliott	1976

CHAPLAINS

A. D. Crake	1865
A. L. C. Heigham	1878
G. F. Garwood	1881
A. L. C. Heigham	1883
W. A. Marshall	1885
R. A. Ransom	1889
H. Wigan	1891
V. T. Kirby	1900
E. J. Crombie	1902
H. R. Willimott	1904
B. M. Maynard	1909

H. R. Willimott	1910
T. G. Blofeld	1917
H. R. Willimott	1926
T. P. Backhouse	1927
L. F. Andrewes	1930
R. D. Hudson	1931
C. C. Barclay	1932
J. S. Douglas	1937
C. G. How	1949
D. Knight	1958
A. J. Gardiner	1958
D. C. Dowie	1964
L. F. P. Gunner	1969

DIRECTORS OF STUDIES

B. A. Clough	1971
N. P. Vinall	1977

BURSARS

H. D. Egerton	1872
C. J. Wilson (O.B.)	1896
L. Jacob	1917
H. G. Morrison	1926
F. A. Stevens	1931
Miss R. A. Garnar	1938
C. A. Jenkins	1955
J. A. H. Wolff	1964
D. L. V. Hodge	1977

HOUSEMASTERS
Wilson (formerly Head's)

Revd F. H. George	1920
V. L. Armitage	1925
W. F. J. Knight	1928
F. G. L. Crawshay	1936
C. A. Hodgkinson	1938
F. V. A. Harmer	1942
J. N. Shaw	1946
G. H. Bletchly	1947
A. D. Pickering	1963
K. A. Spring	1967
M. J. Folliott	1969
F. R. Ullmann	1974

Wilberforce		Merton (VIth-form girls)	
C. N. Lawrence	1920	B. A. Clough	1973
G. M. Bolton	1938	Mrs C. Hall	1977
D. J. Skipwith	1948	*Preparatory School*	
D. G. Longden (O.B.)	1956	Mrs Van der Gucht	1919
J. V. Fiori	1963	Miss Spackman	1921
Crake		Miss Penney	1922
Revd T. G. Blofeld	1920	Miss Green	1926
E. C. Smith	1926	*Junior House*	
L. H. Sutton	1928	K. T. Dewey	1927
K. T. Dewey	1932	B. O. Wheel	1932
R. A. Cruse	1939	J. C. Pallister	1934
E. J. Kahn	1941	(No junior house, 1938-9)	
B. B. Kemp	1956	*Egerton (Junior)*	
R. L. Stein	1978	E. J. Kahn	1940
Egerton (Senior)		E. F. Hodge (O.B.)	1941
E. J. Kahn	1956	T. G. H. Asher	1942
E. P. Gibbs	1961	G. R. Watts	1943
D. G. Guard	1968	D. G. Longden (O.B.)	1946
P. R. Mayes	1973	(Closed, 1956)	
Raymond		*Stone Hill*	
F. J. Willy	1971	N. C. W. Furley	1976
M. C. V. Cane	1974	M. J. Tideswell	1978

PROVOSTS

Canon E. C. Lowe	1896
Rt Revd Hon. A. Lyttleton, bp of Southampton	1898
Canon H. K. Southwell	1903
Preb. E. M. Lance	1921
Rt Revd H. K. Southwell, bp of Lewes	1926
Canon K. E. Kirk (later bp of Oxford)	1937
Canon A. R. Browne-Wilkinson	1944
Rt Revd J. H. L. Morrell, bp of Lewes	1961

CHAIRMEN OF COUNCIL

Until 1925 the Provost usually also acted as Chairman of the Council

J. M. Sing	1925
F. B. Palmer (O.B.)	1926
Professor H. A. Smith (appointed but unable to serve)	1940
F. B. Palmer (O.B.)	1940

From 1941 to 1946 the Provost acted as Chairman

Canon R. C. Mortimer (later bp of Exeter)	1946
H. L. Agnew	1948
G. D. Parkes	1960
J. B. Schuster	1967
L. G. Stocks	1975

OLD BLOXHAMIST SOCIETY

CHAIRMEN
Before the revival of the Society in 1946-7 there was no formal office of chairman. The president (Egerton or the provost) or a senior committee member took the chair at the dinner meeting.

R. M. Raymond	1947
S. G. Lester	1961
D. D. Zvegintzov	1969
S. G. Lester	1971

SECRETARIES
Annual Dinner

R. J. G. Read	1875
A. V. Clarke	1884
W. R. Miles	1889
F. G. Clarke	1891
C. L. Clarke	1893

Old Bloxhamist Society

C. L. Clarke	1896
A. C. Mutter	1899
J. T. Read	1907
R. J. G. Read	1909
Revd H. R. Willimott, St J. M. Young	1911
Revd H. R. Willimott	1914
(None, 1917-20)	
T. R. Taylor	1920
D. D. Zvegintzov, F. W. Boissier	1930
T. R. Taylor	1931
T. R. Taylor, R. M. Raymond	1934
T. R. Taylor	1935
A. E. Snow	1936
E. S. Moore	1939
(None, 1940-46)	
S. G. Lester	1947
F. D. Boss	1961

RESIDENT SECRETARIES

C. J. Wilson (O.B.)	1896
K. T. Dewey	1936
D. G. Longden (O.B.)	1939
E. F. Hodge (O.B.)	1941
R. R. A. Martinek (O.B.)	1942
D. G. Longden (O.B.)	1947
J. M. Lerrigo	1969
S. McLoghry	1977

ACKNOWLEDGEMENTS

The publication of this History has been commissioned jointly by the Old Bloxhamist Society and the School Council, largely due to the persistence of Spencer Lester, successively secretary and chairman of the Society from 1947 to 1978. Both he and the headmaster, Derek Seymour, have given me much encouragement and advice during its compilation. I have also received a great deal of recent unobtrusive help and information from Sam Kahn, and it seems proper to record here the more distant inspiration derived from him as my former housemaster and from the late K. T. Dewey, headmaster, and G. H. Bletchly, historian and history master.

Many people have contributed towards this History and their names have been given under the Bibliography. Inevitably, I fear, there are omissions, particularly of those engaged in conversation on many occasions. In a few cases I have been allowed to consult private papers and wish to acknowledge this special privilege: Mrs G. Gloag and Miss M. Ward for loan of diaries of the Revd G. H. Ward, former headmaster; Mr C. A. Hodgkinson for letting me read his unpublished memoirs on Bloxham; Mr R. S. Thompson, former headmaster, for loan of correspondence files.

I am especially grateful to those present and former members of the Council, staff and Old Bloxhamist Society who read the *History* in draft and made many useful comments, adding new material, correcting matters of fact and gently pointing out false first impressions: Revd P. V. M. Allen (O.B.), F. D. Boss (O.B.), M. J. Folliott, E. J. Kahn, S. G. Lester (O.B.), J. B. Schuster, D. R. G. Seymour, L. G. Stocks, Mr and Mrs R. S. Thompson, T. M. Walker (O.B.). The mistakes that remain are mine alone.

The source of the illustrations has been acknowledged whenever it could be ascertained from endorsements on the original photographs. Many of the earlier ones have already been published in the first *History* (1910) and the centenary booklet. The maps were drawn by Mr P. E. Day of Gloucester, based respectively on the Bloxham inclosure map of 1802, plans of the school lent by the bursar and maps of building developments between 1952 and 1977 by Richard Askwith.

A preliminary task was to sort and catalogue the school archives, among which a collection of about 300 photographs have been mounted for better preservation by Miss Ann Rhodes of Churchdown, Gloucestershire. And for patiently bearing with most of my spare time for three years being devoted to research and writing about Bloxham I owe a large debt to my wife and family.
Brian S. Smith
Coldharbour
Oxenhall
Gloucestershire

BIBLIOGRAPHY

The main sources for the history of the school are quickly described. The story of Hewett's venture is chiefly contained in manuscripts at the Bodleian Library, Oxford. The period when Egerton was headmaster, Warden and Founder is well documented in the archives at the school kept in the Old Bloxhamist Society office. Before 1875 this evidence is supplemented by the files of the Banbury newspapers, and after 1875 by *The Bloxhamist*, together with the jubilee *History* (1910) and its *Supplement* (1925). The aims and activities of succeeding headmasters and the school from 1900 are less well recorded. Few personal papers survive. However, there are three complementary sources. The Council minutes and accounts cover policy and background material, the principal events are reported in *The Bloxhamist* and personal memories become increasingly useful, especially those of old boys for the 1920s and 1930s and of staff from the 1940s.

SECONDARY SOURCES

History of education

T. W. Bamford, *Rise of the public schools* (1967).
K. Evans, *The development and structure of the English educational system* (1975).
B. Gardner, *The public schools* (1973).
B. W. T. Handford, *A history of SS. Mary and Nicolas College, Lancing, 1848-1930* (1933).
B. Heeney, *Mission to the middle classes: the Woodard schools, 1848-1891* (1969).
K. E. Kirk, *Story of the Woodard schools* (2nd edn, 1952).
G. Wilson Knight, *Jackson Knight, a biography* (1975).
Sir J. Otter, *Nathaniel Woodard, a memoir of his life* (1925).
B. Simon and I. Bradley, *The Victorian public school* (1975), especially A. C. Percival, "Some Victorian headmasters".

Oxfordshire history

H. M. Colvin, *History of Deddington* (1963).
Kelly's Directories of Oxfordshire, particularly 1877 and 1883.
R. K. Pugh ed., *The letter-books of Samuel Wilberforce, 1843-68* (Oxfordshire Record Society, Vol. XLVII, 1970).
Ordnance Survey 25-inch map of Oxfordshire (1881).
J. Sherwood and N. Pevsner, *The buildings of England, Oxfordshire* (1974).
Victoria County History of Oxfordshire, Vol. IX (1969).

Bloxham

History of All Saints' School, Bloxham, 1860-1910 (1910). [The anonymous author was the Revd S. Boulter (O.B.)].

Supplement to the History of All Saints' School, Bloxham, 1910-1925 (1925). [The anonymous author was the Revd G. H. Ward].

All Saints' School, Bloxham, 1860-1960: brief history of the school and its progress (1960). [The anonymous author was G. H. Bletchly].

D. Christie-Murray, *The arms of the Revd Philip Reginald Egerton, founder of Bloxham School* (1966).

J.S.W.Gibson, "All Saints' Grammar School, Bloxham, 1853-1857", *Cake and Cockhorse,* Vol. 2, No. 6 (Nov. 1963).

D. W. Harrington, 'The Egerton family of Adstock in the county of Buckingham', *Family History,* Vol. IX, Nos. 53/56 (Nov. 1975).

The Bloxhamist, from 1875.

This has been one of the main sources for this History, reflecting the termly activities and attitudes of the school. The magazine was issued usually ten or eight times a year in quarto format from 1875 to 1915 (Vols. I-XLI, Nos. 1-375). It was then reduced in size and frequency of publication originally because of the war (Vols. XLII- LX, Nos. 376-438), appearing in octavo size from 1915 to 1935; photographs were regularly included in the 1930s. F. V. A. Harmer changed the style and reverted to quarto in 1936 (Vols. LXI-LXV, Nos. 439-462) with the magazine coming out only once a year in war and post-war years. From 1953 changes became more frequent, the plain octavo issues twice yearly from 1953 to 1963 (Vols. LXVI-LXVII, Nos. 463-483) being followed in 1963 by one issue (Vol. LXVII, No. 484) in a pictorial cover before R. C. Theobald introduced the attractive series of booklets running from 1964 and continued by M. J. Folliott to 1970 (Vol. LXVII, Nos. 485-499). With No. 500 (undated but published 1971) the new editor, B. M. Joplin, chose offset-litho printing with many textual illustrations, turning the approximately metric A4-sized magazine landscape-wise, to make it perhaps more suitable for display than the bookshelf. A similar shape but returning to a more traditional lay-out was chosen with No. 511 in 1976.

The contents have also changed over the century. Until 1897 there was a correspondence column and literary contributions were included (except for the period of the Great War) until 1940; articles reappeared regularly for about ten years between 1963 and 1973. Since about 1970 the reduction in detailed factual reporting has made the magazine more readable (if a less useful record for the historian) and No. 504 won a *Birmingham Post* competition for school magazines.

PRIMARY SOURCES

Bloxham School archives
School Council minutes, from 1901.
Correspondence, accounts, commonplace books, notebooks and sermons of Revd P. R. Egerton, 1855-1911.
Log book of Revd F. S. Boissier, 1887-98.
Headmasters' correspondence, 1868-1971.
School prospectuses, from *c.* 1865.
Admission registers, rolls and school lists, from 1860.
Historical notes, newspaper cuttings and miscellaneous papers, from 1864.
Appeals circulars and appeal fund accounts, 1873-1970.
MS biography of Revd A. D. Crake, *c.* 1910.
Examination register, 1864-1929.
School calendars and programmes, club and society programmes, minutes of societies, from 1862.
Sporting fixture cards and programmes, cricket score books, from 1871.
Old Bloxhamist Society registers, minutes and correspondence, from *c.* 1871.
Photographs, from 1863.

Lancing College, Sussex
Woodard papers and letters, 1849-1900.

Bodleian Library, Oxford
Collection of publications of J. W. Hewett, 1853-65, with some MS letters (MS. Top. Oxon. f.40).
Legal papers and correspondence of J. W. Hewett (MS. Oxf. dioc. papers. c. 1736).
Bloxham parish registers, bishop's transcripts (MS. Oxf. dioc. papers. c. 403).
Catalogue of books presented to school library by J. W. Hewett (Gough Adds. Oxon 8° 72).
Calendar of All Saints' Grammar School, 1856 (Cal. Oxon. 8° 480/1856).
Banbury Guardian file, 1854-55 (NGA Oxon. a.6.).

Oxford Central Library
Banbury Guardian, (microfilm), from 1857.
Banbury Advertiser (microfilm), 1855-57.

Oxfordshire Record Office
Inclosure map of Bloxham, 1802 (photo 85).

Mrs G. Gloag, East Sheen, London
Diaries of Revd G. H. Ward, 1911-16.

R. S. Thompson, Clifton upon Teme, Worcestershire
Headmaster's correspondence, reports to Council, 1952-65.

Personal reminiscences

Information has been given by the following members or former members of the school Council and staff — G. M. Bolton, Dr M. C. V. Cane, J. V. Fiori, M. J. Folliott, Miss R. A. Garnar, Revd L. F. P. Gunner, D. L. V. Hodge, C. A. Hodgkinson, D. E. Hood, E. J. Kahn, S. McLoghry, P. R. Mayes, A. D. Pickering, J. B. Schuster, D. R. G. Seymour, L. G. Stocks, R. S. Thompson, F. R. Ullmann, J. A. H. Wolff.

The following Old Bloxhamists have similarly given information — Revd P. V. M. Allen, W. J. B. Anderson, C. J. W. Apps, R. W. Armstrong, R. E. Bateman, F. M. Best, F. D. Boss, A. M. Brassington, L. D. W. Buckle, G. W. R. Caine, P. M. Chambers, B. M. R. Gale, P. H. George, A. J. Greenway, R. A. H. Hartwell, F. D. Hibbert, P. M. Kirk, D. G. Longden, C. H. Mead, E. S. Moore, Lt. Col. D. E. D. Morris, R. M. Raymond, M. C. Riley, T. M. Walker, Group Capt. F. H. Woolliams, H. T. Woolnough, Brigadier D. D. Zvegintzov.

In reply to specific research questions I have also had assistance from Mr Bernard Palmer of the *Church Times,* Mr I. R. McNeil, divisional bursar of the Southern Division of the Woodard Corporation and Mr B. W. T. Handford of Lancing College, Mr D. Maland, headmaster of Denstone, and the Revd. R. V. Douglas, vicar of North Cray, Kent. I should also like to acknowledge the help of the librarians and archivists of the Bodleian Library and Keble College, Oxford, and the Oxfordshire County Library, the Oxfordshire, Buckinghamshire, Devon and Kent Record Offices, Bexley Public Library, Colchester Museum, the Wiltshire Archaeological Society, the Science Museum, London.

INDEX

203